Flyfisher's 1st ed.

Texas Gulf Coast

W9-BJK-718

Fishing Titles Available from Wilderness Adventures Press, Inc.™

Flyfishers Guide to™

Flyfisher's Guide to Alaska

Flyfisher's Guide to Arizona

Flyfisher's Guide to Chesapeake Bay

Flyfisher's Guide to Colorado

Flyfisher's Guide to the Florida Keys

Flyfisher's Guide to Freshwater Florida

Flyfisher's Guide to Idaho

Flyfisher's Guide to Montana

Flyfisher's Guide to Michigan

Flyfisher's Guide to Minnesota

Flyfisher's Guide to Missouri & Arkansas

Flyfisher's Guide to New York

Flyfisher's Guide to New Mexico

Flyfisher's Guide to the Northeast Coast

Flyfisher's Guide to Northern California

Flyfisher's Guide to Northern New England

Flyfisher's Guide to Oregon

Flyfisher's Guide to Pennsylvania

Flyfisher's Guide to Saltwater Florida

Flyfisher's Guide to Texas

Flyfisher's Guide to the Texas Gulf Coast

Flyfisher's Guide to Utah

Flyfisher's Guide to Virginia

Flyfisher's Guide to Washington

Flyfisher's Guide to Wisconsin & Iowa

Flyfisher's Guide to Wyoming

Flyfisher's Guide to Yellowstone National Park

Best Fishing Waters™

California's Best Fishing Waters

Colorado's Best Fishing Waters

Idaho's Best Fishing Waters

Montana's Best Fishing Waters

Oregon's Best Fishing Waters

Washington's Best Fishing Waters

Anglers Guide to™

Complete Anglers Guide to Oregon

Saltwater Angler's Guide to the Southeast

Saltwater Angler's Guide to Southern California

On the Fly Guide to™

On the Fly Guide to the Northwest

On the Fly Guide to the Northern Rockies

Field Guide to™

Field Guide to Fishing Knots

Fly Tying

Go-To Flies™

Flyfisher's Guide to™ the

Texas Gulf Coast

Colby Sorrells

Flyfisher's Guide to™ Series

Wilderness
Adventures
Press, Inc.™

Belgrade, Montana

Published by Wilderness Adventures Press, Inc.™
45 Buckskin Road
Belgrade, MT 59714
866-400-2012
Website: www.wildadvpress.com
email: books@wildadvpress.com

First Edition 2009

ISBN 978 -1-932098-66-2

Table of Contents

Tips On Using This Book

This book is primarily aimed at the near-shore fishing opportunities along the Texas coast. A brief section on offshore fishing is included.

First, we'll go through the different fish and forage species in or near shallow water. I'll discuss techniques for catching the fish and make a few recommendations about tackle.

Texas has 367 miles of gulf shoreline and 3,300 miles of bay shoreline in 18 counties. Over 360 public boat ramps connect anglers to the coastal waters. The Texas coast is made up of many public, state and national parks, and reserves. It also has large areas that are privately owned. The many wildlife reserves and large blocks of private land help insure that the Texas coast remains viable and pristine.

Texas is also an oil state. Oil rigs dot the entire Texas coastline. Luckily for all of us, there seems to be a current trend to make the coast work for all users.

The Texas coast is divided into eight major bay regions: Sabine Lake, Galveston Bay, Matagorda Bay, San Antonio Bay, Aransas Bay, Corpus Christi Bay, Upper Laguna Bay, and Lower Laguna Bay. Each system is then divided into minor bays and areas.

Texas coastal waters offer a wide range of fishing experiences, from fishing for tailing redfish on pristine coastal flats to snook fishing in what one Texas captain calls the "world's ugliest fishing hole", the Brownsville Ship Channel. Fishing experiences along the Texas coast will be as varied as the coast itself. Fishing Sabine Lake is closer to fishing some of the waters off Louisiana while fishing the far Lower Laguna Madre is closer to fishing the Florida Keys. That is the great thing about fishing Texas coastal waters. There is always something to fish for, every month, no matter when or where you decide to fish.

Each of these major bay systems is unique. The bay systems in east Texas are wetter and muddier than the bays in far south Texas. As anglers work their way west, the regions get dryer and sand takes over for mud in the coastal bend.

Within each major bay system are listed major and minor bays, boat ramps, state parks, national wildlife reserves and hub cities. It is always best to check with local sources about expected conditions when planning a trip.

While most of inland Texas is privately owned, large portions of the Texas coast are publicly owned. There are numerous access points along the entire coast. Some destinations require use of a boat to reach a fishing location while others offer walk-in access.

Texas offers the small boat owner or kayak user numerous access points to excellent fishing waters. Kayak fishing is really hot on the middle Texas coast. There are even marked kayak trails in some of the bays.

Regional hub city information includes airports, car rental, lodging, restaurants, fly and tackle shops, guides, and other helpful tips. The hub city listing also includes several smaller towns. These smaller towns are the jump off points for some excellent fishing. If you're going to fish Texas coastal waters, you're going to have to do some driving. Take this opportunity to enjoy some of the best birding and wildlife observation the state has to offer.

Use the Guide section as part of your fishing arsenal. Texas coastal guides are hard working folks and they know what they're doing. Hire a guide. You will learn a lot about the area you fish.

No matter how you get there, boat, kayak or just walking, Texas offers many flyfishing and light tackle opportunities for the angler. Get out there and fish. The good old days are now.

Saltwater Fishing Licenses

A saltwater fishing license is required to fish the Texas coast. Check the regulation booklet or the Texas Parks and Wildlife website at www.tpwd.state.tx.us. Individual species regulations change too often to make them realistic to list here.

Saltwater fishing licenses are sold at over 1,700 locations throughout the state. Some of the smaller Texas coastal towns, however, may not have a local license retailer. Saltwater licenses are available by phone or through the Internet.

Licenses by phone: Call 800-895-4248 9 am to 6 pm, Monday through Friday.

Online Licenses: www.tpwd.state.tx.us - Go to Buying Licenses and follow the directions.

You will need a credit card to buy licenses by phone or online.

Toll free information: 800-792-1112

Resident Saltwater: $33

Senior Saltwater: $16

Non-Resident: $60

One Day All Water: $15

Weather

Tropical storms and hurricanes hit the Texas coast on a regular basis. In 2008, Hurricane Ike hit the Galveston Bay Region, and many facilities were destroyed. Some will take several years to repair. Be sure to check with local sources listed in this guide before planning a trip to any Texas Coastal Region.

Game Fish

The inshore or near shore fisherman of Texas is blessed with a variety of game fish to pursue. Three fish — redfish, speckled trout, and flounder — garner the most attention but there are other worthy adversaries for the coastal angler.

Texas coastal game fish include:

Redfish	Tarpon
Speckled trout	Florida pompano
Flounder	Striped bass
Black drum	Tripletail
Sheepshead	Sand trout
Gray snapper	Bonito or little tunny
Ladyfish	Cobia or ling
Crevalle jack	King mackerel
Gafftopsail catfish	Spanish mackerel
Snook	Bluefish
Whiting or southern kingfish	Dolphin

This book is intended for the inshore fisherman and most offshore species will not be covered. Some of these fish are considered incidental catches not normally pursued on purpose and therefore will be covered lightly. For those adventuresome anglers wanting heavier fish to chase, Texas offshore waters offer most familiar ocean dwelling fish from marlin to tuna.

Fish like cobia, tripletail, and kingfish are covered because the Texas coastal angler will probably run into these fish while fishing near natural passes or the several man-made entrances to the Gulf of Mexico. The clear, blue water of the Gulf of Mexico makes an annual appearance along the Texas coast sometime in August and stays close to shore for six to eight weeks. During this time, the Texas coastal fisherman has a chance at these fish species normally associated with much deeper water.

The game fish of Texas have food and habitat preferences just like any fish, and understanding these preferences will greatly increase an angler's catch. For example, the best time to catch big black drum is in the early spring when the bigger fish enter from the Gulf of Mexico as part of their annual spawning ritual. Anglers can also find these large fish in the fall making a last effort to gain weight before winter sets in.

The discussion on Texas coastal fish starts with the red drum or redfish, as Texans call them.

RED DRUM

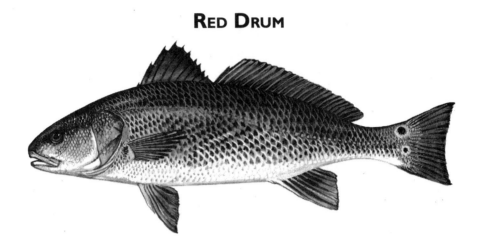

Red drum, or redfish, is the most sought after fish on the Texas coast. Just one short generation ago, if you polled Texas coastal anglers about their target, the speckled trout would have been the choice. The "Redfish Wars" (the late-1970s fight over redfish regulations) occurred to protect one of their favorite fish and ever since, redfish have dominated the Texas coastal scene.

Once you've seen your first tailing redfish you'll never forget it. The bright blue-tipped tail with the big black spot gently swaying back and forth in water not more than 10 inches deep is usually all it takes to make any coastal angler a life long fan of the redfish. After that first sighting, your nights will be haunted by tailing redfish.

Nothing tests the angling skills of a Texas coastal fisherman like a tailing redfish, unless it is a bull red. Bull redfish, the largest members of the redfish family, are the large female redfish, the great spawners of the species. Redfish are like most fish in that the female is the larger of the two sexes. Very big redfish are called "bull redfish" not because they are the males of the species, but because they pull like a bull.

Large schools of redfish over 40 inches long regularly patrol the Texas shoreline. Schools containing over 1,000 fish are not unheard of along the Texas coast. When these large schools of redfish arrive on the scene, there is only one thing to do: FISH. They'll quickly engulf a school of baitfish and be gone to some unknown depth almost as quickly as they appear.

Redfish are distinguished by one or more large black spots on the base of their tails. They get their name from the dark coppery or "red" color but the color can range from a light silver to dark copper. The tip of the tail is often a beautiful aqua blue. Their mouth is located on the bottom which allows them to root and dig for crabs and shrimp. They often make "muds" by sucking in mud, sand, and anything else located on the bay floor and then blowing everything out but what they want to eat. This creates a ring of fine silt circling a depression that often holds pieces of crabs or shell.

Redfish live their first several years in the bay systems before moving to the Gulf of Mexico. Texas may not have the giant redfish of 90 pounds known along the eastern coast of the United States but schools of 40- to 46-inch redfish are plenty for the Texas inshore fisherman to get excited about.

Redfish are caught year round in Texas coastal waters, but fall is the best time to find them in shallow water.

Habitat

Texas redfish are found in almost all coastal waters. Twenty-seven-inch redfish can disappear in 10 inches of water right in front of an anxious fly caster. They are found along the man-made entrances to the Gulf of Mexico on a regular basis. Every creek, cut, lake, and shallow-water flat is a possible home for a redfish. Anglers should anticipate finding redfish almost every trip they make to the Texas coast.

Redfish are also found along muddy shorelines and oyster-covered reefs. They regularly patrol the areas adjacent to the three natural passes of Texas and the many manmade jetties found up and down the coast. Large fish cruise along the gulf shoreline and way back in the many small lakes that dot the Texas landscape. Redfish can be found anywhere there is saltwater and even in most brackish water areas. They are the true equal opportunity fish of Texas.

Prey

Fortunately for Texas fly and light tackle anglers, redfish will eat almost anything. They may prefer small crabs, but will readily attack shrimp, mullet, pinfish, worms, eels, gold spoons, and flies. Usually anything that comes within 8 inches of a redfish nose is considered table fair. They are not picky eaters.

Flyfishing: Tactics, Techniques, and Tackle

Flyfishers always prefer to sight cast to their target. Redfish often oblige fly anglers with great opportunities to practice their art. Texas is blessed with innumerable shallow-water flats made just for redfish and flyfishers chasing them.

Flyfishers have three ways to pursue Texas redfish. Most fly anglers are familiar with casting from the front of a shallow-water flats boat. These boats are designed to maneuver in water less than a foot deep and often as shallow as 4 inches. Flats boats, fished everywhere from Florida to the tip of Texas, often weigh less than 500 pounds. These boats allow guide and angler the chance to approach shallow water flats in relative quiet. Fly anglers familiar with Florida-style bonefish trips will feel right at home on a Texas flats boat. Guides either pole or use a trolling motor to get in close to the fish.

The second way for Texas anglers to get close to redfish is by wading. Anglers most often take a boat close to their favorite Texas flat, anchor the boat and get out and wade. If there is more than one angler in the boat a leapfrog method is used where one angler is let off the boat to a wade a stretch of flat and the second angler goes a couple of hundred yards farther down the flat. The second angler sets the boat anchor and continues wading down the flat. When the first angler gets to the parked boat he retrieves the boat and leapfrogs past the first angler another couple of hundred yards farther down the flat. This process is followed until the entire flat has been fished. Anglers are able to cover large areas in a single day using this leapfrog method.

The third method of fishing for redfish along Texas' many coastal flats is by small watercraft (kayaks and canoes), which have become very popular along the Texas coast. These small watercraft are even quieter than the wader. Kayaks allow the Texas coastal flyfisher to gently glide right in close to tailing reds without alarming them. Kayaks being quietly paddled into shallow water do not disturb most fish and birds.

The kayak also offers Texas coastal anglers a way to avoid the many muddy shore areas that are difficult to wade. As Texas shorelines are eroded wave by wave, the heaviest sediment falls out first. This is the tightly packed sand found near the deepest water out from the grass. These areas are easy to wade and redfish often patrol these areas looking for anything washed up by the waves.

As the waves continue farther inshore the lighter sediments drop out leaving the lightest sediments to fall at or very near the grass shoreline. That also means the closer the wading angler gets to the grass, the muddier the wading gets. Areas closest to the grass will be the most difficult to wade through with anglers often sinking up past their knees or even deeper in the mud. That is where the kayak flyfisher really has an advantage, gently gliding over the muddy areas.

Anglers finding themselves in mud too soft to wade through may have to swim or float back out. Just remember to go back out, not farther inshore. The farther the wader goes in toward the shore the softer the mud will be.

Whether by wading, or fishing from a flats boat or kayak, flyfishers have a great advantage over other types of tackle. Fly anglers can gently drop a relatively small fly right next to a tailing redfish. Fly anglers should choose one single fish to target if they run into a group or school of redfish. By specifically targeting one fish, fly anglers can often catch several fish out of the group.

Cast the fly in front and slightly to one side of the redfish if possible. If there are several fish schooled up together, try to work fish on the outside of the group first. The fly needs to land close to the targeted redfish because they will most likely have their heads down burrowing in the mud looking for something to eat.

The burrowing redfish makes a cloud of sediment or "mud" in the area they're digging. Redfish flare their gill plates, sucking in sediment and prey, and then blow out anything they don't want. This creates a circular mud hole where they've been. Seeing several of these muds tells the angler they are looking in the right spot. A mud will often have a ring of soft mud with broken shell in the center. This is very similar to the way bonefish feed.

Once the flyfisher hooks a redfish, every effort should be made to try to force the fish away from other fish in the school if possible by applying sideways pressure with the rod. If the hooked fish is separated from the other members of the school, the flyfisher can often catch other fish from the group after releasing the first fish.

Flies used to catch redfish include small crab patterns, Clouser Minnows, Lefty's Deceivers, Bend Backs, shrimp patterns, gold spoon flies, and small poppers. Most Texas flats are best fished with weedless flies due to the abundance of floating grass in the area. Redfish have an inferior mouth on the bottom side of their head and they have difficulty getting poppers into their mouth so remember to actually feel the fish tug before setting the hook when using poppers.

Fly anglers should also look for moving schools of mullet in the area. Redfish will often trail these schools searching for a wounded fish or something spooked by the cruising mullet.

One thing redfish anglers need to be cautious of is moving too fast. Redfish will often tail for long periods of time followed by intervals when their tail is not exposed. If the tail of a redfish is readily visible, the fish is feeding and fly anglers can get very close to the fish as long as they are careful not to move too much water with their boat or feet. Go slow. The redfish are not in a hurry and will remain in the area unless spooked.

Another thing anglers are guilty of, particularly boating anglers, is running past a flat covered with redfish because the boater cannot see any fish. Redfish, like most fish, move. They'll have their tails exposed one minute and then quietly disappear in 8 inches of water.

The Texas angler seeking redfish is better served by going to a productive area and working the area slowly and thoroughly. Watch for birds feeding along the shoreline — a sure sign there's plenty of food in the area. A stealthy approach is always best when seeking redfish.

No matter how much caution anglers use in their approach to redfish, other unseen fish will be close by. It is often these unseen fish that spook the tailer. Move slowly and give the area time to get accustomed to your presence. Stand still and just watch for awhile.

Anglers can also catch redfish by blind casting, but should limit their efforts to areas known to hold fish. Look for areas with depressions slightly deeper than the surrounding area.

Redfish often give themselves away by making noise chasing shrimp or baitfish. Be aware of these situations and watch what the fish are doing. Position yourself so you can make an accurate cast in front of the fish. Lined fish will spook.

It's rarely necessary for a fly caster to use a full sinking line when going for redfish, as they seldom need to get to depths greater than 5 feet. A sink tip line will occasionally be useful for the fly caster.

Redfish are not leader shy so use a 0X or heavier leader when going after reds. Leaders of 9 to 10 feet work best.

Eight- or 9-weight rods work for most redfish situations. Four-piece travel rods allow anglers to travel with ease and today's modern multiple-piece fly rods are great.

Fly reels should have a good, smooth drag and hold at least 150 feet of backing. Most redfish will turn with steady pressure applied in the opposite direction of the way they want to go.

Light Tackle: Tactics, Techniques, and Tackle

When fishing with light tackle, make sure you have gold and copper weedless spoons in 1/8-, 1/4-, and 1/2-ounce sizes. Redfish love gold and copper spoons like kids love ice cream. Spoons don't look like anything alive in nature but may look close enough to crabs and small prey fish in the area to entice redfish to strike. Whatever redfish think a spoon is, they like them.

Spoons and most lures are best run with a short leader of 18 inches or less. Attach a leader of 17- to 20-pound test line to running line of 10 to 12 pounds using a small, quality barrel swivel. The swivel allows the spoon to wobble back and forth instead of spin. Fluorocarbon and monofilament both work well as leader material. Connect the leader to the spoon with a Palomar knot.

Soft plastic worms and baitfish imitations used with a jighead also work well on redfish. Jigheads should be from 1/16- through 3/4-ounce weights. Use the lightest weight possible for the fishing situation. If the angler is working shallow-water flats of less than 3 feet in depth, a jighead of 1/16 or 1/8 will be plenty. If the angler is working a cut or channel with fast moving water, heavier weights may work better.

Redfish will also hit topwater lures but light tackle anglers need to be sure they actually feel the fish before they pull back on the rod. A steady pull works better than a hard jerk when fishing for reds with topwater lures. Larger lures, such as large spoons up to 3 ounces, work best for schooling bull reds. They will also hit large topwater plugs.

Rods for reds should be at least 6 feet in length and cast lures from 1/8 ounce to 5/8 ounce in weight. Redfish are not shy about hitting lures, so strikes are easily felt.

Straight handle rods work better than pistol grip type casting rods. Several rod manufacturers include measurement marks on their rods so anglers can quickly measure any fish they might want to keep.

Reels, whether casting or spinning, need a smooth drag and need to be fairly resistant to saltwater. Most reel manufacturers offer saltwater models that work great for catching redfish.

Season

Redfish up to 3 years old inhabit coastal bays year round on the Texas coast. Once a redfish fully matures it migrates through natural and man-made passes to the gulf where it remains for the rest of its life.

Shallow Texas coastal flats warm quickly even in the winter. These clear water areas offer redfish feeding opportunities throughout the year. Prime redfish season is April through early December. Redfish are harder to find after winter cold fronts cool the coastal waters. Winter anglers will do better by letting the flats warm up, starting their fishing in mid-morning to mid-day rather starting at first light.

SPOTTED SEATROUT

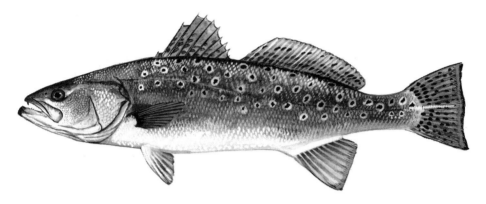

Spotted seatrout, also known as speckled trout, trout, or specs in Texas run a close second to redfish in popularity. Many anglers will argue they are still the top species. Speckled trout were the most sought after coastal fish by the generation of anglers before the current redfish trend. No matter which you prefer, they are both great game fish.

Speckled trout have silvery sides showing a great rainbow of colors when closely examined. They also have black spots down each side and on their tail. The biggest female fish have a bright yellow color inside their mouths.

Dedicated big speckled trout fishers know they're looking for one fish just like big bass fanatics. Big speckled trout are almost always loners and female. Any speckled trout over 24 inches is most likely a female. The very large fish are typically found along grassy shorelines in bays with quick access to deep water. Where redfish will most often be up close to the grass in water less than 18 inches deep, speckled trout will be out where the flat drops off to deeper water. Most Texas bays are less than 10 feet deep and speckled trout like the cover deeper water provides. Speckled trout, except the largest females, are most often school fish. If the angler catches one fish, stay in the spot. The chances of catching another trout are very good.

Speckled trout have two large canine teeth in the upper jaw that should be avoided. Anglers can either use a landing net or grasp the trout with thumb and forefinger right at the top of the gill plates. I prefer to net trout, especially large trout. The net helps control the fish while the angler prepares to remove the hook.

Speckled trout are part of the weakfish family, so called because of their soft mouth. Speckled trout are often lost right when the angler gets it close by shaking its head and setting the hook free. By using a net, anglers increase their chances that the fish will not get away if it shakes its head.

Habitat

As mentioned earlier, speckled trout prefer deeper water than redfish. Once anglers have finished catching redfish they can go to the nearest deeper water and often find speckled trout.

Speckled trout are travelers often moving several miles within one day. A Texas Parks and Wildlife Coastal Fisheries employee once told me a story about a speckled trout they tagged one day and found 21 miles away the next day.

The same flats holding redfish hold trout, just in deeper water. Also, trout are found in guts running throughout the bays. These guts are several inches or feet deeper than the surrounding area and are most often created by moving water.

Speckled trout prefer to be in moving water created by incoming and outgoing tides. Texas coastal waters rise and lower about one foot due to the movement of the tide. Wind plays a larger role along the Texas coast than tidal movement. Wind-driven changes can create water level differences much greater than moon-created tides. Couple the two together and Texas coastal waters move more than enough to entice speckled trout to bite.

Trout face into the current to feed regardless of how it's generated. Strong currents coming into natural and manmade connections to the Gulf of Mexico trigger speckled trout to bite. The currents wash shrimp, crabs, and prey fish back and forth throughout the day. Speckled trout know this and position themselves to take advantage of this food movement.

The big females spawn in the early spring, usually February through April. This is the time big trout chasers are on the flats. Big female trout prefer to spawn in sandy areas, called potholes, in grassy areas along the shorelines. You can often see big female trout sitting parallel to the grass at the edge of the pothole.

These largest fish spook easily and will leave the area with any disturbance. When chasing the big females, coastal anglers should do a lot of looking and cast only when they see a target.

Oyster reefs are an ideal area to find speckled trout. Any shell on the bottom will attract prey species that trout prefer. Smaller trout prefer eating shrimp and switch almost exclusively to prey fish as they mature. Add a nearby deep-water escape route and you've got a prime trout hideout.

Many anglers are familiar with chasing fish under birds and this is true with speckled trout. A group of birds diving into the water should be investigated. Most of the time it will be small trout — less than 15 inches — under the birds.

Texas trout anglers often look for "slicks". These are the slick or oily-looking areas on the water's surface created when trout regurgitate after overfeeding. A small-sized slick means it has just been created and the fish are most likely still nearby. Once the slick gets to be larger than a hula-hoop, the fish may be hard to find. Anglers also need to consider which way the wind is blowing when targeting a slick. The fish will be located at the head of the slick not at the wind blown tail.

The area around a slick smells like watermelon or strawberry pop. I've often smelled slicks before I could actually see them. Other fish, like gafftopsail catfish, create slicks so don't be surprised if the slick you find doesn't hold any trout.

Prey

Speckled trout eat almost anything that gets in their way, but they do have preferences. Trout up to 20 inches in length like shrimp. Once a trout gets over 20 inches it prefers small fish like piggy perch, croaker, mullet, and mud minnows. Trout are cannibals and a really big sow trout will eat a 15-inch relative.

Flyfishing: Tactics, Techniques, and Tackle

Flyfishing for speckled trout requires more blind casting than fishing for redfish. Anglers should concentrate on locations where the water depth drops from 18 inches to over 4 feet in depth. These drop-offs are natural train tracks for trout. They'll follow the drop-off from deep water to shallow just like a train going down the track.

Anglers should position themselves back from the drop-off within easy casting distance. The best cast will be almost parallel to the drop-off. Do not stand in the drop-off zone because that is where the fish want to travel.

Any jetty area is a good place to blind cast for trout from a boat. Don't be afraid to cast right into the rocks. The current will quickly move the fly away from the rocks. Trout often hang out in just enough water to swim around the jetty rocks. This is a good place to cast Clouser Minnows, Lefty's Deceivers, and Bend Backs with floating lines. Areas where currents bring food past islands, into guts, out of lakes, and past grass patches, are all prime locations for speckled trout. Waders or fishers in kayaks should concentrate on these areas.

Small topwater poppers also catch trout. Try working the popper slowly at first, making a single pop and pausing several seconds before making the second pop. If this doesn't entice a strike, try casting the popper and retrieving with a rapid series of pops, one right after another, until the popper has moved a couple of yards. Then let the popper sit. Repeat the popping sequence after several seconds pause until the popper is retrieved.

For the larger fish, try a Lefty's Deceiver or Clouser at least 4 inches in length. Work the fly like a large prey fish with an irregular cadence. Keep the rod tip right at the water's surface. Strip-strike any fish that hits and be prepared to give line quickly. Make sure all fly hooks are very sharp.

Eight- or 9-weight rods are perfect. Anglers should have both floating and full sinking lines available when fishing for speckled trout. Reels for speckled trout are the same as for redfish.

It is possible to catch a large speckled trout on fly tackle. The current world record — over 15 pounds — was caught on the Texas coast.

Light Tackle: Tactics, Techniques, and Tackle

Light tackle was made for speckled trout fishing. Lines of 10- or 12-pound test are all the trout angler needs. I like to use an 18-inch leader of 17- to 20-pound test with a small, quality swivel to connect the line to the lure.

Lures for speckled trout include silver spoons, jigheads with soft plastics, and hard-bodied lures. Jigheads of 1/8 through 3/4 ounce should be carried. Use the lightest jighead possible, depending on the fishing situation. Heavier jigheads are required when fishing fast-moving water around jetties and inlets where tides flood the bays. Lighter jigs work better when wading down a long grass-lined flat.

Anglers will notice a better feel when using a casting outfit than a spinning outfit. The better sensitivity is necessary because speckled trout will often make a gentle bite on soft plastics. If using spinning tackle, try filling the reel with one of the modern super lines now on the market. A braided line offers better sensitivity and evens the playing field with the casting crowd.

I prefer a slightly longer rod when fishing for speckled trout. A casting rod of 7 to 9 feet seems to work better. Also, the rod should be able to handle the lighter jigheads associated with sometimes finicky trout.

A wading angler should be prepared to cover lots of shoreline when fishing for speckled trout. If trout are not found in one area, move. If you find them, stay with them until you don't get any more bites. Try to figure out which direction the school is traveling and get in front of the school if possible. When fishing with another angler, remember to use the leapfrog method described in the redfish section.

The best speckled trout fishing is most often early in the morning during the warm months. Many seasoned trout anglers end their day by 11 am. During the cold months trout often don't bite until the sun has had a chance to warm the water —often after 9 am — and then stop biting as the sun heads toward the horizon. Sleep in and fish the middle of the day during winter months.

Night fishing for speckled trout is a way to increase your odds of catching large fish. Try to get to the chosen location before sundown and familiarize yourself with the area. Take along a small flashlight and know where the boat is if you're wading. Try to locate funnel areas where currents flow and bring food past waiting trout.

Many speckled trout are caught with a popping cork and live shrimp. The popping cork gets the attention of any nearby fish closely resembling the sound made by feeding trout. Anglers often drift fish with popping corks. Piggy perch and finger mullet are also used to catch speckled trout. A recent trend is to use small croaker.

My preference is to use lures instead of bait — they usually out fish live bait plus the angler doesn't have to spend time or money for bait.

Season

In most Texas bays, speckled trout really start showing up in numbers in April and May. The Laguna Madre area has speckled trout throughout the year. Fishermen prefer to use waders during most of December, January, and February. Typically the water begins to warm up in March throughout most of the state to the point it becomes comfortable to wade wet for speckled trout.

Flounder

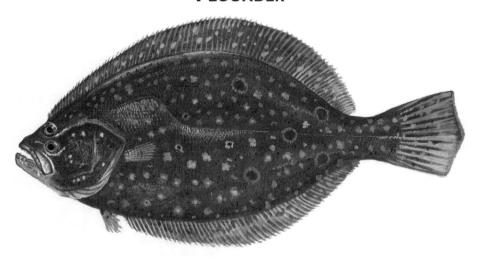

The third member of the Texas Big Three is the southern flounder. Although Texas has three species of flounder, most are southern flounder. Flounder are often found in the same areas as redfish and speckled trout. The serious flounder flyfishers have to have a way to increase their chances of catching flounder because most are caught blind casting.

Flounder like to use the same locations year after year so, if you happen to locate flounder, remember the location because they'll be there again. Flyfishers can improve their chances of catching a flounder by concentrating on known locations and likely spots. Drop-offs with good current movement are great places to locate flounder. Guts and channels feeding small lakes are also good locations for flounder.

Flounder are true predator fish and will rise several feet off the bottom to attack a well-placed fly or lure. They have sharp teeth and fight well, making them a perfect fly-rod fish.

Flounder tend to be class-year fish, meaning some years anglers catch respectable numbers and some years anglers may not catch any. Weather conditions, amount of trawl activity, amount of shrimp harvested, and other factors determine a good class year from a bad year. If you start catching flounder early in the year you'll probably catch them throughout the year. I've had both many-fish years and single-fish years.

If there is one fish Texas anglers prefer to eat, it has to be flounder. They're wonderful fish for the table, but are currently feeling pressure from commercial fishermen, and young flounder are often killed in shrimp trawls. Controlled breeding efforts by conservation groups have not successfully raised flounder to any great extent. Anglers should consider keeping only the fish they will eat fresh and releasing all others.

Habitat

Flounder are bottom-dwelling fish. They spend almost their entire lives looking skyward. They camouflage themselves by matching the colors of the bottom where they're resting. Most are a sandy brown color but can vary in shades from almost black to dark brown to light cream depending on the substrate in the area.

Flounder can be found in almost all of the areas where redfish and trout are located. They prefer ambush locations where prey fish and shrimp are carried past them on a daily basis.

During the fall, flounder make a migration to the gulf to spawn. During this time they congregate in large numbers close to entrances to the gulf.

More flounder are caught on the eastern part of the Texas coast than the rest of the coast. The Texas flounder record is over 13 pounds and was caught in the Sabine Lake area, a real flounder hotspot.

Prey

Opportunistic feeders, flounder will eat shrimp and many different types of prey fish. Mud minnows or striped killifish are favorites of flounder.

Flyfishing: Tactics, Techniques, and Tackle

Flyfishers will most likely sight cast to very few flounder. By concentrating on known locations and likely spots flyfishers can greatly increase their flounder catch.

Try deeper guts where water quickly exits back bays and lakes. Work anywhere there is cover: around boat docks, under overhanging tree limbs, around old pilings and boat wrecks. Other likely locations are around abandoned duck blinds and muddy areas inside oyster reefs.

Since flounder live on the bottom, the flyfisher should fish for them with a sinking line. Work the fly with very short strips of 2 to 3 inches in length. Keep the fly as close to the bottom as possible without hanging up on grass or shell.

My favorite flounder fly is the Lone Star Tiger Rattler. This fly incorporates a loud rattle and bright colors to entice flounder. It closely represents a Flounder Pounder, a soft plastic lure used by light tackle fishermen.

Clouser Minnows in chartreuse and white, tan and all black also work well on flounder. The simple olive or solid black woolly bugger will also take its share of flounder. Just make sure the fly hook is very sharp when fishing for flounder.

A landing net is a good idea when fishing for flounder, as they're notorious for letting go of flies and lures when they see a fisherman. One trick that often helps is to drag the hooked fish onto the shoreline if possible. They don't want to let go of the fly and before they know it they're out of the water.

Rods in 6- to 9-weight work great for flounder. A full sink line helps get the fly down to the flounder strike zone. They are not leader shy so a strong leader is recommended. Flounder are also not shy of fly lines so if you run the line right over the fish it most likely won't spook.

A flounder that is hooked and gets off before the angler can handle it will remain in the area. They simply settle down to the bottom and remain in that location. Don't move! Remember where the flounder came off the hook and let the spot rest a few minutes. After resting, recast to the area where the flounder was. Make numerous casts. If the flounder is there it will often hit the fly again.

Light Tackle: Tactics, Techniques, and Tackle

Light tackle used for catching redfish will work fine for catching flounder. Don't be afraid to aggressively set the hook on a flounder.

Jigheads with soft plastics work great. Eventually any angler fishing for flounder will have one spit out a soft plastic just like it never had the hook in its mouth. One solution to this problem is to use a smaller soft plastic or switch to a slightly different lure like a Flounder Pounder. The Flounder Pounder is about 3 inches in length versus most soft plastics that are 5 inches long.

If you happen to use soft plastic grubs for freshwater bass, you can use them for catching flounder as well. They are great lures for flounder. As always, make sure the hook is really sharp and check the point several times during the day and especially after catching a flounder.

Favorite colors for flounder are fire tiger, punkinseed with chartreuse tail, smoke with red tail, and red flash shad. Flounder seem to prefer the fluorescent orange tail, green body with yellow belly, and gold glitter of fire tiger over other colors, but whatever color you have for speckled trout will probably work.

Season

Flounder are found in Texas bays except during the cold winter months. They make a big spawning run in the late fall, stacking up around entrances to the gulf.

BLACK DRUM

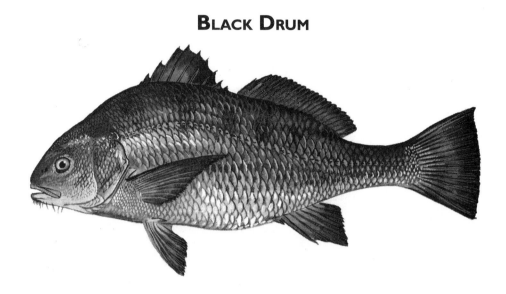

Black drum, or simply drum, are cousins of redfish and are easily distinguished by the barbells or whiskers on their lower jaw. Young black drum often have a series of faint vertical bars down the side of the body. Some of the larger fish may have a coppery tint to them making them look similar to large redfish, but the barbells and their body shape give them away. Large black drum are much more compact than large redfish. Black drum often make a drumming sound while being released.

Large black drum are some of the first fish to return to the bays in early spring. Large fish, up to 60 pounds, ride in on currents during March. These are the big breeders. Some of these fish are over 25 years old and should be released quickly.

Black drum cruise the lower depths of the bays and are usually caught feeding on the bottom. Some areas of the Texas coast, from Port Aransas southward, offer many chances at sight casting to black drum.

Shallow-water black drum are ideal targets for the fly and light tackle fisher. They hit almost any fly and are aggressive fighters. Their near transparent dorsal fin often gives them away as it sticks out of the water.

Black drum don't have teeth. They have crushers in the back of their throat to pulverize whatever they take in. Their mouth is relatively soft so it's best to keep a steady pull on black drum and avoid strong hooksets.

Black drum offer inshore anglers a chance at catching the largest fish of a lifetime. The state record is over 80 pounds.

Habitat

Black drum seem to prefer something to swim around. They're often found around old pilings. Once you find them, they will return to that same site time after time. Small black drum, called puppy drum, can be found cruising shallow flats. They make muds or blow holes similar to redfish. Puppy drum often invade an area leaving it looking like the surface of the moon with numerous craters where they explored for food.

Prey

Black drum most often feed directly on the bottom. They will eat almost anything they can find including shrimp, crabs, worms, and cut bait. A favorite food is the blue crab.

Flyfishing: Tactics, Techniques, and Tackle

Flyfishers target black drum much like they do redfish. Sight casting to visible fish is the preferred method. These are strong fish. A black drum of 5 to 7 pounds is a great adversary for the flyfisher.

During March, flyfishers can sight cast to much larger fish coming in for their annual spawn. Work drop-offs near passes and jetties where the fish come in from the gulf. These fish can be easily spooked but will readily hit a well-placed fly.

Solid black flies like Captain Corey Rich's Little Black Fly are ideal for catching black drum. Try to intercept the fish's path with your cast and avoid casting directly over the fish.

Rod selection is the same as for redfish. A sinking line is required to get flies down to the bottom zone these fish inhabit while around old pilings and docks. Floating line should be used when casting to visible fish.

Light Tackle: Tactics, Techniques, and Tackle

Light tackle used for redfish also works well for black drum. They will hit lures, although they prefer bait such as live shrimp, crabs, and cutbait. The larger fish prefer blue crabs. Use a circle hook on blue crab up to tennis ball size. Passes or channels with deep water are ideal locations for black drum. Just be prepared to fight the fish for a while.

If you're fishing for the really big black drum (fish over 20 pounds), be sure to have a large landing net and keep the fish in the water as much as possible while removing the hook. Take a quick photo or two and release the fish in good shape. Although black drum over 31 inches must be released, anglers should consider releasing any fish over 26 inches.

Season

Mature black drum return to the bays in March and most of the big black drum are caught in March and April. Puppy drum live in the bays year round and can be caught throughout the year.

Sheepshead

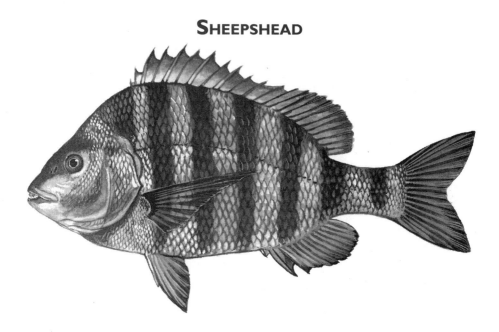

Sheepshead inhabit the same waters as redfish and black drum. They get their name from their sheep-like teeth and mouth. They are hard to hook with flies but it can be done. Sheepshead are considered by some to be the bluegill of the coast. They fight with everything they have once hooked just like freshwater bluegill. They grow to over 25 inches in length and have an excellent white fillet. Everything on a sheepshead either sticks or bites, so handle them with care.

Flyfishers are sometimes fooled by sheepshead due to the dark vertical stripes on their sides. They may resemble small black drum in coloration, but that's all. Sheepshead have a much more compact body and very large teeth. Black drum don't have any teeth and a soft mouth.

Habitat

Sheepshead are found along coastal flats and around deep-water jetties. They live around boat docks and old piers.

Prey

Sheepshead prefer barnacles. That's what those big teeth are designed for. They also eat shrimp, crabs and cutbait.

Flyfishing: Tactics, Techniques and Tackle

Sheepshead will give the fly angler all they can handle on an 8- or 9- weight system. Use a heavy leader and expect to get cut off several times. When casting to visible sheepshead, don't move the fly once cast. Remember, sheepshead are designed to eat barnacles and barnacles don't move.

A simple chartreuse-and-white Clouser works about as well as anything. A Green Weenie is also a good fly. Cast in front of a sheepshead to intercept the fish's path. Cast well before the fish can see the fly land, or they will spook and rapidly leave the area.

Fish for sheepshead anywhere deep water enters a bay system. The largest fish spawn in early spring usually in March. Like most of the other fish, if you find one sheepshead, you'll probably find several.

Light Tackle: Tactics, Techniques, and Tackle

Sheepshead make a great target for the light tackle crowd. Tackle used to catch redfish works well on sheepshead. Live shrimp or shrimp pieces are the bait of choice for light tackle fishers targeting sheepshead.

The largest fish cruise shallow flats near gulf openings in early spring. These fish grow larger than 25 inches, and a sheepshead that size is a lot of fun on light tackle. Kahle hooks work best when fishing for sheepshead. It's best to apply steady pressure with the rod and don't make a quick hook set.

Sheepshead like to pick at their food and they'll quickly nip any shrimp off the hook. One of the best techniques for sheepshead is to move the bait very slowly and gently, once a bite is felt. Keep the bait moving very slowly. The sheepshead will eventually eat most of the bait leaving just a small amount on the hook. That's when the light tackle angler will likely hook a sheepshead.

Season

Sheepshead enter the bays in the early spring, usually in February or March. Large fish come onto flats to spawn at that time of year. The largest sheepshead leave the bays shortly after the spawn and retreat to much deeper water. Smaller sheepshead are found almost year round at jetties and anywhere a barnacle might attach itself.

GRAY SNAPPER

Gray snapper are increasing in numbers all along the Texas coast. A recent report of gray snapper populations presented by the Coastal Fisheries Division of the Texas Parks and Wildlife system showed gray snapper inhabiting almost all of the Texas coast. Prior to 1990 they were only found in a few locations.

Gray snapper hit flies well; they taste great and are now widely spread throughout the entire coast. Most will not exceed 14 inches but fish over 25 inches have been caught. The current state record is over 18 pounds.

Habitat

Gray snapper live around boat docks and jetties.

Prey

Gray snapper are not choosy eaters. Small blue crabs, shrimp and small fish are all food sources for this fish.

Flyfishing: Tactics, Techniques, and Tackle

Fishing for gray snapper with fly tackle is a great way to introduce kids to coastal flyfishing. Anywhere there is a pier or boat dock will have gray snapper. Pilings around fish cleaning stations are also great places to fish for gray snapper.

A simple chartreuse-and-white or solid white Clouser works great for gray snapper. Like several other coastal species, if you find one gray snapper you'll find several. I once fed three hungry fishers on Clouser-caught gray snapper. When the fishing was over there was nothing left of the fly except the eyes and the hook, but the fish were still hitting it!

Rods from 4- through 7-weights work great for gray snapper. Take your lightest tackle and have fun.

Light Tackle: Tactics, Techniques, and Tackle

Anything from the kid's snoopy rod to light spinning tackle works for gray snapper. Use a slightly larger leader when fishing near barnacle-covered piers and pilings to avoid being cut off. A split shot clamped on the line, a small hook, and a shrimp is all that's needed. Be prepared to tie on several hooks because gray snapper will often take a baited hook right down into nearby rocks.

In far south Texas, large specimens readily hit solid white or white and gold soft plastics on jigheads in deeper channels. This is where the largest fish are caught.

Keeping your snappers presents a great opportunity to teach your kids how to clean fish. Then have a meal made of gray snapper fillets and wonderful memories.

Season

Gray snapper appear in the late summer, usually around the first of August. They disappear with the first cold weather, usually by the end of October.

LADYFISH

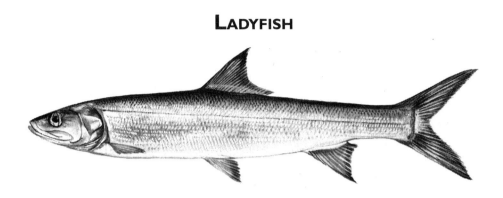

Ladyfish are cousins of tarpon and they prove it when hooked. Very few flyfishers seek out ladyfish on purpose and that's too bad. They're great fish to catch on fly tackle and readily hit flies. They pull hard and fast, make great runs similar to a bonefish, and often make spectacular leaps as high as a boat.

While they are fun to catch, all are released because — like their cousin the tarpon — they are not worth eating.

Ladyfish rarely exceed 3 pounds and the current state record is just less than 5 pounds.

Habitat

Ladyfish prefer to hang out in moving water. Check around old pilings or near cuts entering the gulf.

Prey

Ladyfish eat shrimp and prey fish.

Flyfishing: Tactics, Techniques, and Tackle

Ladyfish are found almost anywhere along the coast. They prefer areas with old pilings, around piers and openings to the gulf. Large schools can be seen swimming in slightly deeper water just off coastal flats.

Six- to 9-weight rods work well. They make fast runs and most often work free from any hook. Any fly reel with a smooth drag and 150 feet of backing will work for ladyfish. If you locate a group of ladyfish, downsize your tackle to a 6-weight for some real fun.

Fly hooks should be very sharp. Check the hook point for sharpness by running it down your thumbnail. It should dig in instead of gliding smoothly down the nail. Ladyfish mouths are very tough so use a strong leader of at least 15-pound test. Ladyfish are not leader shy.

Flies attracting ladyfish include Clouser Minnows, Bend Backs, and Lefty's Deceivers. Pink is a favorite color of ladyfish and any fly tied in pink will not be refused. The Scates' Hot Butt Bend Back is an excellent fly for this fish.

Light tackle: Tactics, Techniques, and Tackle

Ladyfish hit soft plastics on jigheads, hard-bodied lures like a Mirrolure, and live shrimp.

Normal casting and spinning tackle works great for ladyfish. Use 10- to 12-pound monofilament and a 12- to 24-inch leader of 15-pound fluorocarbon. Ladyfish have rough mouths and will quickly abrade any leader. Check the leader after each fish and replace as needed.

Season

Ladyfish first appear in the early summer and stick around until the first cool weather. Large schools can be seen cruising and chasing needlefish in August and early September.

CREVALLE JACK

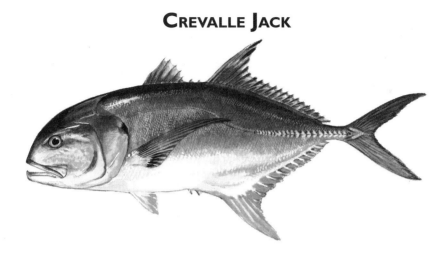

Crevalle jack, or simply jacks, are probably the strongest of the fish found in inshore waters. Seasoned speckled trout anglers hate jacks because they fight hard, make long runs, and often ruin any lure or tackle used in hooking them. Flyfishers love jacks for the exact same reasons. If you want to get someone hooked on inshore fishing, connect him or her with a jack and they'll want more.

Jacks have a dark spot on each side on their gill covers, making them easy to identify. They also have a dark spot on their pectoral fins, a dark gray back, and often a bright yellow area on their belly.

Texas jacks run large with most being over 12 pounds, and the larger specimens exceeding 44 inches in length. They are strong pulling fish and will test any tackle.

The current state record is over 50 pounds. Anglers new to this fish will think they have a record when they hook a 20 pounder.

Habitat

Jacks show up in April or May and leave the coastal waters once the water temperature gets cold, usually in late November or early December. Anglers can find them near openings to the gulf, such as around jetties and natural passes. In the fall, they cruise along flats right at the drop-off chasing baitfish up into the shallows. Jacks often run in small groups of three or four fish. They will school up anywhere there is a strong current pushing prey fish. Jacks run the prey fish into the strong current and aggressively work the balled-up school.

Flyfishing: Tactics, Techniques, and Tackle

Jacks are strong fish. Fly tackle used to pursue jacks should also be strong. Nine- to 12- weight rods give the flyfisher the ability to strongly pull against a jack. Once a jack feels the pull of the line, they pull away horizontally from the angler.

Leaders are critical when using fly tackle for jacks. I like to use the butt sections from old 0X leaders and tie on a 4-foot tippet made of 60- to 80-pound monofilament.

The leader should be 4 feet long and no shorter. Once a jack is hooked, other jacks will slice at the fly in the hooked jack's mouth trying to get the fly. This slicing motion is what cuts leaders. A short 18- to 36-inch leader will be quickly cut. Flyfishers should check the leader and tippet after each encounter with a jack.

Reels need to have smooth drags and at least 200 feet of backing. Jacks will often make runs of over 100 feet before giving at all. They will make more runs until they start to tire and that's when the real work starts.

Try to get back short amounts of line with each working of the rod. Steady pressure works best. Fight the jack with the butt section of the rod not the tip. Pull back and pick up 3 to 4 feet of line, reeling quickly when moving the rod forward.

By the time you get the jack to hand, you and the fish will be tired. Use a large landing net and keep the fish in the water if at all possible. After removing the fly, hold the jack by the tail and work it back and forth to help flush water across its gills. Watch the flutes on the tail. They're sharp and will cut your hand if not gripped properly. Using some type of glove will help.

Jacks are most often encountered when fishing from a boat in one of the natural passes or manmade openings to the gulf. Watch for bird activity early in the morning. Jacks force needlefish, menhaden, and shrimp to the surface and the birds soon see the activity. Make a cast right into the disturbance and quickly get control of the line. A stripping basket helps when chasing jacks as does the two-handed retrieve often used by bluefish and striper anglers in the northeast.

Jacks are also found chasing prey fish in the bay. They usually force the prey fish around some type of structure like an oyster reef or a drop-off along a flat. Single jacks can be found cruising along where the water drops from 18 inches deep to 4 or 5 feet deep.

Fortunately for flyfishers, they'll hit almost any fly that gets in front of them. Large Deceivers, very large Clouser Minnows, large poppers, and large Crease Flies all work well. The Stearns Pinfish is one of my favorite patterns to throw at jacks.

Light tackle: Tactics, Techniques, and Tackle

Casting and spinning tackle work great when going after jacks. They'll hit almost any lure, including large topwater poppers and large metal spoons. The larger fish will most often hit a sinking lure while under the smaller fish on the surface. Running line should be 15- to 20-pound test with a 4-foot leader of 60- to 80-pound test mono or fluorocarbon. Attach the leader to the running line using a triple surgeon's knot. Learn this knot, because if you're jack fishing you'll need to tie it often.

Use a large landing net as described above to help control the fish while removing the hook. Lures with single hooks are much easier to remove than treble hooks, so consider replacing large treble hooks with a single hook.

Season

Jacks show up with the warm water. The water temperature needs to be at least 72 degrees for jack activity. They stay in or near the bays until the cool water of winter arrives.

TARPON

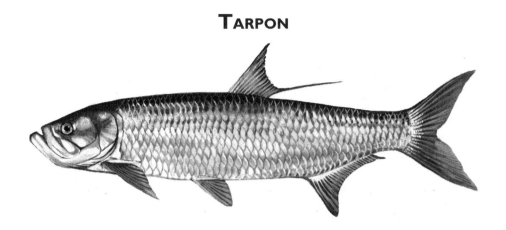

Everyone wants to catch a tarpon. The silver king was once plentiful along the Texas coast; so much so one town was actually named Tarpon. Texas had large tarpon rodeos with numerous boats seeking the silver king. People came from all over the world to fish for Texas tarpon. Even President Franklin Roosevelt made a tarpon trip to Texas in the 1930s.

Local fishing legends like Barney Farley and Hart Stilwell shared numerous stories of Texas tarpon with the public, and Stilwell regularly wrote about catching tarpon along the Texas coast. One of his favorite areas was the mouth of the Rio Grande River, where he caught tarpon both in the river and at its mouth as it entered the Gulf of Mexico. Unfortunately, today the Rio Grande just barely flows into the Gulf of Mexico. Water usage upstream catches almost all of the water that once flowed into the gulf and provided tarpon with the freshwater source they desire. Over harvesting, nets along the Mexican shoreline, and other factors led to a drastic decline of tarpon during the 1950s and 1960s.

Today, with well-enforced regulations, tarpon are starting to make a comeback along the Texas coast. Any tarpon caught should be released regardless of the law. If freshwater inflows can be ensured, Texas tarpon will be around for the foreseeable future.

Habitat

Tarpon show up along the Texas coast in the spring and stay until the water cools down. They are most often found along the natural passes and around manmade jetties and piers. The Padre Island National Seashore is another location that has a regular population of tarpon.

Prey

Mullet are one of the prime food sources of tarpon. They will also eat almost any type of prey fish, including small ladyfish and needlefish. Tarpon also eat crabs and shrimp.

Flyfishing: Tactics, Techniques, and Tackle

If a flyfisher gets serious about catching a tarpon on fly tackle, the best thing they can do is hire one of the guides that are now specializing in tarpon fishing. These guides have the tackle, know the area and how to help the angler succeed.

Classic tarpon patterns, including the Cockroach and Stu Apte's Tarpon Fly, work well. Hooks must be very sharp if the angler is to have any chance of landing a tarpon.

Rod weights of 12 and above work best for tarpon. The pulling strength of these rods is more important than anything. Rods with a front fighting grip will help land the big ones.

The reel needs to have at least 300 feet of backing capacity. The initial run of the tarpon is everything you've read about. Learning to bow or give slack to the line once a tarpon jumps is very important. So is maintaining control of your line and a dozen other things that happen at the same time. Don't expect to bring the first tarpon you hook to hand. They are spectacular fighters and a treasure that deserves to be released.

Light Tackle: Tactics, Techniques, and tackle

Light tackle users most often fish for tarpon with a large mullet for bait, but large lipless diving lures, casting plugs, and spoons are also effective. Tarpon frequent the waters right off the gulf beach in several areas along the Texas coast.

Running line of 20-pound test or stronger works well for tarpon. Use a strong leader of at least 60-pound test. If you're using natural bait, large circle hooks (size 13 and larger) are required.

Special tarpon lures like the Coon Pop consistently catch tarpon. Again for anyone wanting to catch a tarpon, hiring a guide is money well spent.

Season

Tarpon show up sometime in April and stay around until the water starts to cool down. The best activity is during the hot part of the summer.

SPANISH MACKEREL

Spanish mackerel, or just Spanish, are another great fighter available along the Texas coast. Most Spanish will be less than 5 pounds, but occasionally a larger fish is possible. Spanish mackerel are part of the mackerel family and pull just like their bigger cousins, king mackerel.

Spanish are beautiful fish with a rainbow of colors running along their backs and have numerous gold colored spots covering their sides. They have very sharp teeth, so handle them carefully. Using a Boga Grip or similar fish-controlling device when removing the hook is a good idea.

Habitat

Spanish mackerel show up along the Texas coast once the water warms up. They are most often encountered in large schools while chasing prey. They are aggressive feeders and hit almost any fly or lure. They will shy from a heavy wire leader and will quickly cut off any monofilament that is too small. They are powerful swimmers and will test both tackle and angler. The surf along the Padre Island National Seashore is a great place to encounter Spanish mackerel.

Prey

Spanish mackerel feed on prey fish and sometimes squid.

Flyfishing: Tactics, Techniques, and Tackle

There are two primary methods flyfishers can use to catch Spanish mackerel: fishing from a boat chasing a school, or catching them in the surf. Large schools show up once the water warms. Early morning through mid-day seems to be the best time to target Spanish.

Schools of Spanish mackerel slashing through a school of prey fish are often sited along the surf. When the wind lays, Spanish can be targeted in surf areas like the Big Shell area of the Padre Island National Seashore.

Deceivers, Clousers, and Bend Backs are all good flies for Spanish. Flies with chartreuse or chartreuse and white attract them. Use either a short small wire leader or preferably a short section of strong fluorocarbon. Spanish have very sharp teeth and quickly cut most monofilament running lines. Flies tied on Kahle or circle hooks will help flyfishers catch Spanish mackerel and avoid their very sharp teeth. The hook needs to be very sharp.

Flyfishers should use a stripping basket when fishing for Spanish mackerel. Also try using the two-handed retrieve with your rod tucked under your casting arm to increase the fly retrieval speed. Spanish mackerel like fast moving targets and the single-strip retrieve is often not fast enough.

Light Tackle: Tactics, Techniques, and Tackle

Light spinning and casting tackle used to catch speckled trout is also good for Spanish mackerel. Lightweight silver spoons, jigheads with soft plastics, and hard-bodied lures will work, using a short metal or fluorocarbon leader. They have very sharp teeth and quickly cut lightweight running lines used by light tackle anglers.

Spanish mackerel will hit natural shrimp, but they hit small silver spoons so well that natural bait is really not required. Plan on losing several lures when chasing Spanish mackerel. Learn how to quickly tie connecting knots used to attach leader sections. The key to catching Spanish mackerel is to stay in the game with your lure in the water. It is not a bad idea to have several outfits rigged when chasing Spanish mackerel, so you can quickly change to another outfit once a lure is lost.

Cast to the edge of any school seen on the surface, and retrieve the lure as fast as you can. Spanish are accustomed to going after fleeing prey, so you can't work the lure too fast. Try to pull any hooked fish away from the main school to avoid another fish cutting your line above the leader section.

Season

Spanish mackerel arrive with the warm weather and leave once the water starts cooling down.

GAFFTOPSAIL CATFISH

Gafftopsail catfish are true game fish that are plentiful along the Texas coast. A large gafftop puts up a great fight. Look for the large, sail-like dorsal fin to distinguish them from their less-popular cousin, the hardhead catfish. Gafftops are often called tourist trout because they show up about the same time the tourist start thinking about going to the coast. They are also one of the first fish to show up after a cold winter and signal the arrival of other more sought after fish.

Gafftops have a dark blue back and grow up to 8 pounds along the Texas coast.

Habitat

Found in almost all coastal waters, the gafftopsail catfish is most at home on or near the bottom. Deep channels, guts, and the Intracoastal Waterways are likely locations, but you can also find them with a school of tailing redfish on a shallow-water flat. When you locate a spot that consistently has gafftopsail catfish remember it. These fish are tough fighters and are a great source of action for the kids.

As with any catfish, anglers need to handle these fish with caution. They have a protective slime on their skin making them hard to grasp, so use a net if you have one. The ends of the spines are very sharp and cause a sharp pain if they pierce the skin. If you get stuck, try rubbing a little of the fish's slime on the spot. It will often neutralize the pain. Once you get back to the boat or shore, clean the wound and dress it with antibiotic ointment.

Prey

Gafftopsail catfish will hit almost any natural bait including shrimp and small pinfish.

Flyfishing: Tactics, Techniques, and Tackle

Flyfishers should use sinking lines and very slow retrieves when going after gafftopsail catfish. Shrimp patterns and chartreuse-and-white Clousers will entice these whiskered fish to hit. Try using a strike indicator with a fly several feet below to entice these fish to hit. They put up a good fight once hooked.

Light Tackle: Tactics, Techniques, and Tackle

Live shrimp is the bait of choice for gafftopsail catfish. They will also hit cutbait and occasionally silver spoons. Use a Kahle hook and a couple of split shot weights. Gafftopsail catfish usually hit the bait and move, unlike their cousin the hardhead.

Season

Warm weather months, March through September, are the best times to catch these catfish.

Snook

Snook are becoming more plentiful along the Texas coast. Until recent years, the Texas snook population was found mainly in far south Texas. Now snook are found along the entire Texas coast from Port Isabel to Beaumont. The existing Texas snook record is actually larger than the current world record. That 50-plus-pound monster was caught just south of Corpus Christi in the 1950s.

Seasoned anglers often referred to snook as pike, due to the pike-like head and mouth. The long lateral line down the side of the fish helps with identification. Anglers are best served by releasing all snook caught in Texas.

Habitat

Snook like to be around something. Old pilings, water discharge pipes, fence lines, jetty rocks, or any type of obstruction in the water can hold snook. Snook are able to handle very fresh water and will not be far from freshwater most of their lives.

Prey

Snook eat shrimp, crabs, and small baitfish.

Flyfishing: Tactics, Techniques, and Tackle

Flyfishers have the best chance of catching snook in the Brownsville Ship Channel. Dahlberg Divers and Snookeroos are two flies that will attract their attention, and shrimp patterns will also work. A solid white popper works well for a topwater offering. Keep the fly moving because snook like to eat moving targets.

Eight- or 9-weight rods are recommended. Snook are powerful fighters so use a leader of at least 15-pound test. Reels used to catch redfish and speckled trout will also work for snook.

Light Tackle: Tactics, Techniques, and Tackle

Spinning or casting tackle used for speckled trout also works with snook. Use a strong leader of at least 15 pounds, and soft plastic paddletail minnows in white with gold fleck or white with silver fleck work well. Large Mirrolures, Bomber Long A, or Redfins will also take snook as will silver spoons.

Season

Snook prefer warm weather so anglers will find snook in Texas primarily during the warmest months. The snook population in far south Texas is active most of the year, except during unusually cold weather in January and February.

FLORIDA POMPANO

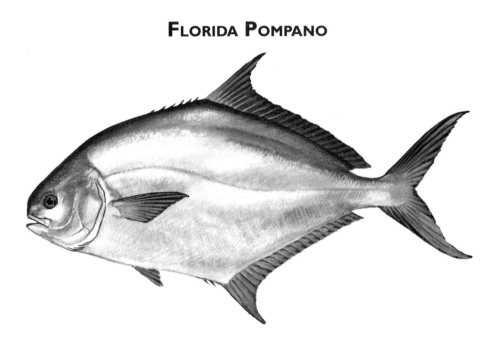

Florida Pompano are sometimes confused with permit. They have the same basic body shape, but there are no permit in Texas. Most Texas anglers associate pompano with the surf but they are also caught inside the bays. Pompano, cousins to jacks and permit, are strong pulling fish and have all of the stamina their larger cousins are known for. They're a lot of fun on fly and light tackle.

Pompano have a forked tail and often have yellow on their belly. Most Texas pompano will not exceed 4 pounds.

Habitat

Pompano are most often taken in the surf in Texas. They will also cruise waters around natural and man-made entrances to the Gulf of Mexico, near oil well footings and pilings. If you find one pompano, you will often find another because they seem to run in pairs.

Prey

Small shrimp, mollusks, and crabs are primary food sources.

Flyfishing: Tactics, Techniques, and Tackle

Pompano in the bays are found in deep water, usually over 4 feet deep, so a sinking line will help get the offering down to the fish. Shrimp, small crabs, and baitfish patterns work best. Try to run the fly right down on the bottom and work a very slow retrieve for best results. Try to imitate the slow movement of a small shrimp or crab, keeping the fly close to the bottom at all times. Fish the surf for pompano with a sinking line and the same flies used in the bays.

Light Tackle: Tactics, Techniques, and Tackle

Small live shrimp and crabs are the best natural bait to catch pompano, using the same rig as used for speckled trout. Reels need a smooth drag because even a hard pulling 2-pound pompano is enough to test your tackle.

Season

Late spring through early fall is when you'll find pompano along the Texas coast.

TRIPLETAIL

Tripletail are large flat-sided fish with extended fins that make them look like they have three tails. They are most often dark gray or brown in color. They are not overly abundant in Texas but some areas do have sizeable populations. They are wary predators that will often slip away with any disturbance.

Habitat

Tripletail are most often seen around floating debris, footings of large oil wells, and old pilings, and they like any shaded area. Floating tripletail are often mistaken for a piece of trash or a leaf floating near something else. The lifeless floating object suddenly comes alive when a live shrimp or shrimp fly is placed near the tripletail. These are strong fish well worth any effort and time spent pursuing them.

Prey

Shrimp and small fish are primary food sources.

Flyfishing: Tactics, Techniques, and Tackle

Strong leaders are called for when targeting tripletail. Most of the fish flycasters pursue will be located around some structure such as oil well footings or crab trap floats. Fly tackle should be strong enough to quickly pull the fish away from any object.

Shrimp and small baitfish flies will entice tripletail. Flycasters need to be able to get the fly close to the target or tripletail will simply ignore the offering. Try to work with the current and place the fly where the water will help move the fly in close to the fish.

Light Tackle: Tactics, Techniques, and Tackle

Light tackle should include a strong leader section of 15- to 20-pound test line to assist in pulling tripletail away from any obstruction they float near. Cast close to the fish but not so close that you spook them.

Season

Warm-weather months.

Sand Trout

Sand trout are very similar to speckled trout but without the spots. They have silvery sides and the same basic body shape as speckled trout. Sand trout found in Texas are usually small with most not reaching the speckled trout's minimum size requirement of 15 inches. They do not pull as hard as speckled trout.

Habitat

Sand seatrout or sand trout are most often associated with large bays and areas with quick access to the Gulf of Mexico. They are sometimes caught when fishing for speckled trout.

The current state record sand trout is just over 6 pounds, caught in the Galveston Bay complex.

Prey

Shrimp and small fish are primary food sources. Sand trout will also eat small crabs.

Flyfishing: Tactics, Techniques, and Tackle

Flyfishers will encounter sand trout while fishing for speckled trout. Use a sinking line with a shrimp or small baitfish pattern. Work the deeper water found in guts and near passes.

Light Tackle: Tactics, Techniques, and Tackle

Light tackle is ideal for catching sand trout — the same tackle used to catch speckled trout. Jigheads with soft plastic tails and live shrimp are the best tackle choices for catching these fish.

Season

Summer months into early fall is when sand trout appear along the Texas coast.

Southern Kingfish or Whiting

Southern kingfish, or more commonly known as whiting in Texas, have a single barbell on the bottom side of the head that helps distinguish them from other fish. They are silvery-gray in color and often have faint stripes on the side. Most whiting weigh less than a pound.

Habitat

Whiting inhabit the same waters as speckled trout. They do not go into shallow waters where anglers find tailing redfish, but the nearby deeper water is a potential location for whiting. They are found in bays near gulf openings. They will most often be encountered while fishing for speckled trout.

Prey

They eat small crustaceans and worms near the bottom.

Flyfishing: Tactics, Techniques, and Tackle

Flyfishers will encounter whiting while fishing for other species. A shrimp imitation used with a sinking line is the best chance for catching a whiting on fly tackle. They have an inferior mouth similar to a redfish, so any fly needs to be small.

Light Tackle: Tactics, Techniques, and Tackle

Live and dead shrimp are primary natural baits for whiting, and they are most often caught while fishing for the big three. They have a soft take but put up a good fight once hooked.

Season

Whiting are most often caught during the warm spring and summer months.

Other Species Found Inshore or Near Inshore Waters

Bonito or Little Tunny

Bonito or little tunny are often found while attacking schools of small baitfish near natural and man-made passes entering the Gulf of Mexico. These fish are strong fighters and will give any flyfisher or light tackle angler plenty to deal with. Small baitfish flies and spoons will catch these little rockets.

Cobia or Ling

Cobia, or ling as they are most often called in Texas, are usually found cruising large jetties feeding into the Gulf of Mexico. During most late summers, blue gulf waters come near or through the jetties, and that is when you'll find ling near shore. Their predominant lower jaw and dusky brown color help identify these strong fish.

Offshore Species

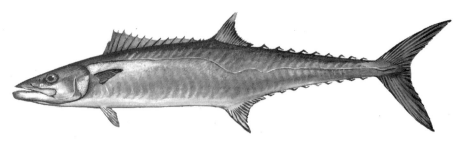

- King Mackerel or Kingfish
- Dolphin
- Bluefish
- Striped Bass

Traditional offshore species like king mackerel and dolphin are found in offshore Texas waters, and are occasionally found in near-shore waters in the warmest months.

Texas has a population of bluefish but these fish are usually very small, often less than 10 inches long. Anglers will most often encounter bluefish by accident and will more likely not be prepared when these toothy fish strike. They are usually found in small schools in areas near gulf entrances, where anglers seek speckled trout.

Striped bass in coastal Texas waters are fish that have made it through freshwater lakes and into the river systems feeding Texas bays. Striped bass are occasionally found in the Sabine Lake and Trinity Bay areas.

All of these fish would be considered accidental catches along the Texas coast and any angler landing one of these fish on fly or light tackle should consider themselves lucky.

A Word About Sharks

I have an agreement with sharks. I don't fish for them and they don't fish for me. Leave the sharks alone. If you get into an area where sharks are taking your catch either on the line or from a stringer, MOVE. Let the sharks have the water. There are plenty of places to fish without having to deal with sharks.

Forage Species

If you want to understand fish, understand what they eat. If there's no food around, there will likely not be any fish around either. Find the food and you'll find the fish.

Texas coastal fish have many different food forms to choose from. Imitate the characteristics of the food and you'll attract fish. Most forage species are prevalent only part of the year and fish target those species when they are most abundant.

SHRIMP

In Texas there are three different groups of shrimp. Each has a definite place it likes to inhabit and a definite time of year when it is prevalent. If you believe in reincarnation you don't want to come back as a shrimp because everything — fish, birds and people — eat shrimp.

Grass Shrimp

The grass shrimp is the predominant shrimp found in Texas bays and estuaries. Grass shrimp in shallow waters are usually about 1 inch long with the largest specimens growing to under 3 inches. They start out life in heavy grass for cover until they mature. This is the little shrimp you see fleeing when redfish are rooting around grassy shorelines.

Grass shrimp are most often colored to blend into their surroundings. They can range from light tan, to dark brown, to olive. These shrimp are around all year long. Go with a nighttime commercial flounder fisherman and see what the lights reveal. You'll see lots of shrimp with eyes that glow.

Flies imitating grass shrimp need to be small, less than 1 1/2 inches long. Try to match the color of the bottom in the area you're fishing to properly imitate the local grass shrimp.

Brown, White, and Pink Swimming Shrimp

This group of shrimp is called penaeid or swimming shrimp. Brown shrimp are the most abundant shrimp along the Texas coast, and white shrimp are the big shrimp found at bait houses and on your dinner table. These shrimp can grow to over 10 inches in length and are often too large to be effective bait.

If you fish shrimp long enough you will eventually see a really large trout swirl on a shrimp-baited hook. Big trout don't like to chase a big shrimp and they will often give up the hunt to an overly actively large shrimp.

Snapping or Pistol Shrimp

The third group of shrimp is the snapping shrimp. These are small shrimp, most often just over one inch in length, that look like small crawfish. The snapping shrimp has one oversized claw. They are most often found around oyster shells, and they make a click, which gives them their name.

CRAB

Blue Crab

The blue crab is a very important part of the food chain in Texas coastal waters. Using the estuaries as a nursery, the female carries a large group or sponge of baby crabs under her belly.

Small blue crabs are eaten by almost all of the game fish species along the Texas coast. Redfish and black drum particularly like blue crab. They are often seen scampering out of the way of waders along long coastal flats.

Mud Crab

Mud crabs are found in shallow waters preferred by redfish. These small crabs are usually a dark olive color and less than one inch wide. When the redfish are eating mud crab they will ignore almost everything else.

FINFISH

Gulf Menhaden

One of the important forage fish species, menhaden can grow to over 8 inches in Texas waters. They have a series of spots down their sides including a large spot just behind their gill plate. The largest specimens will approach 10 inches in length.

Sheepshead Killifish

Sheepshead killifish are shallow-water fish. Flounder really love to eat this little fish, but a redfish or speckled trout will eat them too. They are often referred to as mud minnows. Other similar species are the gulf killifish and the long nose killifish.

Atlantic Needlefish

Needlefish often nip at the tails of multi-colored soft plastic lures used by light tackle casters. If you feel a strike but set the hook into nothing, a needlefish probably nipped your lure.

Needlefish often school, so when you find one you'll probably find several. If you continue to get strikes from needlefish you might want to move, because needlefish will stay in areas as long as predator fish aren't present.

Spanish mackerel like to chase schools of needlefish, as do jacks.

Striped Mullet

Mullet are everywhere along the Texas coast. Large schools are seen in the bays, lazily swimming along until disturbed. Mullet cruise grassy shorelines and are often seen by the hundreds around manmade jetties.

Texas mullet range from just a couple of inches, often called finger mullet, to fish over 18 inches in length. Specimens are reported to 30 inches. The current record fly-caught mullet is just over 7 pounds and was over 24 inches long.

They eat plankton and are often seen mouthing grass stems along the shoreline. Many beginner coastal flyfishers have cast to mullet thinking they were redfish. Their dorsal fin is almost clear, helping to distinguish them from reds.

Mullet are often seen making a series of jumps. Watch any fish you see jumping. If the fish landing back into the water is followed by a big swirl, that mullet was just attacked, probably by a big speckled trout.

Pigfish

Pigfish, or piggy perch, are one of the primary food sources available to Texas coastal game fish. Pigfish are colorful fish and grow to over 14 inches, but most are much smaller. Young piggy perch are found throughout the bays with the larger adults spawning in the gulf.

Pigfish are not as abundant as pinfish along the Texas coast.

Pinfish

Pinfish are common in the bays of Texas, and have very sharp dorsal spines and a single dark spot on their sides located back behind the eyes. Most pinfish will be only a couple of inches long, with mature fish growing up to 8 inches in length.

Pinfish will eat almost any food offering and are notorious bait stealers. Toss a hooked piece of shrimp near any fish cleaning station along the coast and you'll catch pinfish.

Bay Anchovy

Bay anchovy have a light tan or brown back with a pronounced silver side stripe. The body is translucent. Most examples are less than 3 inches long.

Atlantic Croaker

The Atlantic croaker has gained a great following in recent years. Sometimes referred to as a golden croaker, they resemble a small redfish without the large tail spot. Most will be a silvery color with an inferior mouth just like the redfish. Croakers are one of the most important fish in Texas coastal waters.

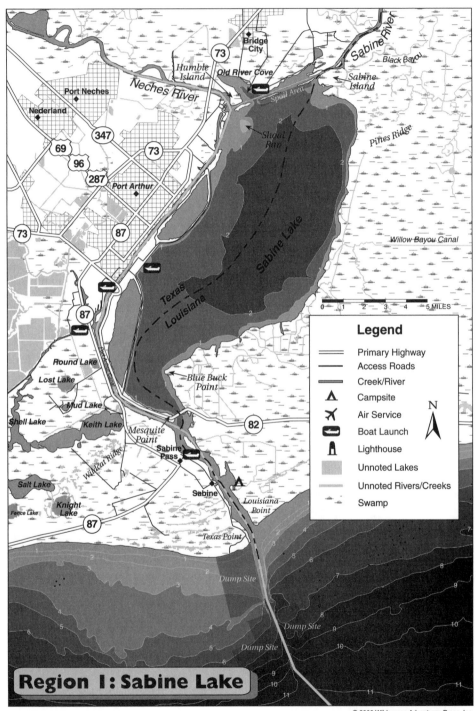

Legend

═══	Primary Highway
────	Access Roads
══════	Creek/River
Λ	Campsite
✈	Air Service
🛥	Boat Launch
🏛	Lighthouse
▨	Unnoted Lakes
────	Unnoted Rivers/Creeks
╌╌╌	Swamp

Region 1: Sabine Lake

Region 1: Sabine Lake

Sabine Lake is on the border of Texas and Louisiana. The Sabine and Neches Rivers flow into the north part of the lake. The lake empties into the Gulf of Mexico at Sabine Pass.

The Sabine Lake Region receives the greatest amount of rainfall of any region in Texas. Annual rainfall in this region is almost twice what the southern part of the Texas coast receives. The Sabine Lake Region is also muddier than the rest of the coast.

Sabine Lake is known as the place to fish for flounder in Texas. The state record flounder weighing 13 pounds came from Sabine Lake.

Anglers holding a valid Texas or Louisiana fishing license can legally fish the waters bordering the two states. However, if you go ashore in Louisiana you will need a Louisiana fishing license.

Highway 87 runs along the Port Arthur Ship Channel. There are numerous petrochemical plants including a large refinery located along Highway 87. Traffic entering and leaving these plants may slow your driving time if you're going to Sabine Pass, so allow extra time.

Seasonal Fishing Chart - Region 1: Sabine Lake

	Jan	Feb	Mar	Apr	May	Jun	Jul	Aug	Sep	Oct	Nov	Dec
Redfish	+	+	++	+++	+++	+++	+++	+++	+++	+++	++	++
Spotted Seatrout	+	++	++	+++	+++	+++	+++	+++	+++	++	++	+
Flounder			+	++	+++	+++	+++	+++	+++	+++	+++	+
Black Drum	+	+++	+++	+++	+++	+++	+++	+++	+++	++	++	+
Sheepshead	+	+++	+++	+++	+++	+++	+++	+++	+++	++	++	+
Crevalle Jack				++	+++	+++	+++	+++	+++	+		
Spanish Mackerel						++	+++	+++	+++			
Gray Snapper						++	+++	+++				
Tarpon						+	+	+				
Pompano				+	+	+	+	+				
Snook												

+++ = Exceptional, ++ = Very Good, + = Available

SABINE RIVER

The Sabine River starts out in northeast Texas and runs south along the border between Texas and Louisiana. Heavy spring rains cause the Sabine to run high and dirty. The river enters Toledo Bend Reservoir south of Carthage and enters Sabine Lake near Bridge City.

Anglers may encounter striped bass or stripers when fishing the river in the winter. The Sabine River and the Trinity River at nearby Trinity Bay are the only two places on the Texas coast where anglers might catch stripers.

Fish the Sabine River for redfish and speckled trout during the cold winter months before the heavy spring rains start.

NECHES RIVER

The Neches River flows from south of Sulphur Springs through the Big Thicket, east of Beaumont and into Sabine Lake. The Neches River brings more silt into Sabine Lake than does the Sabine River. Springtime rains bring freshwater to the coast through the Neches and heavy spring rains can result in a fresh Sabine Lake and poor fishing conditions. The rain tapers off in June and the region gets better as summer progresses.

Fish the mouth of the Neches River in the winter for redfish and speckled trout.

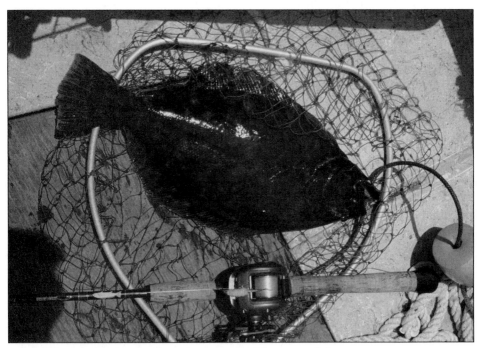

When fishing Sabine Lake, flounder are one of the target fish.

SABINE LAKE

Sabine Lake is the smallest Texas Bay. Sabine Lake is most often fished drifting from a boat as the bottom is often hard to wade. The east side of Sabine Lake is lined with shore grasses and almost no development. The west side of the lake has many petrochemical plants and most of the shoreline is lined with concrete bulkheads.

Fish Sabine Lake drifting from a boat. Oyster shells are scattered over the bottom along the east shore of the lake. Cast parallel to the shore using topwater lures or bait under a popping cork. Fly casters can try small poppers, Bend Backs, or other baitfish imitations. Once you find fish, ease over the anchor and thoroughly work the area.

One fishing technique often used on Sabine Lake is a Carolina rig. Most freshwater bass fishers will be familiar with this method with an egg-shaped weight held in place by a swivel about 2 feet above a soft plastic worm. Sabine Lake fishers often use long, motor oil-colored worms. Cast out the lure and then drift with the egg weight running across the bottom and the worm rising above the bottom.

One fishing guide said about Sabine Lake, "If you see a gull on Sabine, fish it!". That's pretty good advice. If you see birds hovering over the water or diving into bait on the surface, fish the activity. To keep from spooking the fish, try drifting into the location instead of motoring right into the birds. Also look for slicks on the water's surface. Fish the upwind side of the slick for speckled trout.

Fly casters should try sinking flies like a Clouser Minnow with a sink-tip line around the birds or slicks. Jigheads with soft plastics also work well.

KEITH LAKE

Keith Lake is connected to the Port Arthur Ship Channel by a cut at the east end of the lake. Highway 87 runs along the eastern side of Keith Lake. There are often many anglers fishing the cut from the shoreline and parking area next to the cut. The surrounding area is part of Sea Rim State Park and McFadden Marsh National Wildlife Refuge.

Keith Lake is the first in a chain of lakes that run west from the Port Arthur Channel, joining Johnson Lake to the west. Then Shell Lake, Mud Lake, and Salt Lake stretch to the west from Johnson Lake. All of these lakes are connected.

This is a good place to flyfish for redfish. Fish the shallows with a Foxy Clouser or Bend Back. Also, use fly rod poppers to catch redfish in the mouths of the cuts during an outgoing tide. Light tackle casters should use 1/8-ounce weedless gold spoons and 1/16-ounce jigheads with soft plastics.

Look along the shallow grassy shorelines for redfish. Fish the mouth of the cut during tidal movements using live bait or jigheads with soft plastics. Anglers can also expect to catch flounder while fishing Keith Lake.

There is a small public boat ramp with limited parking located at the Highway 87-Keith Lake intersection. This ramp is for launching small boats only. Be careful when entering or leaving the parking area. The road curves near the parking area and it is difficult to see oncoming traffic around the curve, especially during the busy shift changes at the nearby petrochemical plants.

A paved, private ramp big enough for larger boats is located on the east edge of Keith Lake. There is a small fee for using this ramp.

Pleasure Island

Pleasure Island is a long island bordered by the Port Arthur Ship Channel and the Sabine–Neches Canal, making the western boundary of Sabine Lake. Large ships regularly travel the channels. The MLK, Jr. Causeway connects Port Arthur and Highway 82 east to Pleasure Island.

Two large spoil areas can be found on the eastern side of Pleasure Island. These spoil areas are bordered to the east by a deep ditch. Fish the ditch during very hot or cold weather.

The shoreline of Pleasure Island is lined with large rocks where anglers can fish. There are also two short fishing piers located along the east side of the island.

To the north of Highway 82 is the Pleasure Island RV Park. A bait camp is located at the park entrance.

Boat Ramps

Parrothead Marina, 901 T.B. Ellison Parkway / 409-982-2811
JEP's Emporium Boat Ramp, Pleasure Island / 409-983-3822 (gas and bait)
Pleasure Island RV Park, 540 South Spoil Levee Rd / 409-982-6368

Mesquite Point

Mesquite Point is located at the far southern end of Pleasure Island. Waters from the Port Arthur Ship Channel and Sabine Lake come together at Mesquite Point. Highway 82 crosses the Sabine Pass Causeway at Mesquite Point.

There is a paved public boat ramp at Mesquite Point, but parking is limited. Across Highway 82 is the Walter Umphrey State Park and RV Park. The park is managed by Jefferson County. Currently, there is road construction in the Mesquite Point area due to Hurricane Rita so be cautious of the traffic in the area.

Boat Ramp

Walter Umphrey State Park / 409-736-2851

Sabine Pass, Texas Point, and West Jetty

Sabine Pass connects Sabine Lake with the Gulf of Mexico. The Port Arthur Ship Channel runs through Sabine Pass. Anglers with boats can fish the West Jetty rocks for redfish, speckled trout and sheepshead. Flounder are also found along the jetty rocks. Fishers can wade along the Texas Point surf, west of the jetty.

Anglers need to be aware of the large ships that use the pass to reach docks farther inland. These ships make big waves, so be sure to anchor far enough away from the jetty rocks to allow for the wave movement of the boat.

Fish Sabine Pass for black drum in the early spring with live crabs or crab pieces. Remove the claws and use a large circle hook with a sliding spider weight. Work the jetty with light-weighted jigheads or light flies. Cast parallel to the jetty and be sure to cast into any gaps or spaces in the jetty rocks. Anglers can also cast flies and topwater lures right next to the jetty rocks for redfish and speckled trout. Fish Sabine Pass during the colder months when fish seek out the warmth of deeper waters.

Fish the shallows around the spoil islands inside the pass for redfish and flounder.

Amenities

Boat ramp at end of Broadway Street
Sabine Pass Motel, 5623 Greenwich St / 409-971-2200
Sportsman's Supply, 5310 S Gulfway Dr / 409-971-2535, gas, tackle and bait
Lighthouse Deli, 5140 Gulfway Dr / 409-971-9166
Tammie's Olde Tyme Diner, 5404 S. Gulfway Dr / 409-971-2573
Drop on in RV Park, 5241 Greenwich St / 409-971-0191
Stay-A-While II RV Park, 4901 Broadway / 409-728-3981

Large black drum are caught in Sabine Pass during the early spring.

SEA RIM STATE PARK

Sea Rim State Park, located south of Port Arthur, suffered severe damage during Hurricane Rita. The park, about 10 miles west of Sabine Pass, is currently closed for reconstruction. The park phone has a message about the park's operations and potential re-opening. Call before venturing to Sea Rim State Park (409-971-2559).

Sea Rim State Park includes over 4,000 acres of marshland and more than 5 miles of beach along the Gulf of Mexico. A large portion of the park is covered with water. Fish the shallow areas for redfish and flounder. Anglers can also access the surf from the park.

Keith Lake is an ideal place for using flies for redfish.

Sabine Lake Hub Cities

BEAUMONT
Population: 113,866
County: Jefferson

ACCOMMODATIONS

Best Western Jefferson Inn, 1610 I-10 South / 409-842-0037 / 119 rooms / $59-$89 / www.bestwesterntexas.com

Comfort Inn, 1590 South I-10 / 409-840-2099 / 52 rooms / $59-$209/ www.comfortinn.com

Days Inn, 2155 N 11th Street / 409-898-0078 / 152 rooms / $59-$89 / www.daysinn.com

Econo Lodge, 50 I-10 North / 409-835-8800 / 35 rooms / $60-$90 / www.econolodge.com

Holiday Inn, 3950 I-10 South / 409-842-5995 / 253 rooms / $109-$375 / www.holidayinn.com

Howard Johnson, 2615 I-10 East / 409-832-0666 / 42 rooms / $59-$89 / www.hojo.com

La Quinta, 220 I-10 North / 409-838-1266 / 122 rooms / $79-$109 / www.lq.com

CAMPGROUNDS

Gulf Coast RV Park, 5175 Brooks Rd / 409-842-2285 / www.gulfcoastrvresort.net

East Lucas RV Park, 2590 East Lucas / 800-280-2579 / www.eastlucasrvpark.com

Birdsong RV Park, 7209 Hensley Rd / 409-860-3290

RESTAURANTS

Black Eyed Pea, 6455 Phelan Blvd / 409-866-2617 / www.theblackeyepea.com

Chili's, 110 IH-10 / 409-832-1253 / www.chilis.com

Dairy Queen, 3755 College St / 409-838-4723 / www.dairyqueen.com

Fuddruckers, 4545 Dowlen Rd / 409-898-8973 / www.fuddruckers.com

Outback Steakhouse, 2060 IH-10 S / 409-842-6699 / www.outback.com

Waffle House, 3865 IH-10 S / 409-842-0860 / www.wafflehouse.com

Whataburger, 6930 College St / 409-866-2364 / www.whataburger.com

SPORTING GOODS

Gander Mountain, 5855 Eastex Freeway / 409-347-3055 / www.gandermountain.com

AIRPORT

Southeast Texas Regional Airport, 4875 Parker Dr / 409-722-0251

FOR MORE INFORMATION

Visit www.beaumontcvb.com

Orange

Population: 18,643
County: Orange

Accommodations

America's Best Value Inn, 2208 Lutcher Dr / 409-883-6701 / 72 rooms / $50-$65 /
www.bestvalueinn.com

Best Western, 2630 I-10 W / 409-883-6616 / 59 rooms / $59-$89 /
www.bestwesterntexas.com

Executive Inn & Suites, 4301 27th Street / 409-883-9981 / 50 rooms / $45-$60

Holiday Inn, 2655 I-10 East / 409-882-9111 / 73 rooms / $99-$149 /
www.holidayinn.com

Quality Inn & Suites, 2900 I-10 West / 409-988-0105 / 87 rooms / $56-$85 /
www.qualityinn.com

Ramada Inn, 2610 I-10 / 409-883-0231/ 100 rooms / $65-$90 / www.ramada.com

Super 8 Motel, 2710 I-10 West / 409-882-0888 / 50 rooms / $65-$95 /
www.super8.com

Campgrounds

Cypress Lake RV Park, 109 E Lutcher Dr / 800-241-6390 /
www.cypresslakervpark.com

Oak Leaf Park, 6900 Oak Leaf Dr / 409-886-4082

Restaurants

JB's Barbeque Restaurant, IH-10 W at US 90 Bus / 409-886-9823

McDonalds, 3000 W Cedar / 409-886-0641 / www.mcdonalds.com

Novrozsky's, 501 N 16th St / 409-988-0200 / www.novrozskys.com

Quizno's Subs, 175 Strickland Dr / 409-886-4681 / www.quiznos.com

Robert's Steakhouse, 3720 W Park Ave / 409-886-4507

Wendy's Hamburgers, 2205 S Hwy 62 / 409-745-2664 / www.wendys.com

For More Information

Orange Convention and Visitors Bureau
409-883-1011
www.orangetexas.org

PORT ARTHUR
Population: 57,755
County: Jefferson

ACCOMMODATIONS

Comfort Inn, 7800 Memorial Blvd / 409-729-0500 / 58 rooms / $55-$150 / www.comfortinn.com

Hampton Inn and Suites, 7660 Memorial Blvd / 409-722-6999 / 72 rooms / $85-$119 / www.hamptoninn.com

Holiday Inn, 2929 Jimmy Johnson Blvd / 409-724-5000 / 164 rooms / $99-$175 / www.holidayinn.com

La Quinta Inn, 5820 Walden Road / 409-842-0002 / 65 rooms / $69-$109 / www.lq.com

Ramada Port Arthur, 3801 Highway 73 / 409-962-9858 / 123 rooms / $75-$95 / www.ramada.com

CAMPGROUNDS

JEP's RV Park Pleasure Island, 1900 Martin Luther King Drive / 409-983-3822

RESTAURANTS

IHOP, 8685 Memorial Blvd / 409-721-6310 / www.ihop.com

Luby's Cafeteria, 8680 Memorial Blvd / 409-724-0043 / www.lubys.com

McAlisters Deli, 8393 Memorial Blvd / 409-729-3354 / www.mcalistersdeli.com

Tequilas Mexican Restaurant, 4231 Gulfway Dr / 409-983-7545

Texas Roadhouse, 8575 Memorial Blvd / 409-722-2246 / www.texasroadhouse.com

Waffle House, 2940 Jimmy Johnson Blvd / 409-724-2141 / www.wafflehouse.com

SPORTING GOODS

Academy Sports, 8453 Memorial Blvd / 409-723-6800 / www.academy.com

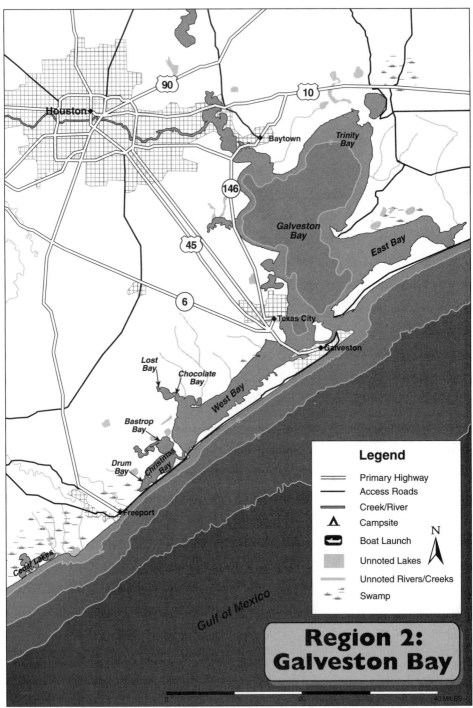

Legend

Primary Highway
Access Roads
Creek/River
△ Campsite
Boat Launch
Unnoted Lakes
Unnoted Rivers/Creeks
Swamp

N

Region 2:
Galveston Bay

© 2009 Wilderness Adventures Press, Inc.

Region 2: Galveston Bay

The Galveston Bay Region is dominated by Galveston Bay, which is Texas' second largest bay. This part of the Texas coast includes some of the first areas settled in the state. Natural passes and large bays provided a deep-water port for early explorers.

Many bays make up the Galveston Bay Region, including Galveston Bay, Trinity Bay, East Bay, and West Bay. Farther to the west is Christmas Bay. Galveston Island is about 30 miles long and 3 miles wide at its widest point. Galveston Island has seen many changes throughout the years including raising the entire downtown area after the Great Hurricane of 1900. The concrete seawall, built after this famous storm, protects the area from high waves still today.

The western end of Galveston Island, only a few feet above sea level, is much lower in elevation than the area protected by the seawall.

Galveston Bay has many diverse uses. Large tankers regularly cruise through the bay as do small shallow-water fishing boats. Vast industrial complexes are also found along the western part of Galveston Bay.

The eastern part of the bay, including areas around Smith Point, is very rural in nature. Over 70 percent of the oysters harvested in Texas come from Galveston Bay.

Seasonal Fishing Chart - Region 2: Galveston Bay

	Jan	Feb	Mar	Apr	May	Jun	Jul	Aug	Sep	Oct	Nov	Dec
Redfish	+	+	++	+++	+++	+++	+++	+++	+++	+++	++	++
Spotted Seatrout	+	++	++	+++	+++	+++	+++	+++	+++	++	++	+
Flounder			+	++	+++	+++	+++	+++	+++	+++	+++	+
Black Drum	+	+++	+++	+++	+++	+++	+++	+++	+++	++	++	+
Sheepshead	+	+++	+++	+++	+++	+++	+++	+++	+++	++	++	+
Crevalle Jack				++	+++	+++	+++	+++	+++	+		
Spanish Mackerel						++	+++	+++	+++			
Gray Snapper						++	+++	+++				
Tarpon						+	+	+				
Pompano				+	+	+	+	+				
Snook												

+++ = Exceptional, ++ = Very Good, + = Available

Galveston Bay is home to many petrochemical plants along the western shoreline. The northern part of the Houston Ship Channel is also lined with chemical companies. Perhaps nowhere else along the entire Texas coast do so many diverse users collide in one bay.

Most of Galveston Bay, other than the channel, is less than 12 feet deep with many areas being less than 6 feet deep. Galveston Bay is fed freshwater by the Trinity River through Trinity Bay and the San Jacinto River through northern Galveston Bay. Heavy spring rains in the Dallas-Fort Worth area bring much of the freshwater into Trinity and Galveston Bays.

During years with heavy spring rains, Galveston Bay becomes difficult to fish. Most of the rains are over by June and the start of summer. Summertime and fall are the best times to fish Galveston Bay.

There are more public access points to the Galveston Bay area than any other bay region in the state, with over 40 access points to the beach and gulf along Galveston Island.

Anglers using bait should consider that Galveston Bay is the most crowded of the Texas bays. If you want bait, you've got to get to the bait stand early. In the summer months that may mean you have to be there when the doors open, sometimes as early as 4am.

The Galveston Bay complex covers a large area. Be sure to adjust any tide times for the distance between the tide-chart location and the spot you're fishing. In some areas, the time difference can be well over one hour. Areas like Sylvan Beach, at the far north end of Galveston Bay, have much different tide movements than those at Seawolf Park.

Also consider the effect the wind plays on the tides. A strong wind will increase or decrease the speed of a tide depending on the direction of the wind and the tide. Texas has a wind-driven coast, so the wind plays a major role in fishing Galveston Bay.

When fishing the many reefs in the Galveston Bay Region look for something different on the reef: like an old shipwreck, a gut, hump, or cut. Anything that makes the water do something different when flowing across the reef will attract fish. A minor difference may be all it takes to attract fish to a particular spot.

Hanna Reef, for example, is a very large reef with portions exposed and other sections under 6 feet of water. Look for color variations in the water to help locate areas with deeper water.

Anglers can use the wintertime low tides to research potential summertime fishing spots. Take along a digital camera and photograph the areas you want to fish when the water is at its lowest point. You can use this information when the higher tides of summer arrive and the reef is covered with water. A little research during the winter can pay off big during the summer.

During recent years anglers fishing Galveston Bay have caught tripletail. Tripletail look like very large sunfish and strike hard. They like to lay in the shade by oil well footings. Cast to any fish you run across next to these footings and hold on. Tripletail are known for their pull. Get the fish away from the structure as fast as you can or risk losing it to a cut line.

East Bay

The eastern most part of the Galveston Bay complex is watched over by High Island. High Island, not an actual island, is the top of a salt dome and is the highest point on the entire Texas coast. High Island is a bird refuge for those species making the long trek across the Gulf of Mexico. The area has heavy bird watcher activity March through May. High Island has numerous large trees that are used as resting places for birds after crossing the gulf. Look for the water tower and large oaks to help locate High Island.

The land extending along the Gulf of Mexico west of High Island is Bolivar Peninsula. Point Bolivar is at the far west end of the peninsula. East Bay is located between Bolivar Point and Smith Point. State Highway 87 is located on the peninsula between the Intracoastal Waterway and the Gulf of Mexico.

Gulf currents enter East Bay at Rollover Pass and Rollover Bay to the east and Point Bolivar and Bolivar Roads to the south. Bolivar Peninsula offers anglers fishing access to both East Bay and the surf along the peninsula. There are several fishing piers located along the gulf side of the peninsula and anglers can fish the surf along the beach.

Goat Island is located along the southern edge of East Bay and is divided from the peninsula by the Intracoastal Waterway (ICW). Fish both the East Bay side and the ICW side of the island.

Most of East Bay is less than 7 feet deep, although much of the shoreline along the far eastern end of East Bay is too muddy to wade. Areas east of Rollover Pass are best fished from a boat.

East Bay can also be accessed from the far eastern end by a public ramp at the Intracoastal Waterway and Highway 87 intersection. The ramp is paved but the parking area is limited and gets muddy during the rainy season.

East Bay is somewhat protected from the strong southeastern winds. Look to catch redfish, flounder, and speckled trout.

Boat Ramps

Ben's Trading Post, 1484 Highway 124, High Island / 409-286-2231
High Island RV Park, 1921 4th St / 409-286-2294 / www.highislandrvpark.com

ROLLOVER PASS

Rollover Pass connects East Bay to the Gulf of Mexico. Rollover Pass, surrounded by the small community of Gilchrist, is 7 miles west of High Island or 20 miles east of the Bolivar ferry landing. Highway 87 crosses over the pass and provides access to both sides. The water around Rollover Pass can be strong when the current is running. There is no boat traffic through the pass due to the low bridge crossing.

The east side of the pass has unpaved parking. There is paved parking on the west side of the pass. The concrete bulkheads lining the pass are often slick from wash over, so be careful when walking on the wet pavement. The bulkheads on both sides are wheelchair accessible. Anglers fish off each end and the middle of the pass.

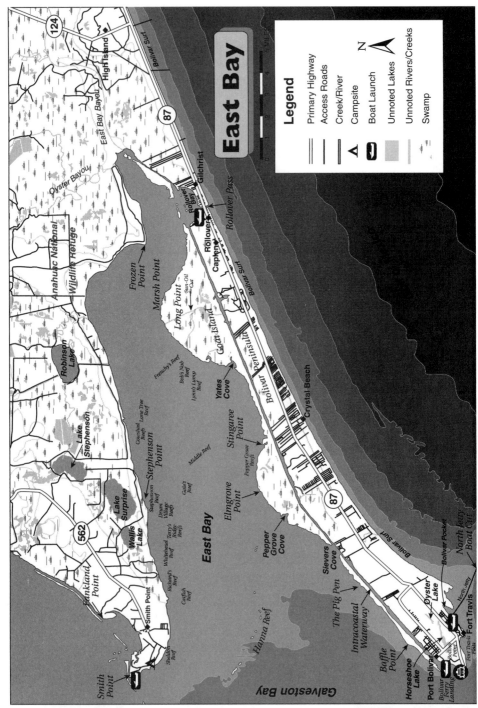

East Bay

Legend

Primary Highway

Access Roads

Creek/River

Campsite

Boat Launch

Unnoted Lakes

Unnoted Rivers/Creeks

Swamp

N

© 2009 Wilderness Adventures Press, Inc.

The pass offers good fishing for redfish, speckled trout, flounder, and sheepshead. Live and cut bait is often used. Use a heavy weight to get the bait down in the fast moving water of the pass.

Rollover Pass is a favorite location for fishing the fall croaker run. Although the croaker run is not as strong as it was in years past, there are still plenty of people fishing Rollover Pass at this time. Use small shrimp or pieces of shrimp when fishing for croaker.

The period when a tide movement starts or ends and the current is not at full speed is often the best time to fish the pass. Slack-water periods are most often the least productive periods.

Also fish the ends of the pass. Some anglers wade out at the south end, but the strong currents in the area suggest this is not a good idea.

The islands on the bay side offer good fishing. For anglers with a boat or kayak, the islands are only a short run across the Intracoastal Waterway. These islands have both shell and grass lining the water. Try the shallow areas for redfish and flounder. Pay attention to barges traveling through the area as they may affect the water level. Be sure to fish when the barge pulls the water away from the shoreline and then pushes it back. Fish will often react to the water movement created by the passing barge just like they react to tidal movement.

There is a boat ramp on the northwest side of the pass. The Dr. Lloyd K. Lauderdale public ramp is paved and parking in the area is limited. The unpaved parking area becomes very muddy after a heavy rain.

The Intracoastal Waterway has a big bend just east of the pass. Anglers can use this area to get out of a strong wind and fish the waterway.

Waters entering Rollover Pass bring bait and fish into East Bay.

Amenities/Boat Ramps

Dr. K. Lloyd Lauderdale Boat Ramp, Bolivar
Bayside RV Park / 409-286-2151
Four Star Quality RV Park / 409-286-5712
La Palmas RV Park / 409-286-5612
Nature's Best RV Park, 1015 Yacht Basin / 409-286-5434
North End Bait / 409-286-5067
Quality Bait Camp / 409-286-5712
Rollover Pass Bait / 409-286-5562
Sunrise Grocery, 1995 Hwy 87 / 409-286-5335

BOLIVAR SURF

The surf along Bolivar Peninsula offers anglers a chance for good fishing. There are several private fishing piers along the beach including Rocky's Fishing Pier. Pay attention to all warning signs in the area. The dunes bordering the beach are protected and driving or parking on the dunes is prohibited.

Many private boardwalks have been erected over the dunes to allow foot traffic to the beach. Use only the public boardwalks unless you pay for the use of a private path to the beach.

Many beach anglers use big spinning tackle with a very long rod to help get their baited hook out farther into the surf. Some anglers use a kayak to paddle out and drop their baited rig in the surf.

When the winds permit, anglers can fish closer in to the shoreline. Look for a slightly deeper hole near the sand beach. Even a small variation in water depth can indicate a good fish-holding location. Don't be surprised by the size of fish caught along the beach. Redfish, speckled trout and jack crevalle are often caught inside the first gut.

Most Bolivar beaches have signs posted about sea turtles. Please report any sightings or nests of sea turtles. Avoid disturbing any turtle nests or nesting turtles. Sea turtle populations are on the rebound along the Texas coast due to strict conservation measures.

Boat Ramps

Rocky's RV Park Fishing Pier, 1260 Hwy 87 / 409-286-2245
Lloyd's Gulf Coast RV, 1900 Hwy 87 / 409-684-0499

BOLIVAR POCKET

Bolivar Pocket, located east of the North Jetty, is shallow and easily fished. Grass is spread throughout the area and anglers will often see birds wading, looking for a meal at low tide. This is a good area for anglers new to kayaking to try out their craft. The North Jetty protects this area from wind, so Bolivar Pocket is often calm all the way to the North Jetty boat cut.

For best fishing results plan to arrive at Bolivar Pocket just as an incoming tide starts to flood the grass or as an outgoing tide is ending. Flounder and redfish are found around the grass.

Fly anglers can use spoon flies and Bend Backs close to the grass for redfish and flounder. Also try a saltwater popper for speckled trout around the grass during the highest water times. Conventional tackle users can try gold spoons around the grass for redfish. Also try a topwater walk-the-dog type lure for speckled trout during high tides. Bait anglers can try live shrimp under a popping cork or rattling alameda rig.

NORTH JETTY

The North Jetty is one of the longest in Texas. Large ships use the nearby channel to take their cargo to docks along the western shore of Galveston Bay. The ship traffic is continuous and it is not unusual to see several ships waiting in line to enter Galveston Bay like airplanes stacking up to land at a major airport.

The North Jetty is partially topped by a flat concrete surface that allows anglers to walk out on the jetty. During calm periods the top will be dry. During high tides and windy periods the top will be covered with water and can become slick. Travel this area with caution.

The long North Jetty protects the channel and provides a great fishing spot.

Farther out on the jetty the smooth concrete path gives way to large granite rocks. Be careful hopping from one rock to the next. The North Jetty has a boat cut about a fourth of the way out limiting foot traffic to the end of the jetty. Shallow draft boats can maneuver through the cut, but use caution.

The Erman Pilsner Boat Ramp is located just to the west of the North Jetty. The ramp is paved and parking is limited. Boaters need to pay attention to the many No Parking signs. During low tides there is also a small sand beach next to the ramp but this area is covered with water when the tide is high or there is a strong south wind. Park above the high tide area to avoid water damage to your vehicle.

The North Jetty is a favorite fishing location and will be crowded during summertime weekends and holidays.

Anglers can fish right off the jetty. The Bolivar Roads side is deeper and the Bolivar Pocket side is shallow, closer to the jetty. Anglers should remember the jetty is much wider at the base than at the top. Be prepared to lose some tackle to the rocks.

Fly anglers can cast parallel to the jetty with Bend Backs, shrimp patterns, and Clouser Minnows. Be sure the tippet is made of a lighter weight material than the fly line in case the fly must be broken off when hung in the rocks. Fishing with live shrimp or cut bait are also favorite methods for fishing the jetty. Try a popping cork to avoid hanging up in the rocks.

Boat Ramps

Erman Pilsner, 15th Street
North Jetty Bait Camp / 409-684-3857

FORT TRAVIS FLATS

The area south of old Fort Travis is a small, protected pocket with some excellent fishing opportunities. This area is often overlooked but, if the wind allows, this can be an excellent speckled trout area. Watch for slicks made by trout. Redfish patrol the grassy areas closer to shore.

Boat traffic through nearby Bolivar Roads is busy with large ships traversing this area constantly. Boat to the Fort Travis flats area with caution.

Fly anglers can cast into the shallow area with a Foxy Clouser and floating line. Work the areas farther out for speckled trout with a Clouser Minnow and sinking line.

Fish for speckled trout with a Super Spook Jr. or TopDog. Also try jigheads with soft plastics or a silver Sprite spoon. Bait casters can try live shrimp under a popping cork or free shrimp with only a split shot for weight.

Fish closer to the shore for redfish and flounder.

BOLIVAR FERRY

The Bolivar ferry runs 24 hours a day, 365 days a year. The ferry system is operated by the Texas Department of Transportation as part of the highway system. Ferry boats pick up cars and passengers at the Bolivar Peninsula side and the Galveston Island side. Once on Galveston Island, motorists can use Highway 87 to connect with IH-45 and the mainland.

During summer weekends and holidays the ferry system will be loaded with passengers. If traveling through the area at this time expect a wait. The boat ride takes approximately 15 minutes to cross the channel and loading and unloading passengers adds to the time.

During busy holidays allow extra time for the ferry ride. The Highway Department workers do an excellent job getting cars and people across as quickly as possible. Several ferryboats are working at all times of the day to minimize the wait.

The traffic from the Bolivar Peninsula side is always less than traffic coming from the Galveston Island side.

Boat Ramps

Crystal Canal RV Park & Bait, 1900 Monkhouse Rd / 409-684-6624 /
www.crystalcanal.com
Bluewater Bait Camp, 1133 Chapman's Point / 409-684-2248
Bolivar Yacht Basin RV & Bait, 4312 Boyt Rd W / 409-684-6700

The Bolivar Ferry runs 24 hours a day, seven days a week.

HANNA REEF

Hanna Reef is one of the largest reefs in the Galveston Bay complex situated between Bolivar Point and Smith Point. Hanna Reef has several arms shooting off the main reef. Some areas of the reef are as shallow as 1 foot deep, while other parts of the reef lie in water up to 6 feet deep. During the lowest tides some parts of the reef are exposed.

The water along the south side of the reef drops off close to the reef. This area is the first stop for many of the fish entering East Bay from the Gulf of Mexico.

Hanna Reef is best fished from a boat. Work the many arms stretching out from the main reef. Look for areas where there is a slight difference in the way the water flows around the reef. A small gut or cut can hold fish even though it may be only a few inches deeper than the surrounding reef. Any type of structure change in the reef will hold more fish.

Boaters need to use caution when working the area and look for shallow parts of the reef. Many anglers drift fish around the reef using soft plastics on jigheads.

EAST BAY SOUTH SHORELINE AND REEFS

The south shoreline of East Bay has two land points — Long Point and Elmgrove Point — extending out into the bay. Long Point is just west of Rollover Pass, and the Sun Oil Cut runs through the middle of it. Farther west is Elmgrove Point. Both of these areas have cuts and channels stretching inland toward the Intracoastal Waterway. Anglers with shallow draft boats can use these cuts to fish the numerous flats on the points.

Work the grassy shallows for redfish and flounder. Fly anglers should use Foxy Clousers and Bend Backs. Conventional tackle anglers should use weedless gold spoons and light weighted jigheads with soft plastics.

There are numerous reefs close to the south shoreline of East Bay. Middle Reef, Frenchy's Reef, Kelly's Reef, and others will hold speckled trout. Try to find a cut or depression in the reef where the water is slightly deeper than the surrounding reef and fish the deeper water.

Fly anglers will need to use sinking lines and heavy Clouser Minnows to fish the deeper water. Cast jigheads with soft plastics to the deeper holes.

Farther to the west is the Pig Pen area just north of the Intracoastal Waterway. Since the Pig Pen area is across the Intracoastal Waterway, anglers will need a boat to get there. Anglers can wade fish the Pig Pen shoreline for redfish, flounder, and speckled trout.

Boat Ramps

Stingaree Marina, Stingaree Road / 409-684-9530
Bolivar Bait Camp, Boyt Road / 409-684-4210

NORTH REEFS

Numerous reefs can be found along the north side of East Bay between Smith Point and the Robinson Lake outlet. Reefs, such as Gale's Reef and Drum Village Reef, offer good fishing. Work these reefs for redfish, flounder, and speckled trout.

Try topwater lures like a Super Spook Jr. or a Catch 2000 early in the day. Switch to jigheads with soft plastics as the topwater bite stops and the day progresses.

ROBINSON LAKE

Robinson Lake is on the north side of East Bay. There is a channel on the south side of the lake that connects the lake to East Bay.

Spoons work well for both redfish and speckled trout.

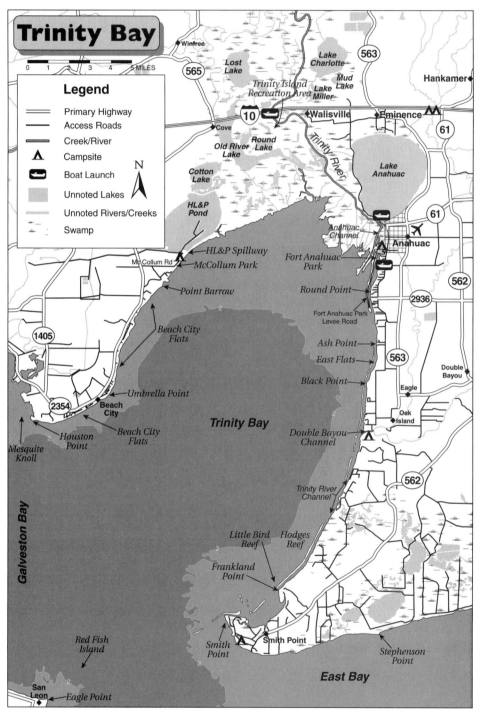

Trinity Bay

0 1 2 3 4 5 MILES

Legend

≡≡≡ Primary Highway
——— Access Roads
▬▬▬ Creek/River
▲ Campsite
⬛ Boat Launch
▨ Unnoted Lakes
≋ Unnoted Rivers/Creeks
⸰⸰ Swamp

N

Winfree

Lost Lake

Lake Charlotte

565

563

Trinity Island Recreation Area

Mud Lake

Lake Miller

Hankamer

10

Cove

Walisville

Eminence

61

Round Lake

Old River Lake

Trinity River

Cotton Lake

Lake Anahuac

HL&P Pond

Anahuac Channel

Anahuac

61

HL&P Spillway

Fort Anahuac Park

McCollum Rd

McCollum Park

Round Point

562

Point Barrow

Fort Anahuac Park Levee Road

2936

1405

Beach City Flats

Ash Point

East Flats

563

Black Point

Double Bayou

Eagle

Umbrella Point

Trinity Bay

2354

Beach City

Oak Island

Houston Point

Beach City Flats

Double Bayou Channel

562

Mesquite Knoll

Galveston Bay

Trinity River Channel

Little Bird Reef

Hodges Reef

Frankland Point

Red Fish Island

Smith Point

Smith Point

Stephenson Point

San Leon

Eagle Point

East Bay

Trinity Bay

Trinity Bay is in the northeast corner of the Galveston Bay complex. The Trinity River enters at the northeast corner. Trinity Bay is located between Smith Point to the south and Houston Point to the north.

The inland area around Trinity Bay is much more rural than the western part of Galveston Bay. Small towns and farms make up most of the area around the bay.

Trinity Bay has numerous oil wells located in the middle of the bay. Many of these wells have oyster shell pads that attract various small creatures that trout like to eat. Fish around these wells for speckled trout and flounder.

SMITH POINT

Smith Point is the long point of land extending into the bay from the eastern shore separating Trinity Bay from East Bay. It is directly across the bay from the large industrial complex on the western shoreline of Galveston Bay. FM 562 leads to Smith Point.

Many private oyster leases are found off Smith Point. These leases are designated by a series of tall, white plastic poles. Perhaps no place on the Texas coast shows the contrast of communities as well as Smith Point. The oyster industry is much the same as it was over 100 years ago, while the petrochemical industry across the bay on the western shoreline is as modern as it gets.

Oyster boats and shrimp trollers work the waters around Smith Point. The oyster fisherman keep nutrients dispersed in the waters by working the oyster reefs. This in turn creates a healthy, food-rich environment that attracts numerous saltwater fish.

Anglers can use the paved boat ramp at James H. Robbins Memorial Park to launch. There is a large unpaved parking area next to the ramp. The Trinity River Channel goes right past the ramp and allows the local oyster and bait trollers access to the bay.

Anglers with kayaks have a short paddle across the boat channel to many fishing spots. Work the small islands across the channel as well as the numerous reefs for redfish, flounder, and speckled trout. Fly casters can try spoon flies, Bend Backs, and Clouser Minnows. Conventional tackle users can try spoons, jigheads with soft plastics, and topwater lures. Bait casters can use live shrimp and mud minnows.

The south side of Smith Point has a grass-lined shoreline with numerous private fishing piers. Fish the edges of the grass and around the old piers for flounder and redfish.

The Van-Ta-Un Grocery store on FM 562 has the only gas in the area and basic supplies, and the Spoonbill RV Park at the end of Hawkins Road sells bait.

Boat Ramp

James H. Robbins Memorial Park

Double Bayou and East Flats

Double Bayou is the water outlet between Fort Anahuac and Smith Point on the eastern shoreline of Trinity Bay. To reach Double Bayou take either FM 563 or FM 564 south out of the Anahuac area. There is a public boat ramp at Double Bayou with limited unpaved parking. Several crabbers use Double Bayou as their home ramp.

Anglers with kayaks can launch at the Double Bayou ramp and make a short paddle to the nearby spoil islands. The entire eastern shoreline of Trinity Bay can be reached for those with enough stamina to make the paddle.

There is a long series of spoil islands on the west side of the Trinity River Channel that offers good fishing. The eastern edge of these islands offers good wade fishing for redfish and flounder. Several reefs located closer to Smith Point, including Hodges Reef and Little Bird reef, also hold fish. Anglers can drift fish around the reefs using lures or live bait.

Double Bayou Channel has deeper water than the surrounding area. Fish the channel during the hottest days and during the winter. Fish the spoil areas around the channel during the early part of the day for redfish, flounder, and speckled trout.

This area is protected from the predominant southeast wind and normally has clear water when the wind is out of that direction. A west wind blows right into the area making it difficult to fish.

Fly casters can fish the shallow waters around the islands with Bend Backs, Clouser Minnows, and spoon flies, and spin casters should try gold spoons and jigheads with soft plastics. Bait fishers can use live shrimp, mud minnows, shad, and finger mullet.

Amenities

Oak Island/Double Bayou
T & D One Stop, 402 W Bayshore Rd / 409-252-4590
Channel Marker 17 / 409-252-4370

Fort Anahuac Park

Lake Anahuac is a large protected lake near the eastern edge of Trinity Bay. FM 563 runs along the eastern shore of Lake Anahuac. Most of the shoreline is private property.

The western side of Lake Anahuac is bordered by the Trinity River and Trinity River Channel. Anahuac is known as the Alligator Capital of Texas and is the county seat of Chambers County. Almost one half of the county is covered in water.

Fort Anahuac Park, just south of Lake Anahuac, has three paved boat ramps and plenty of paved parking. The Trinity River Channel runs along the western side of the park and two ramps enter the Trinity River Channel.

The Fort Anahuac Park Levee Road trail runs about 2 miles south out of the park. The road is closed during wet weather but offers access to both the Trinity River Channel and Trinity Bay.

A third ramp on the west side of the park enters the water on the Anahuac Channel side giving access to the many passes and islands running south from the Trinity River. The Trinity River delta system offers many different locations for fishing.

From Fort Anahuac the shoreline along the northern end of Trinity Bay is made up of many small cuts and islands around to McCollum Park.

The spillway at the end of the H, L & P pond is one of the few places on the Texas coast where anglers can catch striped bass. Be sure to pay attention to the No Trespassing signs in the area. Although striped bass, or stripers, are a saltwater fish they are no longer naturally found along the Texas coast. The stripers found near the spillway are most likely from stocking programs at Lake Livingston or Fort Anahuac. This is one of only a couple of places where Texas anglers can catch redfish, speckled trout, flounder, and striped bass all on the same trip.

The best time to catch stripers is during the spring while the rivers are running. Native stripers prefer cooler water and the early spring is when waters are cool and running.

Fly anglers can use sinking lines with heavy Clouser Minnows for stripers in the early spring. Mud minnows and shrimp are the predominant bait used for fish in the area. Dead shrimp will also attract redfish and catfish.

Boat Ramp

Fort Anahuac Park, 1704 South Main / 409-267-8364

Smith Point in Trinity Bay is a quiet contrast from the busy west side of Galveston Bay.

TRINITY RIVER ISLAND RECREATION AREA

The Trinity River Island Recreation Area is just south of Interstate 10. The recreation area was developed as part of the Wallisville Lake Project. The island is located between the natural river channel and one made by the Corp of Engineers. Entrance to the area is marked. Use exit 806 from IH-10.

The Wallisville Lake Project was designed to keep saltwater from flowing up the Trinity River by using a lock system placed on the river to prevent saltwater encroachment. Boat traffic is allowed through the locks.

Boat Ramp

Corp of Engineers – Wallisville Lake Lock / 409-389-2285

MCCOLLUM PARK

One can reach McCollum Park by taking FM 2354 off of Highway 146 out of Baytown. FM 2354 follows a path along the shoreline from Tabb's Bay around to Houston Point and finally turning back north near McCollum Road.

McCollum Park is located at the end of McCollum Road. The park has a parking area but no boat ramp. Kayakers can launch here, but there is a 25-foot cliff that drops off from the parking area to the bay waters.

The shoreline is bordered with grass and numerous fishing piers. Anglers can work close to the grass for redfish and around the fishing piers for flounder. Be sure to work around the abandoned piers. Many of the piers do not have lights and anglers should use caution during nighttime fishing activities.

A strong southeast wind blows right into the McCollum Park area. Fish here during light winds or when the wind is out of the north for best results.

BEACH CITY FLATS

Beach City Flats is the area between Houston Point and McCollum Park in northwest Trinity Bay. The predominant southeast wind blows right into this section of the bay. This is a good area to fish when the wind is light or when the wind blows out of the north.

There are numerous private piers located along the Beach City Flats and few public access points. Many areas are marked with No Trespassing or No Parking signs. Visitors need to pay attention to these signs or risk vehicles being towed.

The shoreline along Beach City Flats has wide spread shoreline grass beds. Fish near the grass for redfish and flounder, and around the piers for flounder.

Boat Ramp

Beach City RV Park, 9218 FM 2354 / 281-303-0198 / www.beachcityrv.com

Trinity Bay is a good place for trout.

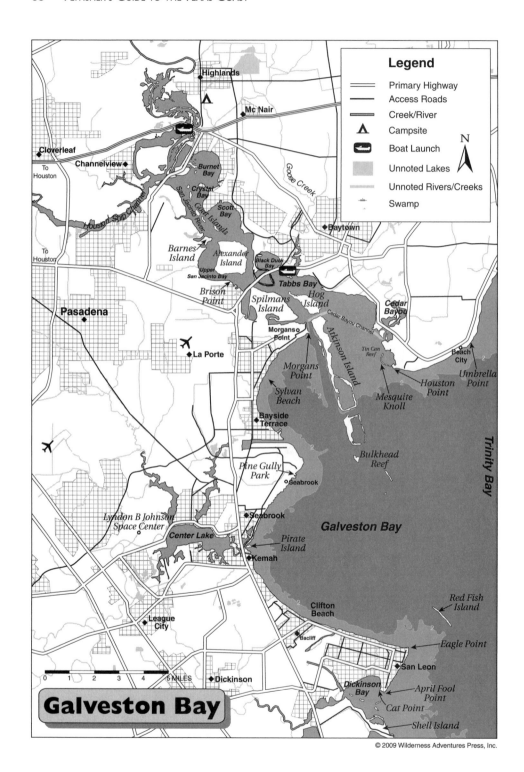

Legend

≡≡≡	Primary Highway
───	Access Roads
⌇⌇⌇	Creek/River
⛺	Campsite
🚤	Boat Launch
▨	Unnoted Lakes
▥	Unnoted Rivers/Creeks
⌁⌁	Swamp

N

Highlands

Mc Nair

Cloverleaf

To Houston

Channelview

Burnet Bay

Goose Creek

Crystal Bay

Scott Bay

San Jacinto River

Gaad Islands

Baytown

To Houston

Barnes Island

Alexander Island

Upper San Jacinto Bay

Black Duck Bay

Tabbs Bay

Cedar Bayou

Pasadena

Brison Point

Spilmans Island

Hog Island

Cedar Bayou Channel

Houston Ship Channel

La Porte

Morgans Point

Atkinson Island

Tin Can Reef

Beach City

Umbrella Point

Morgans Point

Houston Point

Mesquite Knoll

Sylvan Beach

Bayside Terrace

Bulkhead Reef

Trinity Bay

Pine Gully Park

Seabrook

Lyndon B Johnson Space Center

Seabrook

Galveston Bay

Center Lake

Pirate Island

Kemah

Clifton Beach

Red Fish Island

League City

Bacliff

Eagle Point

San Leon

0 1 2 3 4 5 MILES

Dickinson

Dickinson Bay

April Fool Point

Cat Point

Shell Island

Galveston Bay

Galveston Bay

Galveston Bay's history goes back almost as far as Texas' history (certainly most people are aware of the tragic hurricane of 1900). Galveston was a magnet to early explorers in the area and provided a deep-water bay for sailing vessels.

Today, Galveston Bay is home to a vast petrochemical industry. The western shore of Galveston Bay is as modern as any industrial city. With over 2 million citizens located in nearby Houston alone, Galveston Bay is also the bay with the most users.

Large ships travel the ship channel 24 hours a day. The many oil terminals also run 24 hours a day. From the Houston Ship Channel down to the tourist havens of Kemah and Seabrook, the western side of Galveston Bay is continuously busy.

In spite of all of this traffic, parts of Galveston Bay still seem remote. When visiting little Pine Gully Park one feels like one is somewhere else. The park feels more like some of the marshes of Christmas Bay farther to the west than the busy boat-traffic-filled Galveston Bay.

Galveston Bay still produces a lot of oysters for the market every year. This bay also has the highest fish catch rate per-hour-spent-fishing of any of the Texas bays. With extensive mid-bay reefs, numerous private and public piers, and other fishable locations, there are plenty of places for the angler to fish on Galveston Bay.

One of the conservation efforts in Galveston Bay includes re-planting of sea grasses in chosen areas. Galveston Bay sea grasses have suffered over the last five decades but re-planting efforts show signs of success. Only time will tell.

Galveston Bay and its many anglers prove modern man can help conserve our natural resources and have a modern world on its shores.

HOUSTON POINT

Houston Point is where Trinity Bay and Galveston Bay come together. The spoil islands help buffer the waves created by ships traveling through the Houston Ship Channel. The Texas Parks and Wildlife Department is currently working on restoring sea grasses in the Houston Point area.

Most of the water west of Houston Point between Atkinson Island and the Cedar Bayou Channel is less than 4 feet deep. This area is also protected from the predominant southeast winds. Cedar Bayou helps bring freshwater inflows to the area, making it a good place for blue crabs. Generally, where you find blue crabs you find redfish, and Houston Point is no exception. The nearby Cedar Bayou Channel offers deeper water than the surrounding bay. Fish the channel in the winter or on very hot summer days. There are also several reefs including Tin Can Reef in the area. Speckled trout are often found patrolling these reefs.

The road running back to the north where FM 1405 and FM 2354 intersect is a private road. FM 2354, or the Tri-City Beach Road, continues around the northwest side of Trinity Bay.

TABBS BAY

Tabbs Bay, at the far north end of Galveston Bay, can be reached from the Bayland Marina on Goose Creek. The Tabbs Bay side is not as busy as the Morgan Point-Spillman's Island side of the bay.

Anglers with kayaks will find plenty of old piers to fish around in the Goose Creek area. The numerous old pilings in the area prohibit fast boat traffic through the area. Go slow! This area is protected from strong southeast winds.

Amenities

Bayland Park, 2651 Missouri St
Bayland Maritna, 2651 S Highway 146 / 281-420-5076

HOUSTON SHIP CHANNEL

The Houston Ship Channel is a very busy waterway. Large ships and tankers regularly use the channel to transport products to docks on the north and western shore of Galveston Bay.

The pier at Sylvan Beach is a favorite with weekend anglers.

SYLVAN BEACH FISHING PIER

Sylvan Beach Park and Pier are on the northwest side of Galveston Bay. Take Fairmont Parkway off Highway 146 near LaPorte High School to get to the park. With a large paved parking area and several paved ramps the park is very popular and often crowded on weekends and holidays. Mid-week anglers may find they are alone in the park.

The predominant southeast wind blows directly into the Sylvan Beach area. During windy times baitfish are also blown into the area, making it a good location to fish.

There is a fee for fishing from the lighted pier. Redfish, speckled trout, and flounder are often caught along Sylvan Beach.

Anglers can fish from the pier or the nearby bulkhead. Cast lures or flies when there is visible bait working the water. Natural bait, like shrimp, croaker, and mullet —live and dead — works well. Bait fishers should try an egg-shaped weight with a plastic bead placed on each side of the weight. Use a swivel below the weight and attach a leader to the bottom of the swivel. Attach a Kahle hook for the bait.

In the park, Linda's Sylvan Beach bait stand sells bait, tackle, and supplies.

Boat Ramp

Bayshore & San Jacinto Streets
Linda's Sylvan Beach Bait & Tackle / 281-471-5705

BAYPORT SHIP CHANNEL AND REEFS

The Bayport Ship Channel is on the western side of Galveston Bay near the community of Red Bluff. There are several reefs on both sides of the channel. The Houston Yacht Club is nearby and there is plenty of boat traffic in the area so boat through the area with caution.

Anglers can wade fish along the shoreline on both sides of the channel. Fish the nearby reefs from a boat using lures or live shrimp.

ATKINSON ISLAND

Atkinson Island is just east of the Houston Ship Channel. The west side of the island is bordered by the ship channel. The east side of the island is shallow and does not get the strong waves created by ships passing on the west side.

Work the areas in close to the island for redfish and flounder. Work the drop-off farther out for speckled trout.

PINE GULLY FISHING PARK AND PIER

Pine Gully Fishing Pier is located along the western shore of Galveston Bay. Using Highway 146 and Red Bluff Road follow the signs to get to the park. The city of Seabrook manages the park and charges $5 to enter. This small park is very isolated compared to the touristy and often crowded Seabrook area.

There is a small paved parking area in the park. Predominantly southeast winds blow right into the park's fishing pier and surrounding bulkhead.

Anglers fish from the pier with live and cut bait.

SEABROOK AND KEMAH AREA

The Seabrook-Kemah area is a favorite with tourists and there is always plenty of traffic. The Ben Blackledge boat ramp is located under the Highway 146 Bridge. The ramp is paved and has plenty of parking for boat trailers. Nearby Clear Creek Channel leads into Clear Lake and the Clear Creek drainage.

Clear Creek brings freshwater to the western side of Galveston Bay. During heavy spring rains the area waters can become fresh and muddy.

Try to avoid this area during summer weekends and holidays due to the heavy traffic. There are numerous restaurants and seafood shops in the area and always plenty of tourists.

Boat Ramp

Ben Blackledge Boat Ramp under Hwy 146 Bridge

The 18th Street Pier is marked by a large boat sign.

Bacliff

Just south of Kemah is the small community of Bacliff. The Bacliff shoreline along Galveston Bay has numerous private piers extending into the water. This area is somewhat protected from the predominant southeast wind and is usually calmer than the shoreline farther north.

There is a public boat ramp just north of FM 646 with limited parking. The ramp area is very steep. Anglers can work around the piers in the area and fish the nearby reefs farther out.

Farther south, the H L & P Galveston County Bayshore Park has a paved ramp with plenty of parking. The ramp is just south of the H L & P cooling channel and the old Bayside RV Park, which is now closed.

Bayshore Park is a local favorite with land-bound anglers and their families. The park fills up on busy weekends and holidays. Fish the pier with live or cut bait.

This area is protected from a strong southeast wind and gives anglers a chance to fish relatively calm waters. There are also many private piers in the area including a private fee pier at the end of 18th Street farther down the shoreline. The pier is lighted and has a 3-rod-per-angler limit. Look for the large boat at the intersection of 18th Street and FM 646 to help locate this ramp.

Amenities

Bayshore Park, Bayshore Dr. (boat ramp)
18th St. Pier / 281-334-2600

Eagle Point

Eagle Point is the area directly across the bay from Smith Point. The predominant southeast wind blows right into the south side of Eagle Point. The north shoreline of Eagle Point is protected from this wind.

Fish in shallow around the numerous private piers for flounder and redfish.

There are also many reefs located off Eagle Point. Also work the spoil areas near the ship channel. Try drift fishing around the reef with lures and live bait.

Amenities

Eagle Point Fishing Camp, 101 1st Street / 281-339-1131

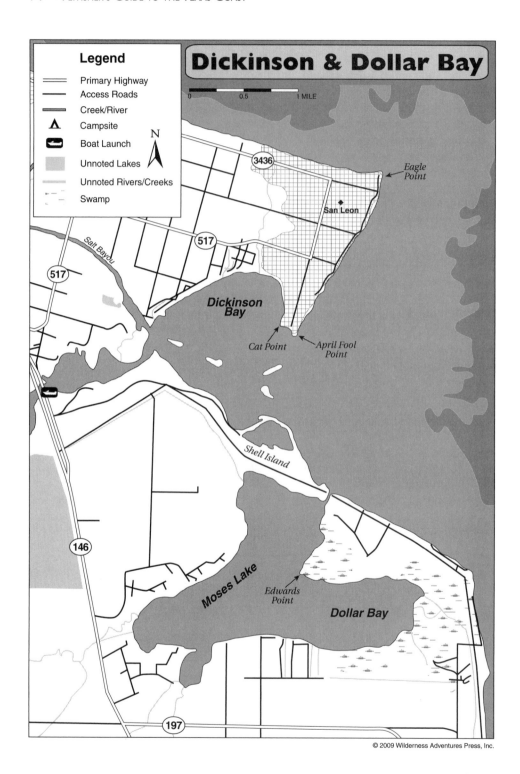

Legend
Primary Highway
Access Roads
Creek/River
Campsite
Boat Launch
Unnoted Lakes
Unnoted Rivers/Creeks
Swamp

N

Dickinson & Dollar Bay

0   0.5   1 MILE

Eagle
Point

San Leon

Salt Bayou

517

517

Dickinson
Bay

Cat Point   April Fool
Point

Shell Island

146

Moses Lake   Edwards
Point

Dollar Bay

197

DICKINSON BAY

Dickinson Bay is located just south of the San Leon area. The mouth of Dickinson Bay is protected by Dickinson Reef, and a deep channel leads from Dickinson Bayou through Dickinson Bay out to Galveston Bay. There is a paved public boat at the Highway 146 bridge and Dickinson Bayou. Pay attention to bacteria signs posted in the areas.

There are several spoil areas located along the channel leading out of Dickinson Bay, which can be fished for redfish and flounder. Fish the intersection of the Dickinson Channel and the Moses Lake Channel, as well as nearby Crescent Reef for speckled trout.

Boat Ramp

Hwy 146 & Dickinson Bayou

Pay attention to the bacteria signs posted along Dickinson Bay.

DOLLAR BAY

Just south of Dickinson Bay are Dollar Bay and Moses Lake. Most of Dollar Bay is less than 4 feet deep. The bay is protected from the predominant southeast wind and the entire bay is surrounded by a large levee.

Automobile traffic is allowed on the levee. Traffic is one way when coming from the Texas City Dike area going north. Past Dollar Point Marina the traffic is two way. You cannot drive across the tide gate at the north end of the levee. Anglers can also fish from this north end. The road to Miller Point gives anglers access to the north side of the levee. The deep channel leading into Dollar Bay is a good wintertime fishing spot where speckled trout seek out the protection of the deeper water.

The entire levee is a favorite during summer weekends and holidays, but there is a ramp fee at Dollar Point Marina.

Amenities

Dollar Point Marina / 409-945-4808

TEXAS CITY DIKE

The Texas City Dike allows land-locked anglers a chance at catching many different saltwater fish. The Dike is about 5 miles long with a long, lighted pier at the end. The Texas City Dike gets crowded on summertime weekends and holidays.

Take 9th Avenue through Texas City from State Highway 146 to reach the dike. Be sure to pay attention to all speed limit signs.

There is large-ship traffic on both sides of the dike. Many anglers prefer to fish the West Bay side of the dike because the water in the Texas City Channel, which runs along the dike, is deeper closer to the dike. Anglers often line the granite rocks with fishing rods.

There are several public boat ramps located along the dike for anglers with boats. The first ramp is near Anita's Bait stand. Farther down the dike are the Noah Welch and Sansom-Yarbrough ramps. All of these ramps are paved. The Sansom-Yarbrough ramp is the largest and has the most parking. The lighted pier at the end of the dike also has a small café and bait shop with 24-hour service.

Many anglers prefer to fish during the night along the dike. Anglers can park their vehicles right next to the granite rocks that make up the dike. Some anglers use large lights powered by generators while fishing at night. The bright light attracts baitfish and shrimp into the area, which in turn attracts predator fish. Some anglers use a kayak to paddle out and drop their baited hook farther into the channel.

The Texas City Dike is also a favorite during the annual spring black drum run. The drum can sometimes be heard making their drumming noise during the early spring. Large drum are caught right off the dike by anglers using blue crab and cutbait. Use a large circle hook, size 13 or greater, and a heavy weight to get the bait to the bottom. All black drum over 31 inches in length must be released.

The Galveston Bay side of the dike is shallower close to the dike. There are several spoil islands located along the Galveston Bay side. Fishers can wade to some of these islands.

Fly casters can also work the shallow with Bend Backs, Clouser Minnows, and spoon flies. Fish the shallow areas with spoons, jigheads with soft plastic, and topwater lures.

Boat Ramps

Anita's Bait & Tackle / 409-945-5727
Curl's Bait Center / 409-948-3894
Noah Welch Ramp, Texas City Dike
Sansom-Yarbrough, Texas City Dike

GALVESTON CHANNEL

The Galveston Channel is the reason this area was developed in the first place. The channel was dredged through one of the original passes located on the Texas coast. The deep channel allowed early explorers access to Galveston Bay and the surrounding areas.

Galveston Channel has gone through many changes since those first explorers. The channel is under constant dredging to insure safe passage by the many large ships and tankers making their way to the petrochemical complex on the north and west sides of Galveston Bay.

Galveston Bay has always been a commercial success but only more recently are local residents realizing the value of the bay itself. The channel has become a controversy due to the mega-ships plying the world's seas. Several attempts have been made to deepen the channel.

As the channel is deepened it allows more salt water into Galveston Bay, which in turn makes the bay saltier. As salinity levels increase, many of the natural organisms that rely on brackish water with lower salinity levels are perishing.

This is important to anglers because many of the creatures that are food for predator fish like redfish, speckled trout, and flounder, live their early lives in brackish water and cannot survive salinity levels that are too high. Young shrimp and blue crabs must have relatively fresh water at the beginning of their life cycle. With a deeper channel and too much salt water, there will be no juvenile shrimp and crabs. Without the juvenile shrimp and crabs, there will be no redfish or flounder and no anglers.

We must all find ways to ensure everyone has access to the channel and the channel serves its many uses.

SWAN LAKE AND CAMPBELL BAYOU

Swan Lake is just west of Snake Island and the Texas City Dike. Swan Lake itself is very shallow. Campbell Bayou is located at the far western end of Swan Lake. The mouth of Campbell Bayou offers good fishing for redfish and speckled trout, especially during tidal flows.

West Bay

Legend

	Primary Highway
	Access Roads
	Creek/River
	Campsite
	Boat Launch
	Unnoted Lakes
	Unnoted Rivers/Creeks
	Swamp

N

0   0.5   1 MILES

© 2009 Wilderness Adventures Press, Inc.

West Bay

West Bay runs from the Galveston Causeway in the east to Mud Island in the west. Galveston Island runs along the southern shoreline. Most of the waters in West Bay are less than 5 feet deep with a slightly deeper area in the middle of the bay.

The area just west of the Galveston Causeway includes several islands and reefs. Tiki Island is located in the northeast corner of West Bay. The area north of the Intracoastal Waterway, called Jones Bay, is shallow in most spots. This is a heavily traveled area and includes boat traffic traveling along the Intracoastal Waterway.

SOUTH GALVESTON JETTY

The South Galveston Jetty is reached from East Beach. East Beach is usually crowded during the summer months, weekends and holidays. There is a beach parking fee. This is one of the favorite beaches in Galveston and there is usually some type of event going on every weekend.

Be prepared for the crowd. Snacks and supplies can be purchased from the beach store. The South Jetty can be fished from a boat or from the jetty rocks. Kayakers can launch directly from the beach. The water on the gulf side is protected from the waves created by the many large ships traveling through the ship channel.

Like all Texas jetties, the jetty rocks are often covered with algae and can be very slick. Walk the rocks with caution. Fly casters can use a sinking line and work parallel to the jetty. Clouser Minnows, Bend Backs, and shrimp patterns work best. Use live shrimp or cut bait to catch sheepshead, redfish, and flounder.

Remember this is a multiple-use jetty, so make sure your cast stays clear of other jetty users.

Amenities

East Beach and Apffel Park, 1923 Boddeker Dr / 409-762-3278

GALVESTON CAUSEWAY

The Galveston Causeway leads from the mainland just south of the Texas City-La Marque area and Virginia Point to Galveston Island. IH-45 is the main road leading into Galveston. IH-45 becomes Highway 87 and then Broadway-Avenue J once on the island.

Anglers with a boat can fish around the causeway itself. The old causeway is located on both sides of the current causeway. The waters running around the many bridge footings are in constant movement and attract many baitfish and predator fish to the area.

Boat Ramp

IH-45 east side

Pelican Island

Pelican Island, just north of Galveston Island, is surrounded by the deep waters of the Intracoastal Waterway to the north, the Texas City Channel to the east and Galveston Channel to the south. With all of the deep water surrounding Pelican Island there is almost always some current flowing.

Some of the eastern shoreline of Pelican Island can be waded. Be sure to pay attention to large ships traversing the area. Other areas are marsh and mud and better fished from a kayak or boat.

The shoreline along the Texas City Channel and the area around Sand Island does not receive much fishing pressure. The west and northwest side of the island is protected from the predominantly southeast winds.

Seawolf Park

Seawolf Park is located on Pelican Island near the intersection of Bolivar Roads and the Galveston Channel. The waters in this area are constantly moving due to the heavy boat traffic, including the Bolivar Ferry boats landing at the Ferry Terminal across the Galveston Channel.

Fifty-first Street runs from Galveston Island across the Galveston Ship Channel and becomes Seawolf Parkway once on Pelican Island.

Anglers can fish right off the bulkhead in Seawolf Park.

A fee is charged to enter and fish Seawolf Park. There is a concrete bulkhead on the southeast point of the park. Anglers can fish directly off this bulkhead. Be aware of the waves the passing ships create. They often crest over the bulkhead making it slippery. Be aware of your surroundings.

The park also has a lighted fishing pier and small bait shop. Anglers are limited to two rods while fishing from the pier.

Anglers can also fish the small cove leading into the park. The street leading into the park, Seawolf Parkway, is lined with No Parking signs, but there are areas where anglers can park. Many landlocked anglers wade into the cove and catch speckled trout and redfish. Since the Bolivar Ferry boats are continuously moving the waters, wade the area with caution and use a life vest.

Amenities

Seawolf Park Bait & Tackle / 409-744-5738

TEICHMAN POINT

Teichman Point is located just west of the Galveston Causeway. Two boat channels follow the southern tip of Teichman Point. The water around the point is shallow and offers good wade fishing for speckled trout and redfish.

Take Teichman Road off Highway 87/Broadway-Avenue J to reach Teichman Point.

Most of the area around Teichman Point is private property and public parking is very limited. Pay attention to the No Parking signs.

OFFATTS BAYOU

Offatts Bayou is located just west of the Galveston Causeway and the far southeastern end of West Bay. Offatts Bayou is a good wintertime fishing spot. Redfish and speckled trout seek out the deeper water when the temperature drops. The water depth in Offatts Bayou ranges from 12 to more than 20 feet deep. The bayou is protected from most of the southeast wind.

Anglers can access Offats Bayou from the 61st Street public ramp. While the ramp is paved, the parking area is gravel with limited spots. The area east of 61st Street is designated for personal watercraft use.

Offatts Bayou is often crowded with pleasure boats, including a paddlewheel cruise boat. Anglers should use caution when boating through it.

Parts of the shoreline are lined with grass. There are numerous private piers located along the shoreline. Some of these piers extend well into the bayou, so boat through the area carefully.

Use 51M Mirrolures, Catch 2000, and other sinking lures, working them slowly through the water. Also use quarter-ounce jigheads with soft plastics. Bait anglers can use live shrimp with a popping cork or free shrimp.

Amenities

Galveston County, 61st Street, boat ramp
Smitty's Bait, 7805 Broadway St / 409-9834
Tuckers Bait & Tackle, 1101 61st St / 409-741-8810

NORTH DEER ISLAND AND SOUTH DEER ISLAND

North and South Deer Islands are located just west of the Galveston Causeway. The water surrounding the islands is shallow and offers good wade fishing. The Intracoastal Waterway goes through the north side of North Deer Island. There are several spoil islands located along the ICW. The area between the islands is covered with many oyster reefs.

JONES BAY

Jones Bay is located north of the Intracoastal Waterway just west of the Galveston Causeway and north of Tiki Island. Anglers can wade the northern shoreline of Jones Bay. Several deep cuts run through Jones Bay offering fish deep-water refuge, but most of the water in Jones Bay is shallow, making this a good area for kayakers.

Boat Ramp

South IH-45 under bridge

One can catch speckled trout in Offats Bayou on hard-bodied lures during the winter.

CONFEDERATE REEF

Confederate Reef is located just south of South Deer Island. There are several guts through the reef. The predominant southeast winds blow across the reef from south to north. Fish the guts and the north side of the reef during strong southeast winds.

Fish for speckled trout early in the day on the crest of the reef and farther out as the day progresses. Fly casters can use light Clouser Minnows or Bend Backs, spin fishers can try topwater lures and light weighted jigheads with soft plastics, and bait fishers can use shrimp under popping corks.

GALVESTON ISLAND SURF

The surf along Galveston Island is often crowded with swimmers, especially closer to town along the seawall. Summer days and holidays find many tourists enjoying the waters off Galveston Island. Try to fish the area during the middle of the week and when school is in session.

There are several granite rock groins and a few piers located along the seawall. Anglers often use these groins to get away from swimmers and get their bait out farther into the surf. Swimmers are restricted to the first 50 yards of water along the beach. Be careful when fishing the rock structures as the constant wave action creates an ideal environment for slick algae-covered rocks.

Pay attention to warning signs posted on the beach.

There is a flag warning system in effect for the beach area. Flags are flown from all lifeguard shacks along the beach warning of high waves and other hazards. Special beach rules are also posted at the lifeguard stations. Observe all warnings.

Winds can create large waves that crash into the seawall. During the windiest times anglers will want to consider other fishing spots such as West Bay. Many anglers fishing the Galveston Island surf use heavy spinning tackle with cut or live bait.

During calmer days the water can be "green to the beach" (clear water that is formed by a calm gulf surf and which usually improves fishing) and fish will patrol right next to the sandy shoreline.

Galveston Island along the southern shoreline of West Bay offers good surf fishing. FM 3005 runs along the Galveston Island shoreline. There are 41 access points along the Gulf. Access Point 41 is located at the tollbooth for the San Luis Bridge.

Fish with live or cutbait when the wind is blowing. Switch to lures or flies on calmer days. Look for deep guts running close to shore. Notice the change in the water color to find the deeper areas. A deep gut next to the beach will look dark green.

GALVESTON ISLAND STATE PARK

Galveston Island State Park is located on FM 3005 about 10 miles from the seawall in Galveston. The park includes a large RV camping area and store. Park properties are located on both sides of FM 3005.

Anglers can use the park to access the beach and surf, to fish in the Gulf of Mexico. Kayakers can enter the West Bay side through Oak Bayou or Dana Cove.

Amenities

Galveston Island State Park, 14901 FM 3005 / 409-737-1222

West Bay South Shoreline

The south shoreline of West Bay has numerous guts, coves, pockets, and islands. This varied terrain gives anglers an almost unlimited variety of locations to fish. Try to stay away from the more populated spots like the Jamaica Beach and West Bay Marina areas, and fish the more secluded areas like Malager Cove, Bird Island Cove, and Snake Island Cove.

All of these areas have grassy shorelines that attract fish. The waters of West Bay are usually clear due to the sea grasses in the area. Anglers can wade the shoreline. Flyfishers can use a spoon fly for redfish along the shoreline. Sheepshead also frequent the area and will hit flies when anglers can get close enough without spooking the fish.

Light tackle casters can also fish the shallows for redfish and flounder. Fish the deeper guts and potholes in the grass for speckled trout. The entire area is protected from the strong southeast wind making it a good area for kayakers to fish.

Boat Ramp

11628 Sportsman Dr
Pirate's Beach Marina, 14302 Stewart Rd / 409-737-9966
16711 Jolly Roger Dr
West Bay Marina, 21706 Burnet / 409-737-3636

Guide

Captain Chris Phillips / 409-935-0208

CARANCAHUA REEF

Carancahua Reef runs north and south down the middle of West Bay. The south end of Carancahua Reef is located across from Jamaica Beach and the Galveston Island State Park on Galveston Island.

At one time, Carancahua Reef was higher than it is today but it has sunk due to subsidence in the area. It has been reported that the Indians living in the area once walked across the reef to reach the mainland. Boats can travel through the area by staying close to either the north or south end of the reef.

The reef offers good redfish and speckled trout fishing. Work gold spoons, soft plastics on jigheads, and topwater lures at the crest of the reef early in the day and fish farther out as the day progresses.

Galveston Island State Park is a great place for fishing in the surf.

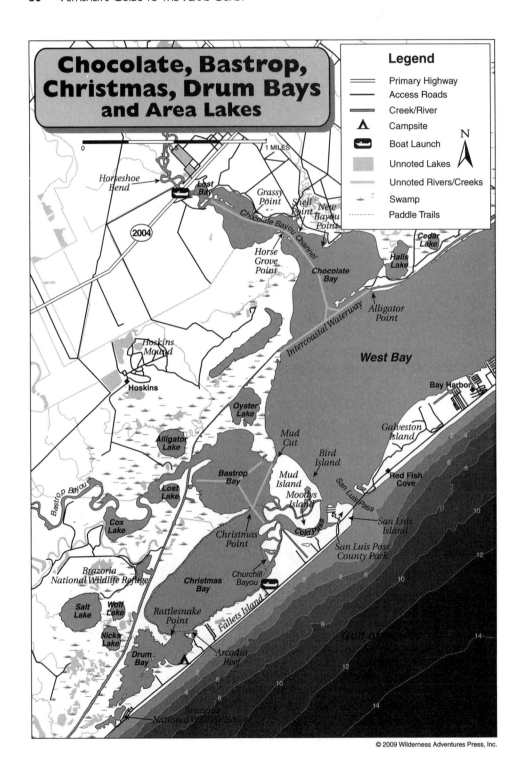

Chocolate, Bastrop, Christmas, Drum Bays and Area Lakes

Legend

═══	Primary Highway
──	Access Roads
──	Creek/River
Λ	Campsite
⊟	Boat Launch
▨	Unnoted Lakes
──	Unnoted Rivers/Creeks
⊣⊢	Swamp
....	Paddle Trails

N

0   0.5   1 MILES

Horseshoe Bend
Lost Bay
Grassy Point
Shell Point
New Bayou Point
Chocolate Bayou Channel
2004
Horse Grove Point
Chocolate Bay
Cedar Lake
Halls Lake
Alligator Point
Intercoastal Waterway
Hoskins Mound
Hoskins
West Bay
Bay Harbor
Oyster Lake
Alligator Lake
Galveston Island
Mud Cut
Bird Island
Bastrop Bay
Bastrop Bayou
Lost Lake
Mud Island
Moodys Island
San Luis Pass
Red Fish Cove
Cox Lake
Christmas Point
Cold Pass
San Luis Island
Brazoria National Wildlife Refuge
Christmas Bay
Churchill Bayou
San Luis Pass County Park
Salt Lake
Wolf Lake
Rattlesnake Point
Fallets Island
Nicks Lake
Drum Bay
Arcadia Reef
Gulf of
Brazoria National Wildlife Refuge

© 2009 Wilderness Adventures Press, Inc.

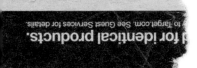

SHELL ISLAND REEF

...ted just west of Carancahua Reef, off Shell Point. Shell Island ...ark for area boaters. The area off the southwest corner is the ...the island.

CHOCOLATE BAY

...north of the western end of West Bay and the Intracoastal Waterway. ...of two Texas bays named Chocolate Bay. The eastern part of Chocolate ...is dominated by a series of reefs and is generally less than 3 feet deep. In the center, the depth drops to over 4 feet.

Near the southeastern corner of Chocolate Bay is an inlet called the Narrows that leads into Halls Lake. The inlet includes several reefs and islands. Halls Lake joins Chocolate Bay in the southeast corner. The eastern shoreline offers good redfish and flounder fishing. Hall's Lake is very shallow with most of the water less than 3 feet deep.

Chocolate Bayou Channel runs the length of Chocolate Bay to the north with numerous spoil islands on each side of the channel. The channel makes a bend to the west between Horse Grove Point to the west and Grassy Point to the east. Fish these spoil areas for redfish, speckled trout, and flounder.

Also, fish the spoil islands near the Intracoastal Waterway. Fish will often locate at the intersection of the ICW and Chocolate Bayou Channel, especially during cold weather.

As the name implies, Chocolate Bay is often muddy in appearance. The predominant south wind blows right down the middle of the bay. Pay attention to the wind conditions when fishing this bay.

Boat Ramp

Chocolate Bayou & Hwy 2004

OYSTER LAKE

Oyster Lake is located between West Bay and Bastrop Bay. The Intracoastal Waterway borders Oyster Lake to the north. The lake is best accessed from the ICW. The waters in Oyster Lake are very shallow with several reefs lining the shoreline. Boaters in Oyster Lake should use caution and travel slowly.

BIRD ISLAND

Bird Island is just inside the mouth of San Luis Pass. There are several guts around Bird Island that feed water in and out of San Luis Pass. The currents flowing through these guts can be swift when the tide changes.

The north side of Bird Island is protected from the wind and offers good wade fishing. Also work around the many sand bars in the area. Work the drop-off using sinking lines with Clouser Minnows, crab patterns, and shrimp patterns. Spin casters should use jigheads with soft plastics for speckled trout and flounder.

SAN LUIS PASS

San Luis Pass is one of the natural passes on the Texas Coast. Strong currents bring water into West Bay through San Luis Pass. The area around the mouth of the pass is continuously changing, forming and eroding sand bars. The water through the pass ranges from about 10 to 40 feet deep. Texas 257 crosses over the pass connecting Galveston Island to Follets Island. The bridge over San Luis Pass connecting Galveston Island to Follets Island is a toll bridge ($2).

San Luis Pass County Park is located on the Follets Island side of the pass. A paved boat ramp and parking area are available in the park. There is also a sand parking area at the pass just outside of the park.

The water running through San Luis Pass can be very strong. Warning signs are spaced along the Galveston Island side of the pass. Pay attention to these warnings. Fish San Luis Pass for flounder in the summer and fall. The pass is also a highway for speckled trout in early summer. Work the many guts running through the pass. Anglers can also fish from the Follets Island side at the San Luis County Park pier.

Boat Ramp

San Luis Pass County Park, 14001 CR 257 / 979-233-6026

Amenities

Bright Lite, 13201 Bluewater Highway / 979-233-8115
San Luis Pass County Park, 14001 CR 257 / 979-233-6026

San Luis Pass is always a good fishing spot.

BASTROP BAY

Bastrop Bay, located to the west of West Bay, is bordered by Christmas Bay to the southwest and the Intracoastal Waterway to the north. Bastrop Bay has two deep channels making a large X through its middle. Another channel lines the southeast side of the bay. These deeper waters offer cold-weather protection to speckled trout and redfish. Anglers should fish these deeper waters during very cold or very hot weather conditions.

Bastrop Bay can be accessed from the east through Mud Cut, from the west by Christmas Point, or from the north at the Intracoastal Waterway. Bastrop Bay is another good area for kayakers. For anglers with a larger boat, load your kayak in the boat, travel to Bastrop Bay and use the kayak to fish the waters surrounding the shoreline of the bay.

Numerous spoil areas line the channels. Fish them early in the day during warmer months and later in the day during cold months after the sun has had a chance to warm the surrounding waters.

Areas along the east and west shoreline are wadeable. Most of Bastrop Bay is less than 3 feet deep.

CHRISTMAS BAY

Christmas Bay is a great place for anyone to get his or her first experience fishing the Texas coast. It's close to Houston and has the modern conveniences to make an easy, first coastal trip. There are several access points for fishermen with or without a boat.

Christmas Bay is made up of seagrass beds, tidal flats, and salt marshes. The seagrass beds are the largest in the Galveston Bay Region. In fact, grass and reeds line the shoreline of most of Christmas Bay. Anglers will see numerous birds when fishing Christmas Bay and where birds fish, there's fish for anglers. Anglers will also find oyster reefs in the bay.

Christmas Bay is only about an hour drive from Houston. At just over 4,000 acres, it's covered extensively with grass flats. Due to the shallow waters, boat traffic is limited, making Christmas Bay perfect for anglers fishing out of a kayak.

It is located just west of West Bay. Most of the bay is less than 3 feet deep with some of the center section over 4 feet deep. Christmas Bay is protected to the south by Follets Island and is bordered to the north by the Intercoastal Waterway and the Brazoria National Wildlife Refuge. Moody and Mud Islands border the bay to the east. Rattlesnake Point separates Christmas Bay at the west end from Drum Bay.

The eastern end of Christmas Bay has a series of small islands separated from Follets Island by Churchill Bayou. Cold Pass is a deep channel that separates the small islands from Moody Island and feeds into San Luis Pass and the Gulf of Mexico.

Christmas Bay has good wade fishing along the north and south shorelines. Work around the small islands at the east end for both redfish and speckled trout. The Arcadia Reef area in the southwest part of Christmas Bay offers good fishing for redfish, speckled trout, and flounder from spring through late fall.

Texas Parks and Wildlife has established a paddling trail around Christmas Bay. The major trail is just over 19 miles long. Two shorter trails are made by circling the east small islands (3.8 miles) or bypassing the islands (10.3 miles). The paddling trails can be accessed from Highway 257 that runs along Follets Island.

Anglers in shallow draft boats can drift through the center section of the bay for speckled trout using topwater lures and jigheads with plastics. Bait fishers can use shrimp under a popping cork or Mansfield Mauler. There are often flocks of birds feeding on shrimp driven to the surface by fish. Stay in front of the birds, taking care not to crash through the area to extend your time around the school of fish. Have at least one outfit rigged with a chrome-and-chartreuse Rat-L-Trap or a swim lure to work the school of fish.

Anglers can access Christmas Bay by using the ramp near Ernie's Bait Barn. Look for the red airplane and sign on Highway 257.

Boat Ramp

Seidler's Landing, CR 257S

Amenities

Ernie's Bait Barn / 979-233-5159 (Bait)

The old airplane for Ernie's Bait also points the way to Seidler's Landing and Christmas Bay.

SALT LAKE AND NICKS LAKE

Salt Lake and Nicks Lake are located just north of the Intracoastal Waterway and Drum Bay. One cut leads into the two lakes from the south side. The water in these two lakes is very shallow. Anglers are best served fishing from a boat or kayak as the bottom of the lakes can be very muddy.

Work the shorelines and the mouths of the cut connecting the lakes.

DRUM BAY

Drum Bay is just to the west of Christmas Bay. Most of Drum Bay is very shallow and a great place for anglers fishing from a kayak. Anglers can access Drum Bay from State Highway 257 along the south shoreline.

The old Intracoastal Waterway cuts right through the middle of Drum Bay. The channel is still there and the deeper water of the channel often holds fish. It is also a wintertime haven for fish trying to escape cold water.

FOLLETS ISLAND

Follets Island offers anglers access to the gulf shoreline. Follets Island runs from San Luis Pass in the east to the Freeport Harbor Channel in the west. State Highway 257 runs the entire length of the island.

Anglers can access the beach through six marked beach access points along Highway 257. Beach traffic goes one way from the west to the east along Follets Island. Kayakers can access Christmas Bay at 257M, but need to abide by the No Parking signs.

There is also a boat ramp at 257S – Seidler's Landing. The ramp is paved and parking is paved but limited.

Several signs along Highway 257 note that water is frequently over the road. Follets Island is not very high in elevation and, during the wettest times, waves from the gulf may drive water over the road.

Follets Island offers a unique fishing opportunity. Anglers can fish in the gulf or go inshore and fish the waters of Christmas Bay. During windy conditions, anglers using a kayak can fish the calmer waters of the bay. When the wind dies down, fish the green water on the gulf side. The distance across the island from the gulf to the bay side is short, giving anglers the chance to fish both waters easily in one day.

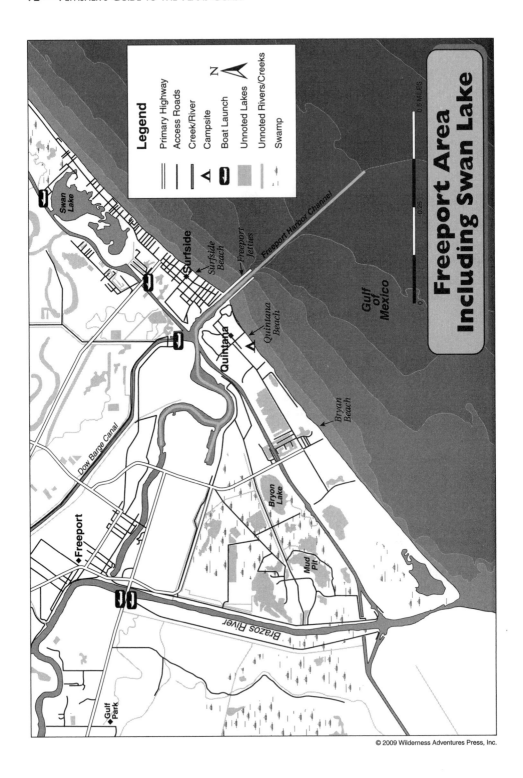

Legend

Primary Highway
Access Roads
Creek/River
Campsite
Boat Launch
Unnoted Lakes
Unnoted Rivers/Creeks
Swamp

N

Swan Lake

Surfside
Surfside Beach
Freeport Jetties
Freeport Harbor Channel

Quintana
Quintana Beach

Gulf of Mexico

Bryan Beach

Dow Barge Canal

Bryon Lake

Freeport

Mud Pit

Brazos River

Gulf Park

0 0.25 0.5 MILES

Freeport Area Including Swan Lake

SWAN LAKE

Swan Lake is located south of the Intercoastal Waterway and east of Freeport. The lake is best accessed from the south along State Highway 257. Anglers can also access the Intracoastal Waterway across Highway 257 from Stahlman Park. There is a paved parking area with three paved boat ramps. There is also a limited parking area near the crabbing pier.

Boat Ramp

Stahlman Park Hwy 257

SURFSIDE BEACH

Surfside Beach offers access to the eastern Freeport Jetty and the surf along the Gulf of Mexico. Highway 257 runs along the beach area. Although a permit is required to park on the beach, there is a free parking area on State Highway 332 at the edge of the beach. You can also enter the beach through Stahlman Park.

Surfside Beach is often covered with sargassum seaweed, a natural part of the environment and should be left in place. Be cautious when driving over the seaweed. It can accumulate over soft spots in the beach and vehicles can become stuck. Also leave any Christmas trees or hay bales where you find them. They are part of the beach erosion control program.

During windier periods, waves can come all the way up the beach to the dunes in the Surfside Beach area, eliminating any area for driving a vehicle. Pay attention to the waves.

Amenities

Pier 30 Bait / 979-233-4250
Perry's Food Store, 2703 Bluewater Highway / 979-239-1610
Surfside Jetty County Park, 427 Jetty View Rd / 979-230-9452

FREEPORT JETTIES

The Freeport Jetties protect the Freeport Harbor Channel from gulf waters. This channel was once part of the Brazos River but now serves the vast industrial area as a deep shipping lane.

The relatively deep waters of the Freeport Channel offer good wintertime fishing. Fish gather in the deeper channel during cold weather. Be aware of the large vessels in the area.

Boat Ramp

Beach Bait & Tackle, 1601 Hwy 332 / 979-233-9509
Bridge Bait, 1011 Casko Rd / 979-239-2248
Cold Pass Marina, 11511 Bluewater Hwy / 979-239-2040

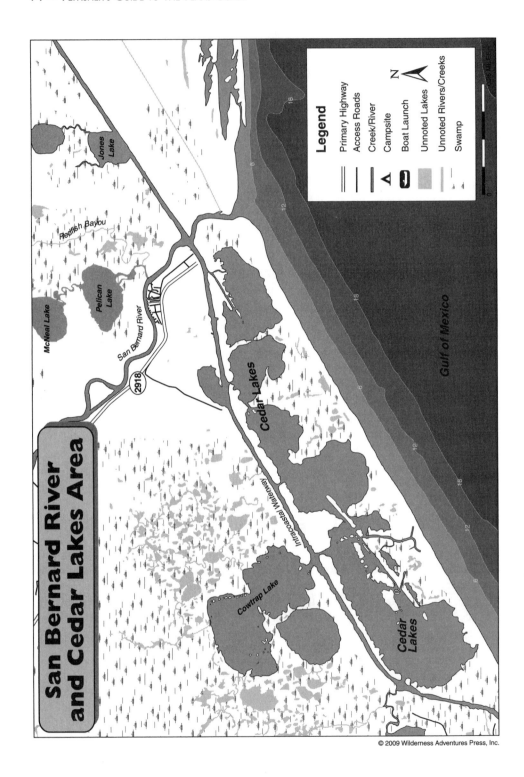

San Bernard River and Cedar Lakes Area

Jones Lake

Redfish Bayou

Pelican Lake

McNeal Lake

San Bernard River

2918

Cedar Lakes

Intracoastal Waterway

Cowtrap Lake

Cedar Lakes

Gulf of Mexico

Legend

Primary Highway
Access Roads
Creek/River
Campsite
Boat Launch
Unnoted Lakes
Unnoted Rivers/Creeks
Swamp

N

© 2009 Wilderness Adventures Press, Inc.

QUINTANA BEACH AND BRYAN BEACH

Quintana Beach and Bryan Beach are located between the south Freeport Jetty and the Brazos River. FM 1495 leads to the bridge over the Intracoastal Waterway. Looking north, you see the vast industrial complex associated with the Brazosport area.

There is a public boat ramp located at the Intracoastal near Quintana Beach with paved parking. Anglers can fish the gulf from the beach.

Brazos River

The Brazos River is one of the longest rivers in Texas. The river flows from the southern panhandle region west of the Fort Worth area all the way to the Gulf of Mexico. Stretching over such a long distance, the Brazos has the chance to gain additional water from runoff almost anytime of the year.

The heaviest rains are in the spring and fall. During spring rains the Brazos River can collect large amounts of water and flood. The water of the river is often a sandy or light brown color from the sediment along its lengthy shoreline.

The Brazos River enters the Gulf of Mexico just west of Freeport. The mouth of the river, just south of the Intercoastal Waterway, is partially silted in. Fishers need to use a shallow draft boat or kayak.

JONES LAKES

The Jones Lakes are a chain of lakes north of the Intracoastal Waterway. The first Jones Lake is located right next to the Intracoastal Waterway just to the east of the San Bernard River. There are many shallow areas and oyster reefs located throughout the lakes. This is an excellent area for anglers with kayaks.

The various Jones Lakes are connected by a small channel. The areas around the lakes are marshy and most of the lakes have reed-covered shorelines.

SAN BERNARD RIVER

The San Bernard River is located between the Brazos River to the east and the Colorado River to the west. The river is best fished during the winter months, and runs into the Intracoastal Waterway to the south and originally went all the way to the Gulf of Mexico.

The area of the river south of the Intracoastal Waterway can change as any river does. There is currently an effort underway to have this area dredged to allow easier gulf access.

COWTRAP LAKE

Cowtrap Lake and West Cowtrap Lake are north of the Intracoastal Waterway and north of the chain of Cedar Lakes. Anglers can enter Cowtrap Lake from the Intracoastal Waterway. Most of Cowtrap Lake is less than 3 feet deep with numerous oyster shell reefs scattered throughout. Some areas have a soft mud bottom, so test the area before wading. This is another good area for kayakers.

CEDAR LAKES

Cedar Lakes has the best fish population in the state, which is a bold but true statement. According to the Coastal Division of the Texas Parks and Wildlife creel surveys over the last 30 years, the Cedar Lakes have the highest concentration of speckled trout, redfish, black drum, and other species that anglers pursue. It's hard to believe these lakes have so many fish and so few fishers.

Cedar Lakes is a chain of lakes on the gulf side of the Intracoastal Waterway. The lakes can be accessed from the public boat ramp at the end of FM 2918 across the Intracoastal Waterway near the San Bernard River.

There are five large lakes, several smaller lakes, and numerous small islands throughout this area. These lakes are ideal for fishing out of a kayak. The short trip across the Intracoastal Waterway leads kayakers to the protected areas of the lakes.

Many parts of the lakes are too shallow for anything but a kayak. Anglers can paddle in and either fish from the kayak or get out and wade. The southern shorelines of First Cedar, Blowout Hole, and the last Cedar Lake offer areas to wade.

As with most of the Texas coast, wind plays a big role in fishing these lakes.

Boat Ramp

End of FM 2918

Amenities

Nelson's River Inn, FM 2918 / 979-964-3814

Surf fishing along Follets Island.

Galveston Bay Hub Cities

BAYTOWN
Population: 66,430
County: Harris

ACCOMMODATIONS

Best Western, 5021 I-10 East / 281-421-2233 / 50 rooms / $80-$90 /
www.bestwesterntexas.com

Comfort Suites, 7209 Garth Rd / 281-421-9764 / 61 rooms / $80-$200

Hampton Inn, 7211 Garth Rd / 281-421-1234 / 70 rooms / $115-$149 /
www.hamptoninn.com

La Quinta Inn, 52151 IH-10 East / 281-421-5566 / 104 rooms / $72-$79 /
www.lq.com

Quality Inn, 200 South Highway 146 Business / 281-427-7481 / 109 rooms /
$50-$109 / www.qualityinn.com

Super 8 Motel, 9032 Hwy 146 / 281-576-6521 / 56 rooms / $60-$199 /
www.super8.com

CAMPGROUNDS

Houston East RV, 11810 IH-10 East / 281-383-3618

Lost River RV, 8407 N FM 565 / 281-576-2617

Pine Lakes RV, 6600 Hwy 146 / 281-573-9975 / www.pinelakesrvresort.com

RESTAURANTS

Bud's Barbeque, 4505 Garth Rd / 281-422-4715

Cracker Barrel, 5173 IH-10 East / 281-421-5091 / www.crackerbarrel.com

IHOP, 5001 Garth Rd / 281-421-9555 / www.ihop.com

Outback Steakhouse, 5218 IH-10 east / 281-421-9001 / www.outback.com

Tortuga Coastal Cantina, 4710 IH-10 East / 281-839-3902

Whataburger, 1930 Garth Rd / 281-428-7257 / www.whataburger.com

FREEPORT
Population: 12,814
County: Brazoria

ACCOMMODATIONS

Country Hearth Inn, 1015 W 2nd St / 979-239-1602 / 40 rooms / $49-$55 / www.countryhearth.com

CAMPGROUNDS

Ks & Js RV Park, 8333 CR 400, Brazoria / 979-798-2726
Way Station RV Park, 14462 Hwy 36, Brazoria / 979-798-6560 / www.waystationrvpark.com

RESTAURANTS

B&B Seafood, 1515 Brazosport Blvd / 979233-1340
Hammerhead Bar & Burger, 10 Surf Dr / 979-233-1200
On the River, 919 W 2nd / 979-233-1352
Talk About Good, 2105 Brazosport Blvd / 979-233-0665
Windswept Seafood Restaurant, 105 Burch Circle / 979-233-1951

FOR MORE INFORMATION

Visit www.brazosport.org

GALVESTON
Population: 57,247
County: Galveston

ACCOMMODATIONS

America's Best Value Inn, 6311 Central City Blvd / 409-740-9001 / 50 rooms / $45-$300 / www.bestvalueinn.com

Best Western, 5914 Seawall Blvd / 409-740-1261 / 150 rooms / $43-$260 / www.bestwesterntexas.com

Comfort Inn, 102 E Seawall Blvd / 409-766-7070 / 63 rooms / $80-$164

Days Inn, 6107 Broadway / 409-740-2491 / 88 rooms / $40-$160 / www.daysinn.com

La Quinta, 8710 Seawall Blvd / 409-740-9100 / 71 rooms / $65-$239 / www.lq.com

Quality Inn, 5924 Seawall Blvd / 409-740-1088 / 91 rooms / $80-$199/ www.qualityinn.com

Hawthorn Suites, 6300 Seawall Blvd / 409-744-3801 / 230 rooms / $90-$304 / twww.hawthorne.com

CAMPGROUNDS

Bayou Shores RV Park, 6310 Heards Lane / 888-744-2837 / www.bayoushoresresort.com

Dellanera RV Park, 10901 San Luis Pass Road / 409-740-0390 / www.dellanerarvpark.com

Galveston Island RV Park, 2323 Skymaster / 409-744-5464

Galveston Island State Park, 14901 FM 3005 / 409-737-1222 / www.tpwd.state.tx.us

RESTAURANTS

Brodie's Beach Hut, 401 Broadway / 409-765-6855

Casey's Seaside Café, 3828 Seawall Blvd / 409-762-9625 / www.gaidos.com

Denny's, 1410 Seawall Blvd / 409-763-5954 / www.dennys.com

Fuddruckers, 111 23rd St, 409-765-8000 / www.fuddruckers.com

Gaido's Seafood, 3900 Seawall Blvd / 409-762-9625 / www.gaidos.com

Landry's Oyster Bar, 2100 Harborside Drive / 409-762-4747

Luby's, 6125 Central City Blvd / 409-744-8788 / www.lubys.com

Queen's Bar-B-Que, 3428 Ave S / 409-762-3151

Quizno's Subs, 23rd St & Market / 409-762-5700 / www.quiznos.com

McDonalds, 517 Seawall Blvd / 409-750-9945 / www.mcdonalds.com

Saltgrass Steakhouse, 1502 Seawall Blvd / 409-744-6000 / www.saltgrass.com

Whataburger, 6327 Stewart Road / 409-744-6344 / www.whataburger.com

SPORTING GOODS

Academy Sports, 4523 Ft. Crockett Blvd / 409-941-6550 / www.academy.com

HOUSTON
Population: 2,009,834
County: Harris

ACCOMMODATIONS

Best Western Greenspoint, 14753 North Freeway / 281-873-7575 / 50 rooms / $65-$195 / www.bestwesterntexas.com

Best Western Hobby Airport, 8600 Gulf Freeway / 713-910-8600 / 49 rooms / $60-$100 / www.bestwesterntexas.com

Clarion, 500 N Sam Houston Pkwy / 281-931-0101 / 220 rooms / $100-$210 / www.clarionhotel.com

Comfort Inn Greenspoint, 12701 North Freeway / 281-875-2000 / 97 rooms/ $65-$120

Hilton Hobby Airport, 8181 Airport Blvd / 713-645-3000 / 303 rooms / $100-$280 / www.hilton.com

Holiday Inn Intercontinental, 15222 JFK Blvd / 281-449-2311 / 415 rooms / $89-$179 / www.holidayinn.com

La Quinta, 15510 JFK Blvd / 281-219-2000 / 132 rooms / $84-$139 / www.lq.com

Quality Inn Hobby, 7775 Airport Blvd / 713-644-3232 / 56 rooms / $60-$149 / www.qualityinn.com

CAMPGROUNDS

Advanced RV, 2850 S Sam Houston Pkwy / 888-515-6950 / www.advancedrvpark.com

Houston Central KOA, 1620 Peach Leaf / 281-442-3700 / www.koa.com

Lakeview RV Resort, 11991 S Main St / 800-385-9122 / www.lakeviewrvresort.com

South Main RV Park, 10100 South Main St / 713-667-0120 / www.southmainrvpark.com

RESTAURANTS

Hobby Airport area

Denny's, 9810 Gulf Freeway / 713-946-0230 / www.dennys.com

IHOP, 6888 Gulf Freeway / 713-847-9908 / www.ihop.com

Pappas Bar-B-Q, 8560 Gulf Freeway / 713-947-9927 / www.pappas.com4

Intercontinental Airport area

Cracker Barrel, 14765 North Freeway / 281-872-0809 / www.crackerbarrel.com

Los Cucos, 9441 FM 1960 West / 281-540-2270

Waffle House, 7106 Will Clayton Pkwy / 281-548-1018 / www.wafflehouse.com

SPORTING GOODS

Academy Sports / www.academy.com
    11077 NW Freeway / 713-613-6300
    19720 NW Freeway / 281-517-3800
    7600 Westheimer / 713-268-4300
    13400 E Freeway / 713-445-4400
    10375 N. Freeway / 281-405-4300
    13150 Breton Ridge Street / 281-894-3700
    10414 Gulf Freeway / 713-948-4100
    8236 S. Gessner / 713-219-3500
    2404 S.W. Freeway / 713-874-6020
    14500 Westheimer / 281-556-3200
Bass Pro Shops, 5000 Katy Mills Circle, Suite 415, Katy / 281-644-2200 /
    www.basspro.com
IFLY, Angler's Edge, 5000 Westheimer Rd. / 713-993-9981
Canoesport, 5822 Bissonnet / 713-660-7000 / www.canoesport.com
Cut Rate Fishing Tackle, 8933 Katy Fwy / 713-827-7762
Gander Mountain, 19820 Hempstead Hwy / 832-237-7900 /
    www.gandermountain.com
Houston Angler / 713-953-1079
Orvis Houston, 5848 Westheimer Rd / 713-783-2111 / www.orvis.com
Sports Authority / www.sportsauthority.com
    1210 Fry Road / 281-599-1944
    2131 South Post Oak Blvd / 713-622-4940
    8625 F.M. 1960 West / 281-807-9020
    10225 Katy Freeway / 713-468-4870
    11940 A Westheimer Rd / 281-493-9190
Tackle Hut, 216 W. Little York Rd #C / 713-694-8008

AIRPORTS

Bush Intercontinental Airport, 2800 N Terminal Rd / 281-230-3100
Houston Hobby Airport, 7800 Airport Blvd / 713-640-3000

KEMAH
Population: 2,333
County: Galveston

ACCOMMODATIONS

Courtesy Inn, 909 Kipp / 281-538-9648 / 3 rooms
Days Inn, 1411 Hwy 146 / 281-538-0077 / 42 rooms / $50-$125 / www.daysinn.com
Kemah Escape Hotel, 617 9th St / 281-538-3200 / 8 rooms / $139-$229

CAMPGROUNDS

Lakeside RV Park, 1017 Marina Bay Dr / 281-334-3036 /
    www.lakesidervparktx.com
Marina Bay RV, 925 Marina Bay Dr / 281-334-9944 / www.marinabayrvresort.com

RESTAURANTS

Cadillac Authentic Mexican, 2003 Blessing of the Fleet / 281-334-9049
Dairy Queen, 1107 Hwy 146 / 281-538-1084 / www.dairyqueen.com
Landry's Seafood, Kemah Boardwalk / 281-334-2513
Saltgrass Steakhouse, 201 Kipp Ave / 281-334-0192 / www.saltgrass.com
Skipper's Café, 1026 Marina Bay Dr / 281-334-4787
IHOP, 401 FM 2094 / 281-334-9888 / www.ihop.com
Wendy's Hamburgers / 325 FM 2094 / 281-538-7774 / www.wendys.com

For more information visit www.kemah.net

LAKE JACKSON
Population: 26,386
County: Brazoria

ACCOMMODATIONS

Comfort Suites, 296 Abner Jackson Parkway / 979-297-5545 / 60 rooms / $108-$180
Holiday Inn Express, 809 Highway 332 / 60 rooms / $82-$105 /
www.holidayinn.com
Super 8 Motel, 915 Hwy 332 / 979-297-3031/ 97 rooms / $69-$89 /
www.super8.com

RESTAURANTS

Cactus Grill, 107 West Way / 979-285-9300
The Cajun Greek, 410 A Flag Lake Dr / 979-297-1000
Charley's Grilled Subs, 100 Hwy 332 W / 979-480-0233 /
www.charleyssteakery.com
El Chico, 100 Hwy 332 / 979-297-4002 / www.elchico.com
Johnny Carinos Country Italian, 106 E Hwy 332 / 979-285-3570 /
www.carinos.com
Luby's, 125 West Way / 979-297-2216 / www.lubys.com
Quizno's Classic Subs, 401 B This Way / 979-297-9929 / www.lubys.com
Riverpoint Steakhouse, 111 Abner Jackson Pkwy / 979-299-7444

SPORTING GOODS

Academy Sports, 120 Highway 332 West / 979-373-5700 / www.academy.com

PASADENA
Population: 158,000
County: Harris

ACCOMMODATIONS

Econo Lodge, 823 Pasadena Freeway / 713-477-4266 / 39 rooms / $69-$149 /
www.econolodge.com

Holiday Inn Express, 2601 Spencer Hwy / 866-270-5110/ 60 rooms / $90-$165 /
www.holidayinn.com

La Quinta Inn, 3490 E Sam Houston Pkwy South / 281-991-7771 / 49 rooms /
$70-$80 / www.lq.com

Super 8 Motel, 5400 Vista Rd / 281-487-8882/ 49 rooms / $60-$70 /
www.super8.com

RESTAURANTS

A&W, 2001 Genoa-Red Bluff / 281-998-2730 / www.a&wrestaurants.com

Chili's, 5548 Fairmont Pkwy / 281-487-7182 / www.chilis.com

Denny's, 4125 Spencer Hwy / 713-947-9902 / www.dennys.com

Gabby's Steaks & Barbecue, 4010 Spencer Hwy / 713-628-3965 /
www.gabbysbbq.com

IHOP, 3605 Spencer Hwy / 713-944-9908 / www.ihop.com

Jason's Deli, 3905 Spencer Hwy / 713-946-3354 / www.jasonsdeli.com

Luby's, 1210 E Southmore Ave / 713-477-2050 / www.lubys.com

Texas Roadhouse, 3033 E Sam Houston Pkwy / 281-998-0779 /
www.texasroadhouse.com

Whataburger, 4831 Fairmont Pkwy / 281-998-1605 / www.whataburger.com

SPORTING GOODS

Academy Sports, 5500 Spencer Hwy at Beltway 8 / 713-947-4000 /
www.academy.com

PEARLAND
Population: 80,000
County: Brazoria

ACCOMMODATIONS

Best Western, 1855 N Main St / 281-997-2000 / 45 rooms / $70-$130 /
www.bestwesterntexas.com

Hampton Inn, 6515 W Broadway St / 832-736-9977 / 61 rooms / $99-$214 /
www.hamptoninn.com

Holiday Inn Express, 1702 Main St / 281-997-2600 / 58 rooms / $80-$199 /
www.holidayinn.com

La Quinta Inn, 9002 Broadway / 281-412-5454 / 55 rooms / $70-$80 / www.lq.com

Spring Hill Suites, 1820 Country Place Pkwy / 713-436-7377 / 91 rooms / $119-$159
/ www.springhillsuites.com

RESTAURANTS

Central Texas Bar B Que, 4110 W Broadway / 281-485-9626

Golden Corral, 9114 Broadway / 281-412-4546 / www.goldencorral.net

Joe's Crab Shack, 3239 Sliberlake Village Dr / 713-436-8880 /
www.joescrabshack.com

Lenny's Sub Shop, 3320 E Broadway / 832-736-9782 / www.lennyssubshop.com

On the Border Mexican Grill, 2728 Smith Ranch Rd / 713-436-7880 /
www.ontheborder.com

Saltgrass Steakhouse, 3251 Silverlake Village Dr / 713-436-0799 /
www.saltgrass.com

SPORTING GOODS

Academy Sports, 2804 Business Center Dr / 713-793-5000 / www.academy.com

Bass Pro Shop, 1000 Bass Pro Drive, 713-770-5100 / www.basspro.com

Fishing Tackle Unlimited (Cut Rate), 12800 Gulf Freeway / 281-481-7762 /
www.fishingtackleunlimited.com

Seabrook
Population: 9,443
County: Harris

Accommodations

Comfort Inn, 2901 NASA Pkwy / 281-326-3308 / 47 rooms / $90-$200

Hampton Inn, 3000 NASA Rd 1 / 281-532-9200 / 70 rooms / $70-$149 / www.hamptoninn.com

Holiday Inn Express, 2720 NASA Rd 1 / 281-326-5871 / 78 rooms / $99-$149 / www.hiexpress.com

La Quinta Seabrook, 3636 NASA Rd 1 Pkwy / 281-326-7300 / 52 rooms / $80-$110 / www.lq.com

Restaurants

Outrigger's Seafood Grill, 101 Bath / 281-474-3474

Pappadeaux's Seafood Kitchen, 309 Waterfront Dr / 281-291-9932 / www.pappas.com

Subway, 2400 Bayport / 281-474-4031 / www.subway.com

Tookies, 1108 Cook St / 281-474-5860

Waffle House, 2102 Seabrook Cir / 281-291-0092 / www.wafflehouse.com

Whataburger, 1408 Bayport / 281-474-2518 / www.whataburger.com

SURFSIDE BEACH
Population: 763
County: Brazoria

ACCOMMODATIONS

Anchor Motel, 1302 Bluewater Highway / 979-239-3543/ 32 rooms / $45-$50
Cedar Sands Motel, 343 North Beachfront / 979-233-1942 / 19 rooms / $73-$119
Surfside Motel, 330 Coral Court / 979-233-4948 / 14 rooms / $70-$120 /
www.surfsidemotel.biz

CAMPGROUNDS

Austin's Landing RV Park, 318 Thunder Rd (12th St) / 979-239-1923
Gottasea RV Park / 979-233-2694
Quintana Beach RV County Park, 330 5th St, Quintana / 979-233-1461
Surfside Beach RV Park, 102 Fort Velesco Dr / 979-233-6919 /
www.surfsidebeachrv.com

RESTAURANTS

Jetty Shack, 412 Parkview / 979-233-5300
Kitty's Purple Cow, 323 Bluewater Highway / 979-233-9161
Castaway's Club & Grill, 110 Ft. Velasco / 979-233-7370
Red Snapper Inn, 402 Bluewater Highway / 979-239-3226 /
www.redsnapperinn.com

Texas City
Population: 41,521
County: Galveston

Accommodations

Best Western Mainland Inn, 10620 Emmitt Lowery Expressway / 409-986-6600 / 52 rooms / $79-$129 / www.bestwesterntexas.com

Crystal Suites, Hwy 146 N / 409-945-0999 / 44 rooms / $69-$89

Fairfield Inn, 13250 E F Lowry / 409-986-3866 / 64 rooms / $90-$104 / www.fairfieldinn.com

Hampton Inn, 2320 FM 2004 / 409-986-6686 / 64 rooms / $99-$104 / www.hamptoninn.com

La Quinta, 1121 Highway 146 North / 409-948-3101 / 121 rooms / $62-$115 / www.lq.com

Restaurants

Bravos, 2525 Palmer Hwy / 409-948-2456 / www.bravosmexicanfood.com

Denny's, 1201 Hwy 146 / 409-935-2252 / www.dennys.com

Grand Prize Barbecue, 2223 Palmer / 409-948-6501 / www.grandprizebarbeque.com

Quizno's Subs, 2028 9th Ave / 409-983-2898 / www.quizmos.com

Subway, 2920 Palmer / 409-935-4996 / www.subway.com

Wendy's Hamburgers, 3805 Palmer / 409-945-4663 / www.wendys.com

Whataburger, 2411 Palmer 409-948-3153 / www.whataburger.com

For More Information

Visit www.texascitychamber.com

Anglers set up special lights to fish the Texas City Dike after dark.

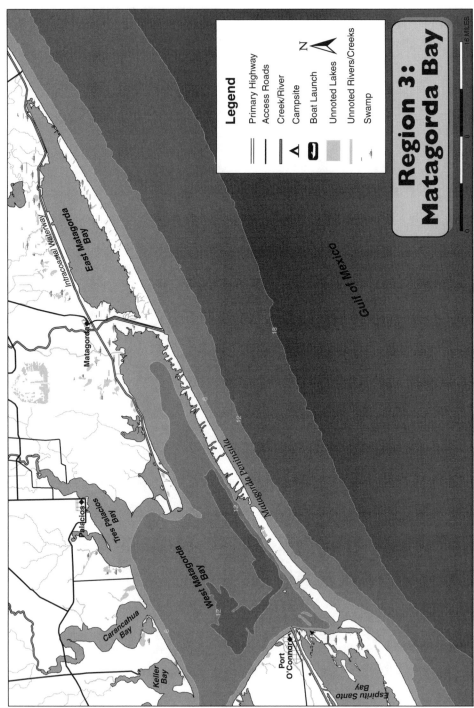

Region 3:
Matagorda Bay

Legend

Primary Highway
Access Roads
Creek/River
Campsite
Boat Launch
Unnoted Lakes
Unnoted Rivers/Creeks
Swamp

N

Gulf of Mexico

Intracoastal Waterway

East Matagorda Bay

Matagorda

Matagorda Peninsula

Palacios

Tres Palacios Bay

West Matagorda Bay

Carancahua Bay

Keller Bay

Port O'Connor

Espiritu Santo Bay

16 MILES

Region 3: Matagorda Bay System

The Matagorda Bay system is the bay directly west of the Galveston Bay complex. Matagorda Bay is surrounded by four smaller bays and the Gulf of Mexico.

The Colorado River intersects the Intracoastal Waterway near the town of Matagorda and splits East Matagorda Bay from Matagorda Bay. Just to the west of the Colorado River is the Mad Island Wildlife Management Area.

Matagorda Bay is fed by several rivers. Tres Palacious River enters Tres Palacious Bay from the northeast. The Navidad River feeds into Lake Texana and into the eastern part of Lavaca Bay. The Lavaca River joins the Navidad River just south of Lake Texana.

Matagorda Bay is big. Anglers need to pay special attention to the weather when venturing long distances in this bay, especially when going to the far south shoreline. Spring and summer thunderstorms pop up and change an easy-to-cross bay into a rolling sea of brown water and spray. It is a good idea to take along a weather radio when boating in any Texas bay, and to check the weather before you head out in the morning. Pay particular attention to any front that will arrive during the day.

Seasonal Fishing Chart - Region 3: Matagorda Bay

	Jan	Feb	Mar	Apr	May	Jun	Jul	Aug	Sep	Oct	Nov	Dec
Redfish	+	+	++	+++	+++	+++	+++	+++	+++	+++	++	+
Spotted Seatrout	+	+++	+++	+++	+++	+++	+++	+++	+++	++	+	+
Flounder				++	+++	+++	+++	+++	+++	+++	+++	+
Black Drum	++	+++	+++	+++	+++	+++	+++	+++	+++	++	+	+
Sheepshead	++	+++	+++	+++	+++	+++	+++	+++	+++	+++	+	+
Crevalle Jack				++	+++	+++	+++	+++	+++			
Spanish Mackerel						++	+++	+++	+++			
Gray Snapper						++	+++	+++				
Tarpon						+	+	+				
Pompano				++	++	++	++	++				
Snook												

+++ = Exceptional, ++ = Very Good, + = Available

If you get caught by a storm, it is often better to ride it out in a safe cove or along a shoreline, than to try to make your way back to the dock.

Anglers fishing in this area need to be aware of the series of locks along the Intracoastal Waterway. These locks were made to help barges and boats maneuver when crossing the Colorado River.

Small boats need to be particularly careful when caught inside a lock with a large barge. The tugboat pushing the barge may cause the water to violently circulate inside the lock. Small boats can get caught up in this current and will have difficulty staying out of the current.

If you haven't traveled through these locks, it's suggested that you hire a guide until you learn how to properly maneuver through this busy section of the Intracoastal Waterway.

The locks on the Colorado River help control area boat traffic.

SARGENT BEACH

The small community of Sargent lies between the Brazosport area and East Matagorda Bay. FM 457 leads directly to the Intracoastal Waterway. Sargent Beach is just south of the Intracoastal Waterway. There is a swing bridge over the Intracoastal that allows barges to move through the area. Normally fishing traffic in the area is sparse except for weekends and holidays. Travelers may be required to wait while the water traffic clears through the area. Expect delays on the busiest days.

Sargent Beach is easily accessed by automobile and a permit is required to park on the beach. The permit can be purchased from local businesses or at the Matagorda County Courthouse. Anglers can fish the surf or the Intracoastal.

There is a paved boat ramp and parking just south of the Intracoastal.

Amenities

Sargent Beach Bait & Tackle / 979-323-0000
Caney Creek RV Park, 108 Socha Rd / 979-245-4735
Caney Creek Marina, 7905 Carancahua / 979-245-3691
Sargent Shores RV, 2237 CR 299 / 713-419-2078
Tuttle's Krusty Pelican, FM 457 / 979-245-0201

EAST MATAGORDA BAY

East Matagorda Bay, at over 18 miles long and 3 miles wide, is made up of a mud and shell bottom with some shell reefs. Many portions of the bay are wadeable but anglers can expect soft muddy bottoms throughout the area. Many light-tackle casters prefer to drift fish using their boat. The bay becomes very busy during the summer months with drifting boats so fishing during the week is recommended.

Waders will do best concentrating on the north and south shorelines and around the many reefs in the middle of the bay. The entire bay is less than 6 feet deep so there is plenty of shallow water for fishing.

Reefs like Long Reef, 3 Beacon Reef, and Half Moon Reef offer oyster-shell bottom surrounded by slightly deeper water. These are prime areas for speckled trout.

Located at the far east end of East Matagorda Bay, Brown Cedar Flats offers good wading areas. This is a very shallow area that fishes best before the hottest summer months and again in fall as temperatures cool down.

Midway along the south shoreline are Catchall Basin, Eidlebach Flat, Oyster Farm, and Kain Cove. All of these areas offer good wading for redfish in the shallows. Waders can try for trout at the deeper water drop-offs.

For anglers wanting to beat the heat of July and August, try fishing around the reefs at night close to a full moon. Thoroughly work one reef before moving to the next. For anyone not familiar with the area, hiring a guide is a good idea.

On the western part of East Matagorda Bay, Raymond Reef is another good area to work. Watch for jumping shrimp and bird activity in East Matagorda Bay. The bird activity increases during the fall months and East Matagorda Bay can get crowded with numerous boats drifting for fish under the birds.

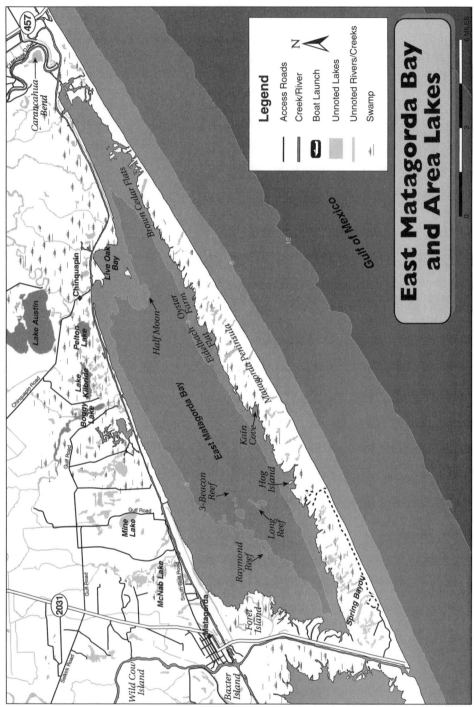

East Matagorda Bay and Area Lakes

Legend

- Access Roads
- Creek/River
- Boat Launch
- Unnoted Lakes
- Unnoted Rivers/Creeks
- Swamp

N

6 MILES

© 2009 Wilderness Adventures Press, Inc.

Menhaden come in from the gulf using the lower Colorado River as an access. Shortly after the menhaden move in, shrimp make their appearance in vast numbers. This offers the lure fisherman a great opportunity to fish hard-body lures, such as Mirrolures, for larger trout chasing the baitfish.

The Colorado River itself can offer excellent fishing when it is not too fresh with upstream runoff.

Guide

Captain Bill Pustejovsky, Gold Tip Guide Service / 979-863-7353

Matagorda Island Surf

The surf along the Gulf of Mexico can be accessed from FM 2031 in Matagorda. Travel south out of Matagorda, crossing over the Intracoastal Waterway. The Matagorda Bay Nature Park and the Colorado River Jetty and Park are located where the Colorado River enters the Gulf.

The Lower Colorado River Authority – LCRA — built the Nature Park and Natural Science Center as well as the Matagorda Bay Nature Park RV Park at the gulf entrance to the river.

A long fishing pier extending into the gulf is located at the park. Fishermen can use live or cut bait to work the surf area at the end of the pier.

Anglers can also fish the surf along Matagorda Island. A beach parking permit is required to park on the beach. Permits can be purchased from area businesses or from the Matagorda County Courthouse.

Beach travelers should travel in tracks made by other vehicles to avoid getting stuck in the sand. Four-wheel drive vehicles are recommended.

Surf fishers can use live or cut bait. Lure and fly casters can concentrate on deeper areas close in to the shoreline.

Anglers can also access areas along the south shoreline of East Matagorda Bay. Three Mile Lake can be reached by four-wheel drive vehicle traveling along the beach and then turning inshore.

LIVE OAK BAY

Live Oak Bay has one of the best redfish populations on the coast according to the Texas Park and Wildlife Department Coastal Fisheries Division annual surveys. It is a small area on the north east shoreline of East Matagorda Bay that has very shallow water with most areas less than 3 feet deep.

Flyfishers working this area should try shrimp and spoon patterns on floating lines. Light tackle casters should try gold spoons and hard-body topwater lures like a Super Spook or Top Dog in Bone.

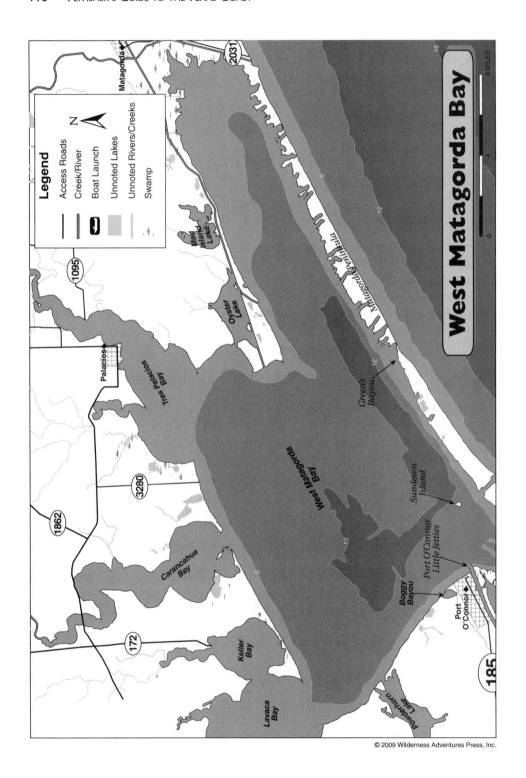

Legend

N

Access Roads

Creek/River

Boat Launch

Unnoted Lakes

Unnoted Rivers/Creeks

Swamp

Matagorda

Mad Island Lake

Oyster Lake

Palacios

Tres Palacios Bay

Matagorda Peninsula

Green's Bayou

West Matagorda Bay

West Bay

Sundown Island

Carancahua Bay

Port O'Connor Little Jetties

Boggy Bayou

Keller Bay

Port O'Connor

Powderhorn Lake

Lavaca Bay

West Matagorda Bay

8 MILES

WEST MATAGORDA BAY

West Matagorda Bay starts just to the west of the Colorado River and goes all the way to Port O'Connor. The south shoreline of West Matagorda Bay offers miles of wadeable fishing.

The area will have a mixture of mud, sand, and grass. There is a good deep water drop-off along the entire south shoreline offering deeper and cooler water to both angler and fish when the hot summer sun bakes the shallows.

Anglers should be aware of sharks in the spring and early summer in West Matagorda Bay. Sharks will eat any fish they can find, including fish on an angler's stringer.

Captain Bill Pustejovsky takes along a 48-quart cooler while wading with his customers to hold any fish caught. He stated even then, he has seen sharks circling the cooler trying to figure a way to get to the boxed fish.

It's simple: If you encounter sharks, move. They're really more interested in the fish you're trying to catch, but why chance it. There are plenty of other places to fish without the toothy cruisers.

Along the south shoreline, places like Green's Bayou, Cotton Bayou, and the Middle Grounds offer excellent wading early in the morning.

Anglers fishing the West Matagorda Bay system should be aware of the recent weather. A heavy rain in the area will take five or six days for the freshwater to settle out of the bay. If the areas farther north near Columbus receive heavy rains causing heavy river runoffs, the bay may not fish well for up to a month.

West Matagorda Bay is one place anglers may encounter sharks during the spring. Frequently empty your stringer or use a Do-Net.

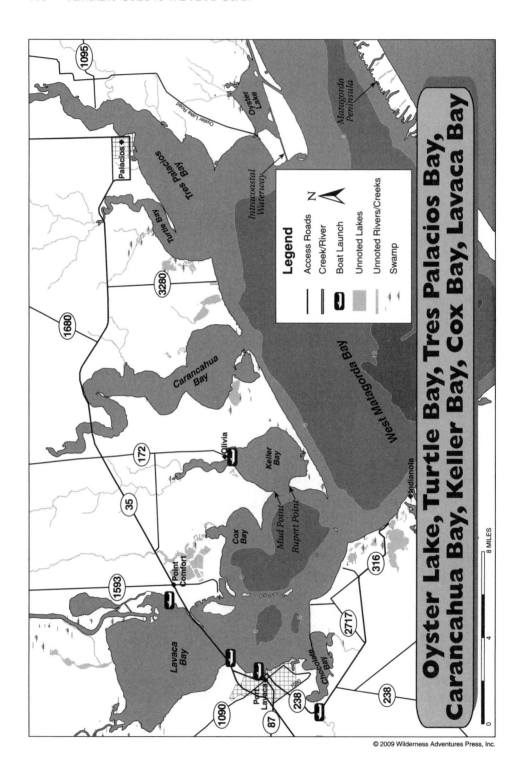

Legend

N

	Access Roads
	Creek/River
	Boat Launch
	Unnoted Lakes
	Unnoted Rivers/Creeks
	Swamp

Oyster Lake, Turtle Bay, Tres Palacios Bay, Carancahua Bay, Keller Bay, Cox Bay, Lavaca Bay

Matagorda Peninsula

Palacios

Tres Palacios Bay

Oyster Lake

Oyster Lake Road

Intracoastal Waterway

Turtle Bay

Carancahua Bay

West Matagorda Bay

Olivia

Keller Bay

Mud Point

Rupert Point

Indianola

Cox Bay

Point Comfort

Lavaca Bay

Port Lavaca

Chocolate Bay

8 MILES

4

0

© 2009 Wilderness Adventures Press, Inc.

OYSTER LAKE

Oyster Lake along the eastern shore of Matagorda Bay offers shallow-water fishing for redfish, but you may decide to stay in the boat because this area can be very muddy. Oyster Lake can be accessed from FM 1095 running south out of Collegeport. The paved road ends just past the First Baptist Church of Collegeport. Don't be tempted by the many shrimp lakes in the area. Mr. Bower (a local shrimp farmer who has warning signs posted) does not like people that take his shrimp. The dirt and gravel road gets slick and bumpy during heavy rains so pay attention to the weather.

Oyster Lake can also be entered from the Intracoastal Waterway to the east. Try to fish during the best tide movements and during a north wind.

Oyster Lake is a good area for flyfishers. Use a floating line and concentrate on redfish using spoon flies, shrimp, and crab patterns. Light tackle casters should use the lightest jighead possible, 1/16 ounce is best. Copper or gold weedless spoons also work well in Oyster Lake.

TURTLE BAY

The western shoreline of Turtle Bay is wadeable. The north shoreline is also wadeable but look to this area when the wind is out of the north. This is also a good area to fish in the fall. There will be plenty of birds working over bait during the hotter summer months.

TRES PALACIOS BAY

Tres Palacios Bay is a small bay on the northeast corner of Matagorda Bay. It is accessed from either the west side at Palacios or from the east at the small town of Collegeport. This secluded bay is a good area for the beginning kayaker. The water becomes brown with a strong south wind. Look to this area during the fall and winter, especially any time there is a north wind.

CARANCAHUA BAY

Carancahua Bay has good fishing when the wind will allow you to fish it. Look to this area when the wind is out of the north. Redfish Lake and Salt Lake are on the southern part of Carancahua Bay and are not heavily fished. Both of these lakes are very shallow with grass-covered bottoms.

KELLER BAY

Keller Bay is very popular and gets crowded on the weekends. There are heavy grass beds with scattered shell and hard-packed sand bottom in the area. The points at the mouth of Keller Bay offer good big trout fishing in the early spring. Mud Point on the north and Rupert Point on the south enclose the mouth of Keller Bay. The Mud Point area offers good wade fishing when the south wind is not too strong.

Keller Bay can be accessed from the ramp at Olivia. It has lots of grass areas inside the bay itself, and the entire area is wadeable via Olivia Park. Sand Point extends from the far southern side of Keller Bay and offers good wading for redfish, but again pay attention to the wind when fishing this area.

Boat Ramps

Florence Bait Camp, End of Second Street, Olivia
Olivia Haterius Park, End of Highway 172, Olivia

Cox Bay

Parts of Cox Bay are off limits to fishing, and the area around Mitchell's Reef is heavily polluted and should be avoided. Signs at local boat ramps display maps showing the restricted areas. Huisache Cove on the north end offers good fishing for redfish. Most of Cox Bay is less than 3 feet deep and best maneuvered in a shallow running boat. Look to Cox Bay for wintertime fishing.

Lavaca Bay

Lavaca Bay is the area north of Indianola and includes several smaller bays and lakes. The far northern part of Lavaca Bay has several oyster shell reefs and is a great winter fishing area. There are scattered shell reefs throughout the area. If there has been a lot of rain to the north, this area may become too fresh to fish. The river area at the north end offers good winter fishing.

Boat Ramps

Alamo Beach on Carrigan Avenue
City Harbor Highway, 238 & Harbor Street, Port Lavaca
City Park, End of Lamar Street, Point Comfort
Harbor of Refuge Boat Ramp, Off Alcoa Road/FM 1090, Port Lavaca
Lighthouse Beach & Bird Sanctuary RV Park, 700 Lighthouse Beach Drive, 361-552-5311, Port Lavaca
Magnolia Beach Park, Margie Tewmey Road & North Ocean Drive, Magnolia Beach
Nautical Landings Marina & Bayfront Peninsula, 106 Commerce Street, 361-553-7041, Port Lavaca
Six Mile Park, End of Royal, Port Lavaca

Chocolate Bay

This is the second bay in Texas to have this name. Chocolate Bay is on the western side of Lavaca Bay. This little bay does not usually hold a lot of fish and anglers would do better seeking other areas.

Boat Ramps

Chocolate Bayou Park, FM 238 at Chocolate Bayou, Port Lavaca

Green's Bayou

Green's Bayou was a cut once open all the way to the Gulf of Mexico. When the Matagorda Ship Channel was dug, nearby Green's Bayou closed. Now Green's Bayou is a series of long grass fingers and shallow water coves.

Most people travel to Green's from Port O'Connor. Head due east from the Port O'Connor Little Jetties until you get near the Matagorda Ship Channel, watching for boat traffic around the busy ship channel. Travel east along Matagorda Island. Look for the long bulkhead just east of the old Matagorda Club Airfield. Green's is just past the bulkhead.

Wading in Green's can be difficult due to the muddy bottom. It is a long way from the nearest boat ramp so take along plenty of drinking water. Make sure someone knows that you plan on going to Green's, and don't get caught here when a Norther or line of thunderstorms blows in.

Green's offers plenty of places for prey fish to hide and also offers a grassy shoreline used by shrimp as a nursery. Redfish, speckled trout, and flounder all call Green's home. Cast shrimp flies right at the grass and watch for any visible signs of prey species, especially fleeing shrimp and nervous mullet.

You may want to avoid Green's during the hottest part of the summer, usually between July 4 and the end of August. The water really heats up and becomes somewhat stagnant during this time. Fish become lethargic and there are unseen hazards in water approaching 90 degrees. If the water feels too warm to be comfortable it's best to fish somewhere else that has better circulation.

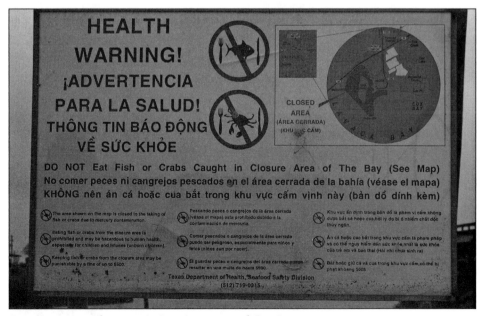

Pay attention to bay restriction signs around Cox Bay.

Port O'Connor Area

Legend

Primary Highway
Access Roads
Creek/River
Campsite
Boat Launch
Unnoted Lakes
Unnoted Rivers/Creeks
Swamp

N

Green's Bayou

Matagorda Peninsula

Matagorda Ship Channel

West Matagorda Bay

Sundown Island

Decros Island

Little Jetties

Middle Grounds

City Slicker Flats

Pass Cavallo

Broad Bayou

Boggy Bayou

Port O'Connor

Saluria Bayou

Matagorda Island

Huckleberry Bayou

Powderhorn Lake

Ranchhouse Flats

185

Intracoastal Waterway

Grass Island

Espiritu Santo Bay

Pringle Lake

MATAGORDA SHIP CHANNEL
(Port O'Connor Big Jetties)

The Matagorda Ship Channel, often called the Port O'Connor Big Jetties, is the major water connection between Matagorda Bay and the Gulf of Mexico. The channel has water over 60 feet deep and acts as a major portal to both Matagorda Bay and Espiritu Santo Bay.

Very large oil tankers regularly travel the channel on their way to Port Lavaca or out into the gulf. These large vessels make waves that can swamp small watercraft. Ships are supposed to travel very slowly through the channel and most do, but pay attention when these shipping goliaths are in the area. Also, first thing in the morning, numerous offshore fishing boats use the Big Jetties as their way to the gulf, so be aware of the wakes they make.

To get to the Matagorda Ship Channel, head due east out of the Port O'Connor Little Jetties crossing West Matagorda Bay. The only obstruction in this section of the bay is a series of lighted pilings around a wellhead. The ship channel is clearly marked with buoys.

On busy weekends fishing boats line the rocks on both sides of the Big Jetties. Be careful when anchoring in the area. Make sure your anchor is stuck firm and anchor far enough away from the rocks to allow for boat movement due to large waves made by the big tankers.

The tide can really run fast through these jetties. The Big Jetties are best fished when the tide is moving but not too fast. Texas coastal waters fluctuate only about a foot, but one foot of water over Matagorda and Espiritu Santo bays is a lot of water. The best jetty fishing is at the start and end of the tide change. Use the large buoys in the area as a marker to help determine current speed.

Flyfishers can cast directly towards the jetties and let their fly drift with the current. Most strikes will occur a couple feet below the surface. Both floating and sinking lines have their place at the Big Jetties. Start with a sinking fly like a Clouser on a floating line and switch to a sinking line with a shortened leader if you don't get any strikes. If you have a problem with flies hanging up in the jetty rocks, try flies with a weedguard.

Large speckled trout, redfish, and sheepshead are all found around the Big Jetties. Clouser Minnows work well as do Lefty's Deceivers and Bend Backs. Shrimp and crab patterns will also entice jetty fish to strike.

The ends of the Big Jetties provide flyfishers with the opportunity to catch species they would not normally catch while wading a shoreline flat. Tarpon are often seen around the jetties as are Spanish mackerel, bonito or little tunny, cobia, and kingfish. All of these fish will hit a white or chartreuse-and-white Clouser or large white Lefty's Deceiver.

The Big Jetty side nearest Matagorda Bay holds bonito during the hot summer months but only when there is a moving tide. They like small white flies including Lefty's Deceivers and Bend Backs.

The Big Jetty side closest to the Gulf of Mexico is more adversely affected by the predominant southeast winds. Use caution when heading out of the jetties. There are often large waves breaking around the jetty ends. Both the north and south side of the outside jetty rocks hold fish.

Cobia and kingfish can be seen from the surface. If you see one, cast right in front of it with a large Lefty's Deceiver or Clouser, but make sure your hook is sharp before you cast. Either one of these fish will test the best fly reels, so make sure you use a reel that has a smooth drag and plenty of backing when fishing for these jetty cruisers.

Tarpon around the jetties are usually in the 25- to 60-pound class. They are often seen just outside the jetties, especially on the outside of the north jetty rocks. This is an area that is protected from the wind and tarpon are seen daisy chaining or gasping for air near the rocks. These fish are cautious and any fly must be quietly placed within the tarpon's eyesight.

Light tackle anglers can use jigheads with soft plastics, spoons, and topwater poppers for fish around the jetties. Redfish and speckled trout will hit jigheads with soft plastic bodies. Try to make the jighead work with the current. Cast in toward the rocks and let the jighead be carried with the current. Most strikes occur after the jighead has reached a depth of several feet. Set the hook anytime a bite is felt and hang on. Large speckled trout and redfish regularly use the strong current around the jetties to help fill their bellies.

For those using bait, a shrimp under a popping cork is often the best bet. Use the popping cork to get the shrimp to the correct depth along the rocks, and don't be afraid to place the popping cork and shrimp right next to the rocks. You're going to lose some hooks no matter where you cast. Sheepshead especially will take the shrimp down into the rocks and cost you a few rigs.

Another method that works well is to use a shrimp on a Kahle hook and a small split shot or two. As the water increases in speed through the jetties, additional split shots may be required to get the bait down into the strike zone. As the water slows down, less split shots allow the shrimp more freedom to swim. When the water is almost slack, the best method is to use just the shrimp and hook. Let the shrimp swim around the rocks. The fish will find it.

I recommend using a 4-foot leader of 17- to 20-pound fluorocarbon or monofilament on all light tackle rigs. The heavier leader will help when working around the jetty rocks and catching toothy fish.

During winter very large sheepshead use the Big Jetties as a staging area for their anticipated early spring spawn. From February through the end of March these large breeders are easy targets for anglers throwing shrimp close to the jetty rocks. Go with plenty of hooks and split shots because sheepshead are notorious bait thieves.

It's always a good idea to have a large landing net with you any time you fish the jetties. Pull any hooked fish into the net at the surface and then bring the net into the boat if it's fish you want to keep. When netting very large fish, like bull redfish and crevalle jacks, it is best to keep the fish and the net in the water. The large net helps control the big fish. By keeping the fish in the water they'll be less stressed and quickly revived when released.

A few anglers actually hop the rocks at the jetties. This can be a dangerous idea because the rocks are often covered with algae, making them very slippery. As a general rule, I don't recommend this activity.

The jetties are also an excellent location for night fishing. Anglers in boats often place large underwater green lights next to their boat to attract small fish and shrimp. It doesn't take long for the big predators to locate the bait.

Flies, lures, and live bait all work when fishing at night. Larger fish cruise the outer edge of the lighted zone. Small white Lefty's Deceivers and Clousers, and soft plastics on jigheads will entice these nighttime fish.

Any time you fish the jetties I recommend wearing a personal flotation device. Even if you're the best swimmer in the world it takes time to pull up the anchor and retrieve someone that has fallen into the water. With the strong current in the area even a good swimmer will quickly be pulled away from the boat.

Ed Jaworowski shown with a nice jack caught on fly tackle in the Matagorda Ship Channel.

SUNDOWN ISLAND (BIRD ISLAND)

Sundown Island, commonly called Bird Island, was originally made from the spoil dredging of the Matagorda Ship Channel. Today, it is a protected bird sanctuary. The once endangered brown pelican uses this as a nursery island, as do many different terns, skimmers, and gulls. The laughing gull is one of the loudest occupants of the island.

Anglers can fish around the island, but aren't allowed to touch dry land. This is a protected island and not made for human footprints. Most anglers fish Sundown Island from a boat.

There are strong currents rushing past the island from the gulf through the ship channel. Be aware of these currents. During the fastest moving currents, it is often hard to get anything less than a half-ounce jighead down to where the fish are. Waders can feel the sand moving under their feet when wading around Sundown Island during the strongest tides. Try to find a spot where the current is not as strong, like the area behind a rock in a mountain stream. That little buffer area is ideal for speckled trout.

Flyfishers need full-sinking lines when fishing this area. Clouser Minnows and Half and Halfs work well. Use a shortened leader of around 4 feet. Let the fly sink as deep as possible. Most of the bottom around the island is firm sand and flies will not get stuck. Once the fly has reached the maximum depth make a slow retrieve trying to keep it as close to the bottom as possible.

Light tackle users can cast jigheads with soft plastics, spoons, and hard-bodied lures like the Mirrolure Catch 2000 or Classic 52M. Use 10- or 12-pound monofilament with a 17- or 20-pound leader.

Let the jighead fall all the way to the bottom before you move it. If the current is strong you may need to use a heavier jighead to get the lure deep enough. Start with the lightest jighead your tackle can cast. If you don't get any bites switch to a heavier jighead. When the current is really moving, a half-ounce jighead may be required to get the lure into the strike zone.

Light tackle fishers will also catch plenty of fish in the area using one of the two bait rigs described in the Big Jetties section. Natural bait anglers are often harassed by ladyfish around the island so be prepared to lose some bait.

DECROS ISLAND

Decros Island is the western end of Matagorda Peninsula between the Big Jetties and Pass Cavallo. Flats on the Matagorda Bay side offer good wade fishing, especially during early spring when large black drum cruise the area looking for a date. Large speckled trout use the many sand potholes surrounded by grassy areas to hide in, but waders must approach these sandy potholes quietly. Be sure you have good polarized sunglasses and look around the perimeter of the potholes for laid-up fish.

As the water warms, trout will seek the deeper water of the bay. Light-tackle anglers are often seen wading this area in water up to their chest. Don't forget to scope out the shallow water within the first 20 yards of the shoreline. Redfish use this shoreline to cruise along looking for small crabs and baitfish.

There are also a couple of large pockets along the Decros shoreline. The farther back you get into these pockets, the muddier the bottom becomes. The deeper cuts feeding these pockets are good places to cast for trout.

Flyfishers can use gold spoon flies, Bend Backs, and shrimp and crab patterns for redfish in shallow water. When going after trout in the deeper water and in potholes, a Clouser on a floating line will work. When the water gets more than 3 feet deep, consider switching to a sinking line with a shortened leader to get the fly in the strike zone quicker.

Light-tackle anglers should use gold or copper spoons in the shallow water for redfish, and jigheads with soft plastics for trout farther out. Take your time and work this area slowly. More fish are spooked by fast waders than by lures.

Ladyfish on a fly are always fun.

POWDERHORN LAKE

Powderhorn Lake is a large, shallow body of water just south of the town of Indianola, which was the site of one of the most devastating hurricanes in early Texas history. This is the place LaSalle came ashore over 300 years ago — the town actually has a large statue honoring the explorer. Indianola is actually lower in elevation than the Port O'Connor area. Strong, predominant southeasterly winds blow water right at Indianola.

Powderhorn Lake is a great place for the beginning kayaker to become familiar with his or her craft. The lake is protected from all sides and offers excellent shallow-water fishing.

Redfish, speckled trout, and flounder are all found in the lake. There is only one boat ramp in the area, so it is a good idea to ask about launching a boat because there may be a fee. Also it is a good idea to ask about parking, and follow the directions.

Kayakers can launch from Magnolia Beach right in town and paddle around to Powderhorn Lake. There are no grocery stores, so take what you are going to need with you.

Boat Ramps

Coloma Creek Highway, 1289 & Powderhorn Lake, Indianola
Powderhorn RV Park, 601 Powderhorn Lane, Indianola / 361-552-7481

The LaSalle statue marks the area where the explorer landed over 300 years ago.

RANCHHOUSE FLAT

Ranchhouse Flat is the area just south of Powderhorn Lake. This is a firm, sandy bottom flat with lots of grass. There are a series of guts or ridges running parallel to the shoreline. Redfish and speckled trout regularly inhabit these guts. This long flat offers plenty of wading and kayaking opportunities. You may want to travel north from Port O'Connor to reach this flat instead of south from Indianola.

Flyfishers should concentrate on the grassy shoreline. Redfish will chase preyfish and shrimp right against the grass. This is an area where flyfishers should be prepared to cover some ground between casts. In order to save your arm, only cast when you see something to cast to.

Look for nervous water or fleeing shrimp. Cast behind any group of mullet, and watch for fish pushing shrimp into the grass. Kayakers can work this area effectively, only stopping for visible fish.

Light-tackle fishers can make long casts parallel to the shoreline. Use a casting or spinning rod with 10-pound running line to get maximum distance. If you don't get any bites, keep moving, and cover as much ground as you can. Once you locate a redfish or speckled trout, thoroughly work the area. Make several casts before moving at all. Many times, the fish in this area are school fish and where you catch one you're likely to catch several.

If you're fishing with several other anglers, position one in each of the guts until the last person is in water over the waist. Work parallel to the shallows. It is usually best to have the person in the deepest water take the lead with the other anglers closer in a few paces back. This moves any fish in towards the other fishermen and acts as a block to prevent fish from escaping to deeper water.

BOGGY BAYOU

Boggy Bayou is just north of Port O'Connor. This small, shallow lake is a great place for the beginning kayaker and birder to learn. The bottom of Boggy Bayou is muddy and difficult to wade, making it perfect for kayakers.

Casters of all types will have trouble with the many oyster shells located on the bottom of this muddy lake. Take plenty of flies, lures, leaders, and line when fishing Boggy.

Take 3rd Street where it crosses Taylor to get to Boggy. The gravel road leads right to the mouth of the bayou. Please carry out all trash you find in this area.

Both sides of the mouth are also good places to fish, and the flats on both sides typically hold redfish and speckled trout.

OIL RIGS IN WEST MATAGORDA BAY

The oil rigs in West Matagorda Bay are one of the few places along the coast that hold tripletail. Many anglers mistake tripletail for floating debris, so look close at anything floating around one of these platforms. Cast a small, white Lefty's Deceiver, shrimp, or crab pattern to any visible fish.

Light-tackle anglers are best served using free-lined shrimp. No matter what tackle you use, be prepared for a strong fight when you hook one of these fish. These tripletail can weigh over 20 pounds. Try to work the fish away from the rig as quickly as possible as these strong pullers can quickly wrap around the rig feet.

Look for tripletail during the warmer summer months. If there has recently been a heavy rain in the area or to the north where the rivers are, you'll probably have a hard time finding them. They do not like freshwater and find other places to hang out.

There are special regulations for tripletail caught in West Matagorda Bay. You may retain only three tripletail over 17 inches per day. The Texas state record tripletail comes from this area.

Speckled trout, as well as other species like pompano and Spanish mackerel, also haunt these rigs.

Oil rigs in West Matagorda are often home to many different species of fish.

PASS CAVALLO

Pass Cavallo is one of three natural passes on the Texas coast. LaSalle, thinking he had reached Galveston Bay, used this pass to explore the region. The pass has partially silted in since the Matagorda Ship Channel (Port O'Connor Big Jetties) was built, but still remains open.

The area around the pass continuously changes. Each hurricane in the area reshapes the surrounding sand. The area northwest of the pass is very shallow and will fool many boaters, so know your path before crossing this area.

Pass Cavallo also offers quick access to the surf. During Texas' warmest months (August and September), the Gulf of Mexico calms down enough to allow boaters to exit Pass Cavallo and run south along the gulf side of Matagorda Island.

When the water is green to the beach, look for cruising schools of speckled trout, redfish, and Spanish mackerel. These fish will hit almost any fly or lure.

MIDDLE GROUNDS

This is the area just inside Pass Cavallo. At one time, this was actually an island — Turtle Island — but the many storms passing through the area keep the bottom constantly shifting and changing. Today, the Middle Grounds, or the "Hump" as locals call it, is a good springtime speckled trout location. Weekends often find the entire area encircled by boats and waders. The water level changes from close to 7 feet to only a foot deep in the shallower areas, providing fish with quick access to deep water. Predator fish take advantage of this water depth change.

Waders should be cautious with any fish they string as numerous small blacktip sharks inhabit this area and are known to steal an easy meal from unsuspecting anglers. Either unload the stringer when you have a couple of fish on, or use a Do-Net to avoid feeding the sharks, instead of yourself.

Fly anglers can try Clousers and Half and Halfs on sinking line with short leaders. Light-tackle anglers can use jigheads with soft plastic tails, DOA shrimp, Mirrolure's Catch 2000, and Catch 5. A double rig made up of a topwater, walk-the-dog-type lure such as a Mirrolure Topdog or Heddon Zara, followed by a light jighead with soft plastic tail will often catch fish when other lures are ignored.

Bait anglers can use shrimp, piggy perch, or croaker in this area.

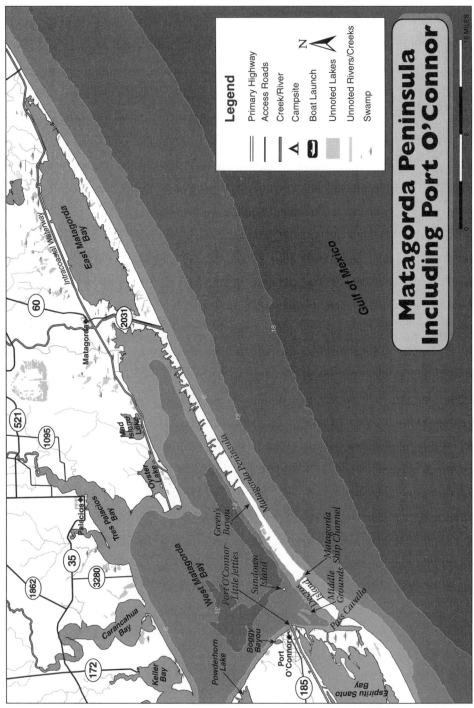

Legend

- Primary Highway
- Access Roads
- Creek/River
- ▲ Campsite
- 🛥 Boat Launch
- Unnoted Lakes
- Unnoted Rivers/Creeks
- Swamp

N

Matagorda Peninsula Including Port O'Connor

16 MILES

East Matagorda Bay

Intracoastal Waterway

Gulf of Mexico

Matagorda

60

2031

521

1095

Mad Island Lake

Oyster Lake

Tres Palacios Bay

Palacios

35

1862

3280

172

Carancahua Bay

Keller Bay

West Matagorda Bay

Green's Bayou

Matagorda Peninsula

Port O'Connor Little Jetties

Sundown Island

Powderhorn Lake

Boggy Bayou

Port O'Connor

185

Matagorda Ship Channel

Middle Grounds

Jetties

Pass Cavallo

Espíritu Santo Bay

© 2009 Wilderness Adventures Press, Inc.

PORT O'CONNOR LITTLE JETTIES

The Port O'Connor Little Jetties were created to shelter the mouth of the Intracoastal Waterway as it enters Matagorda Bay. Both jetties provide shelter for fish, such as sheepshead, flounder, speckled trout and redfish.

Anglers wanting to walk the jetties or "hop the rocks" can do so from Port O'Connor. There is a small parking area located at the corner of Washington Boulevard and Commerce Street. Use caution when walking down the jetty rocks. Moss-like algae grow on most of the rocks and make them extremely slippery.

The jetties are much wider at the base than at the surface. Fly casters can cast out from the jetties and try to retrieve their flies as close to parallel as possible. A sinking line will help get the flies down to the level most fish inhabit. Light-tackle and bait anglers should also try to parallel the rocks and use the currents to move their offerings along the rocks. The Port O'Connor Little Jetties are a favorite with land-locked anglers and weekenders.

The Port O'Connor Little Jetties are a good place for land-locked anglers to fish.

City Slicker Flats

The area between Big Bayou and Saluria Bayou on the shoreline of West Matagorda Bay is called City Slicker Flats. This is a long shallow area that offers plenty of wade fishing. Water depth is less than 4 feet deep and it's close enough to the town of Port O'Connor to make it easily accessible to kayakers.

Fish for redfish close to the grass. You'll find trout in the deeper water close to the channel running between the flats and the Middle Grounds.

This is a good area for beginning flyfishers to hone their skills. There are plenty of grassy areas and large areas of sand and mud that will give the novice wader an overall feel for wading a Texas flat.

The Surf along Matagorda Peninsula

The surf along Matagorda Peninsula can offer some unbelievable fishing. The only problem is that calm surf days are few and far between. Try to hit the surf when the water is sandy green just as it is clearing up. If the fishing is good in a particular area inside the bay, the fishing will probably be good right across the land in the surf.

Surf fishing is best during the hottest months of the year — July through September. Early morning is best, but the action can last all day.

For anglers lucky enough to catch the surf on a calm day, fly and lure selection is not a problem. Surf fish stay hungry and will hit almost any fly or lure. Be prepared with plenty of flies and lures because you'll probably miss numerous fish.

If you've hired a guide and he says you're fishing in the surf, be prepared for the trip of a lifetime.

The surf can be accessed either through Pass Cavallo, the Matagorda Ship Channel, or the Colorado River. Boaters new to surf fishing need to be very careful when anchoring along the surfside, and are best served hiring a guide.

When fishing the Colorado River area, travel south out of the town of Matagorda on TX FM2031 for access to two small-boat ramps along the river. There is also wade-in fishing available once you get to the mouth of the river at the Matagorda Nature Center.

For the Wader and Kayaker

Two areas offer excellent opportunities for the land-bound wader or those fishing out of a kayak. First the area around Palacios Bayou and Oyster Lake offers a unique opportunity for waders and kayaks. FM 1095 goes south off of State Highway 35. From Bay City and the east take FM 1095 south near the small town of Elmaton, and from Palacios and the west, take 521 east to Tin Top and then south on FM 1095.

When approaching Collegeport look for the sign that points to the Collegeport Cementery on the right-hand side of the road right after the S curve coming into town. Turn south on County Road 365. The pavement ends just south of Collegeport, but this dirt road takes you all the way to Palacios Bayou.

There is an area to launch small boats or kayaks at the end of the road. Waders can wade the Tres Palacios Bay side or venture into Oyster Lake through Palacios Bayou. During the week you'll probably be the only person there. The area offers fishing for redfish, trout, and flounder. It is a fairly long drive to reach the area, but well worth it if you're looking for an area away from the crowds. Be sure to take along bug spray, plenty of fresh water, and food because you're a long way from any place with supplies.

The second area is the shoreline from the Port O'Connor Little Jetties north to Indianola. Waders can access the area from the front beach in Port O'Connor or from Boggy Bayou just north of town.

The shoreline is mostly firm sand intermixed with grassy areas and deeper guts. Boggy itself can be difficult to wade but is ideal for the kayaker. Powderhorn Lake is also an excellent location for kayakers.

Take Highway 185 into Port O'Connor, and park anywhere along the front beach or in the areas around Boggy Bayou.

Redfish and trout regularly frequent the shoreline.

Pompano are often caught in the surf.

Anglers Garland Braune, Pete Devaney and Mike Conrad like catching these big reds in Matagorda Bay.

Matagorda Bay Hub Cities

PALACIOS
Population: 5,312
County: Matagorda

ACCOMMODATIONS

The Luther Hotel, 409 S Bay Blvd / 361-972-2312/ 27 rooms/ $90
The Delux Inn, 1505 First St / 361-972-2547/ 28 rooms/ $45
Bay Prairie Lodge, Hwy 111 & 71 at Midfield / 361-588-6565/ 16 rooms/ $35

CAMPGROUNDS

Serendipity Resort & Marina, 1001 Main St / 361-972-5454
Bay Front RV Park, 902 First St / 361-972-3727
Third Coast RV Park, 208 First St / 361-972-3284
Pier Drive Inn RV Park / 361-972-3284

RESTAURANTS

Baytown Seafood Restaurant, 1001 Henderson Dr / 361-972-1020
Palacios Mexican Restaurant, 511 Main St / 361-972-2766
The Outrigger Restaurant, 515 Commerce / 361-972-1479 /
    www.outriggerrestaurant.com
Subway, 307 Henderson / 361-972-2273 / www.subway.com
Los Cucos Mexican Café,1601 First St / 361-972-6024 / www.loscucos.com

FOR MORE INFORMATION

Palacios Chamber of Commerce
    312 Main Street Palacios
    Texas 77465/ 800-611-4567
    www.palacioschamber.com

PORT LAVACA
Population: 12,192
County: Calhoun

ACCOMMODATIONS

Best Western, 2202 Highway 35 / 361-553-6800/ 50 rooms/ $73-$106 /
www.bestwesterntexas.com

Days Inn, 2100 North Hwy 35 Bypass / 361-552-4511/ 95 rooms/ $40-$59 /
www.daysinn.com

Chaparral Motel, 2086 N Hwy 35 / 361-552-7581/ 53 rooms/ $50-$55

CAMPGROUNDS

Gateway RV Park, 1620 W Main / 361-552-1388

Lavaca Bay RV Park, 1818 Broadway / 361-552-4814

RESTAURANTS

El Patio, 548 W Main / 361-552-6316

Green Iguana Grill, 137 E Main / 361-552-3861

Gordon's Bayside Grill, 2615 Hwy 35 / 361-552-1000

Subway 306, Hwy 35 / 361-552-7300

AIRPORTS

Calhoun County Airport / 361-552-2933

FOR MORE INFORMATION

Port Lavaca/Calhoun County Chamber of Commerce
2300 Highway 35
Port Lavaca, TX 77979
800-556-7678
www.calhountx.org

MATAGORDA
Population: 710
County: Matagorda

ACCOMMODATIONS

Casa del Pescador Lodge, CR 251 / 979-863-7130/ 4 rooms/ $60 per person /
www.casadelpescadorlodge.com
Fisherman's Motel, 40 Fisher St / 979-863-0000/ 14 rooms/ $65-$75 /
www.fishermansmotel.com
Matagorda Shell Motel, CR 2031 / 979-863-2520
The Cabins / 979-863-2262
The Full Stringer Lodge, 143 Beach Rd / 979-863-1143 /
www.fullstringerlodge.com
Stanley-Fisher B&B, 107 St.Mary's St / 979-863-2920/ 5 rooms/ $90-$160 /
www.stanley-fisher.com

CAMPGROUNDS

L&L RV Park, 760 Caney St / 979-863-7799
Seabird RV Park / 979-863-2592
Matagorda Bay Nature Park RV Park / 979-863-7120 / www.matagordabayrv.com
Lighthouse RV, 18411 Hwy 60 S / 979-863-7144
Fisherman's RV, 40 Fisher St / 979-863-0000 / www.fishermansmotel.com

RESTAURANTS

River Bend Restaurant / 979-863-7481
Waterfront Restaurant Matagorda Harbor / 979-863-2520
Lighthouse BBQ, 18411 Hwy 60S / 979-863-7303

SPORTING GOODS

Russell's Bait & Tackle, 1 Harbor Dr / 979-863-7620
Rawlings Baitcamp, 205 Beach Rd / 979-863-7669

FOR MORE INFORMATION

Matagorda Chamber of Commerce
979-557-6526
www.matagordachamber.com

Port O'Connor, just west of Matagorda Bay, provides the best access for fishing West Matagorda Bay, the Matagorda Ship Channel, Sundown Island, and Decros Point. A full listing of services in Port O'Connor can be found in the Region 4 Hub Cities.

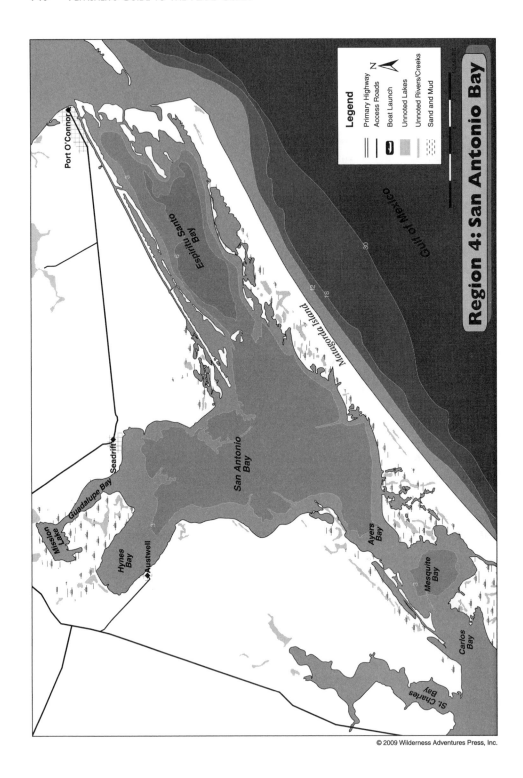

Region 4: San Antonio Bay

Region 4: San Antonio Bay

Espiritu Santo Bay and San Antonio Bay offer a wide variety of fishing opportunities to the saltwater angler: Redfish up to 44 inches, tarpon up to 125 pounds, speckled trout to 10 pounds, and black drum up to 60 pounds. All of these and more await anglers in these two middle coast bays.

The land surrounding these bays is home to a vast array of wildlife including deer, javelina, feral hogs, numerous hawks and birds of prey, and even whooping cranes.

No matter what the weather, there is someplace to fish in these two bays. If the wind is too strong to venture to Panther Reef, work the many inshore pockets and coves around the Big Pocket area near Port O'Connor.

If the wind lets you travel where you want, the many south shoreline lakes including Pringle Lake, Contee Lake, and South Pass Lake offer excellent fishing for speckled trout and redfish.

Long distance travel not in your plans? Travel by kayak to one of the many secluded areas just across from the Intracoastal Waterway. There's even a designated kayak trail in the area.

Whatever your fishing choice, these two middle coast bays offer something for everyone.

Seasonal Fishing Chart - Region 4: San Antonio Bay

	Jan	Feb	Mar	Apr	May	Jun	Jul	Aug	Sep	Oct	Nov	Dec
Redfish	+	+	++	+++	+++	+++	+++	+++	+++	+++	+++	++
Spotted Seatrout	++	+++	+++	+++	+++	+++	+++	+++	+++	++	+	+
Flounder			++	+++	+++	+++	+++	+++	+++	+++	+++	+
Black Drum	++	+++	+++	+++	+++	+++	+++	+++	+++	++	+	+
Sheepshead	++	+++	+++	+++	+++	+++	+++	+++	+++	++	+	+
Crevalle Jack				++	+++	+++	+++	+++	+++	++		
Spanish Mackerel						++	+++	+++	+++			
Gray Snapper						++	+++	+++				
Tarpon						+	+	+	+			
Pompano				+	+	+	+	+				
Snook												

+++ = Exceptional, ++ = Very Good, + = Available

ESPIRITU SANTO BAY

Espiritu Santo Bay is the bay system just south of the small town of Port O'Connor. Take Hwy 185 south out of Victoria. Highway 185 goes through Seadrift and dead ends into Matagorda Bay in Port O'Connor. Almost all of the fishing is across the Intracoastal Waterway from the town, so some type of watercraft is required to fish Espiritu Santo Bay. Port O'Connor has three boat ramps and they're very busy during the summer months, especially on weekends and holidays. One ramp is maintained by Texas Parks and Wildlife and the other two are fee ramps. Parking is very limited in Port O'Connor. Weekenders often get to the ramp well before sun-up to launch their boat and find a parking spot. You may want to take your vehicle and trailer back to the motel or wherever you're staying and ride a bicycle back to the ramp area if you're fishing during the busiest times.

The CCA STAR listings are posted at the Fishing Center so you can see the summer long tournament results. They also collect STAR Tournament entry fees. The Fishing Center has a 4-lane ramp, good parking area, and a launch fee.

Clark's Marina ramp is a single-lane ramp with limited parking space, so be prepared to either get there early or wait in line. If you've got a boat that is hard to maneuver in tight spaces you might want to use one of the other ramps. There is also a ramp/parking fee at Clark's.

Ramp fees are $5 or less which includes your parking if you get there early enough to get a spot. All of these locations offer fish cleaning stations on the water. These cleaning stations are great places to take a kid fishing. The hardhead catfish, piggy perch, gray snapper, pelicans, and sea gulls living near the cleaning stations devour any morsel tossed their way.

In Port O'Connor you can get groceries at the Speedy Stop and the Shamrock Station. The Speedy Stop is much larger and has a much larger variety of groceries than the normal fast stop. They have most types of groceries, meats, drinks, and even some camping supplies. They have a full line of lures and tackle, including flies and frozen bait.

Captain Marty also has a well-stocked tackle store at Byers and Hwy 185. Between these two locations you can find most of what you need to enjoy a day of coastal fishing. The Speedy Stop offers quick breakfast including breakfast tacos and coffee. If you're in a hurry, the Speedy Stop is your best bet.

Espiritu Santo Bay is one of the bays along the Texas coast that has marked kayak trails. The trails start just across the Intracoastal Waterway and proceed through most of the shallow-water areas along the eastern edge of the bay.

These shallow waters are made for kayaking. There are numerous small creeks, cuts, and pockets that will take many anglers a lifetime to thoroughly cover. Most of these waters are too small to be navigated by large boats, making them a safer place for kayakers. Use a warning flag, like those attached to kid's bicycles, to help other anglers spot your kayak. Take a waterproof map and compass when exploring these kayak trails.

POCO Bueno fishing tournament is held annually around the third week in July. The little town of Port O'Connor hosts a crowd that grows to several thousand for this tournament. Motel rooms, RV park sites, and parking spots become scarce during this time.

The town is also very crowded on the Saturday nearest the Fourth of July. The community has an excellent fireworks display that night and thousands of visitors come from the surrounding county and farther. Several of the town streets are blocked off and parking becomes a problem. The Chamber of Commerce will have the dates for these events. Anglers may want to avoid the crowd and plan their trip to the area for another time.

Boat Ramps

Clark's Marina & Restaurant, 7th & Maple / 361-983-4388
Froggies, Byers & Maple Street / 361-983-4466
The Fishing Center, 13th and Water Street / 361-983-4440

J Hook

The J Hook is the area just on the west side of Pass Cavallo. This area offers some excellent fishing for the big three. There is mud nearest the shoreline and firm sand intermixed with mud farther out. Early spring and fall are the best times to fish the J Hook. Fish move through the area when first entering the bay system during the spring and again work back through the area as they leave the bays for the winter.

Look for deeper cuts while wading especially during the hot weather months. A nearby favorite summer spot is Sunday Beach, the area just south of the J Hook. Weekenders often take their boat to Sunday Beach, set up tents and camp for the weekend. There are no amenities so you need to take everything with you including plenty of water or you'll have to make a trip back to Port O'Connor for supplies.

It's an easy walk across Sunday Beach to the gulf but plenty of fish are caught right off Sunday Beach itself. Fish for speckled trout with Lefty's Deceivers, Half and Halfs, and Clousers. A sink tip or full-sinking line will help get the fly down to the fish's level quickly. Light tackle users should try soft plastic tails with jigheads. Live shrimp under popping corks will also get strikes.

Fish Pond

Fish Pond is directly across from Sunday Beach, and is somewhat treacherous to enter. Go slowly and ease into the mouth of the pond. Once inside you've got a fairly large area to fish. As with any trip to Texas inshore waters, do the stingray shuffle with your feet if you get out and wade, as there are plenty of them in Fish Pond. It is like a lot of the middle coast in that it has areas of firm, easy to wade sand and areas of thick, hard to wade mud. A great way to fish the lake is with a kayak. You may also see alligators and even rattlesnakes in this area so pay attention.

Fish Pond often holds good numbers of redfish, speckled trout, and flounder. Crevalle jacks also occasionally make it into the pond. The largest ladyfish I've ever

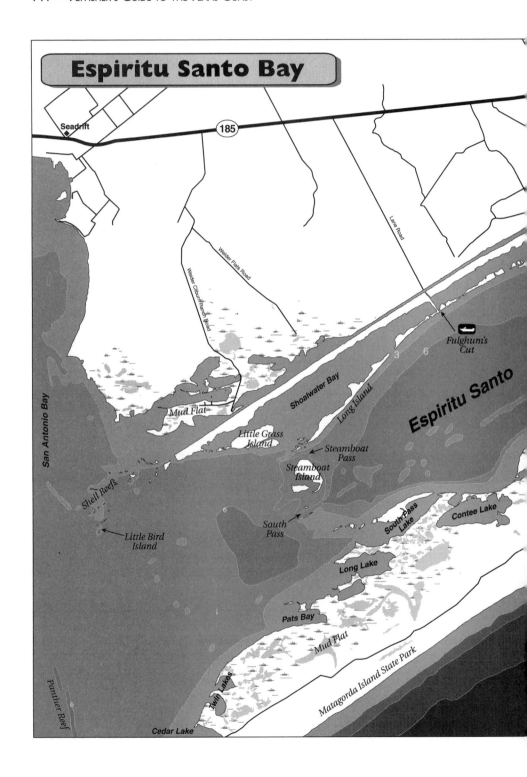

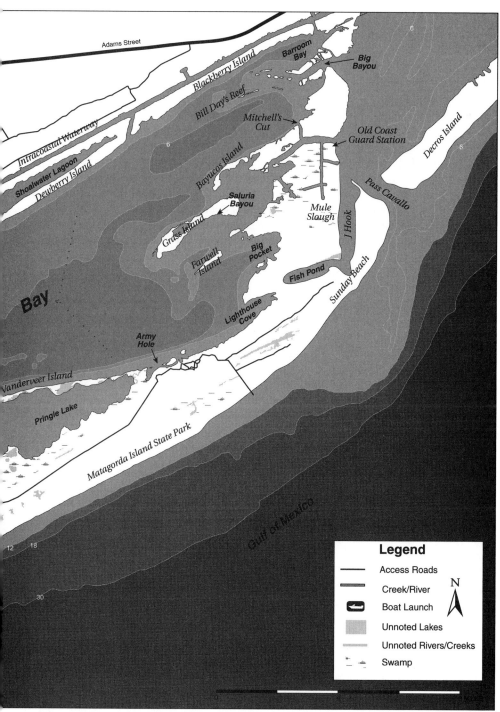

Adams Street

Blackberry Island

Barroom Bay

Big Bayou

Bill Day's Reef

Mitchell's Cut

Old Coast Guard Station

Decros Island

Intracoastal Waterway

Shoalwater Lagoon

Dewberry Island

Bayucos Island

Pass Cavallo

Saluria Bayou

Mule Slough

J Hook

Grass Island

Farwell Island

Big Pocket

Fish Pond

Sunday Beach

Bay

Lighthouse Cove

Army Hole

Vanderveer Island

Pringle Lake

Matagorda Island State Park

Gulf of Mexico

12 18

30

Legend

——— Access Roads

〰〰〰 Creek/River

🛥 Boat Launch

░ Unnoted Lakes

〰 Unnoted Rivers/Creeks

⚓ Swamp

N

© 2009 Wilderness Adventures Press, Inc.

seen was hooked in the back half of Fish Pond so you never know what you're going to catch here.

Flyfishers should concentrate on the grassy shorelines around the perimeter and also work the mouths of the many cuts that enter the lake. The water in Fish Pond really heats up in August making it difficult to fish after mid-morning.

Old Coast Guard Station and Coast Guard Flats

The Old Coast Guard Station was wiped out in 1961 by Hurricane Carla. If you want to see the destruction a hurricane can create, just boat past the old station. There are numerous cement, wood, and metal pilings sitting just under the surface so be careful when boating in the area. The old pilings offer a chance at fish that like to be around structure like ladyfish, flounder, and black drum.

A sinking line fished with a Lone Star Tiger Rattler will catch flounder. Use a solid black fly like Corey's Little Black Fly to entice black drum around the pilings.

Be especially careful if you decide to wade around the old station. There are many underwater obstructions to get both tackle and yourself caught in.

The long flats on the southside of the Old Coast Guard Station are ideal for wade fishing. The bottom is mostly hard-packed sand with a grass covering. There are several guts running through this area so again remember to use the stingray shuffle while wading. The area right across from the J Hook is a large sandy flat that often holds good-sized speckled trout. This is an area that depends on current movement, so check tide charts before planning any trip.

Redfish patrol the shallow water near the shoreline. This is a well-known fishing area that is often crowded on weekends and holidays. If you see more than two boats in the area it is best to seek another spot.

Floating line with spoon flies or shrimp patterns work well. For the lure caster try either a weedless spoon or soft plastics with 1/16-ounce jighead.

Barroom Bay

Sometimes referred to as Hole #2 or the mud hole, Barroom Bay is often overlooked by anglers boating to other areas. This small bay is an easy trip for a kayaker and frequently holds redfish and trout. The bottom can be muddy so kayakers have an advantage fishing this area.

Texas Parks and Wildlife Department Coastal Fisheries Division shows Barroom Bay as having one of the highest populations of redfish and speckled trout in their annual gill net surveys.

Flyfishers should use spoon flies, shrimp imitations, and small poppers for redfish. Speckled trout are caught on Lefty's Deceivers and Clouser Minnows.

Light-tackle anglers can catch redfish on gold or copper weedless spoons. Trout are taken on soft plastic tails and jigheads, Johnson Sprite silver spoons, and live shrimp.

MITCHELL'S CUT

Mitchell's Cut is one of the major cuts through the east end of Espiritu Santo Bay. The area southeast of Mitchell's is very shallow. The shoreline will hold redfish and some flounder. This area is also one of the primary boat lanes connecting several areas, so be mindful of your wake and other anglers. Stay in the marked channel to avoid shallow areas. The water in the middle of the cut drops to over 20 feet deep in some places. In the early spring many boats line up, throwing bait into the deepest part of the cut trying for big black drum. There are almost always porpoise swimming in this deep-water cut, so watch out for them when boating through.

Black drum are caught using either cut bait or blue crab, their favorite. A large spinning rig with a heavy weight and large circle hook baited with a tennis ball-sized blue crab will entice any black drum in the area to hit. It's best to be prepared with a large net to land these early season monsters. Remember to take a quick photo and then release the big drum in good shape — these are the big spawners that keep the species going. Any drum over 31 inches must be released.

SALURIA BAYOU

Saluria Bayou is named for the old town of Saluria that was originally at the location of the Old Coast Guard Station. It's hard to believe that there was once a town that had more than 10,000 visitors during the summer months, with a large Ferris wheel and carnival to entertain visitors, but that was Saluria. This area was hit by several hurricanes in the early 1900s and the town was never rebuilt.

Saluria connects Espiritu Santo Bay to the Gulf of Mexico through Pass Cavallo. The water is over 30 feet in places and best fished from a boat. Big black drum use this as a path to spawning areas during the early spring. You can sometimes hear the fish drumming here.

Saluria is a good place to catch the big three and several other uncommon varieties including Spanish mackerel and crevalle jacks. Work the grassy shoreline and the deep-water drop-off. Waders should be aware of the strong tides that run through this area and the steep drop-off when wading along the grassy shoreline.

KAYAK TRAILS NEAR PORT O'CONNOR

The Texas Parks and Wildlife Department has established three paddling trails in the Port O'Connor area, which are clearly marked with signs. Kayakers should be aware that all of the trails are a long paddle from the Intracoastal Waterway. Novice kayakers may choose to work closer to town until they gain some distance paddling experience or load their kayak onto a large boat to get closer to the trails.

Kayakers can access the trails from the Fishing Center in Port O'Connor or from the Matagorda Island State Park area on the island. There is no shuttle service provided by the park system so kayakers will have to arrange for their own shuttle.

The trail that leads to Fish Pond is just over 12 miles long. The North Loop trail is almost 5 miles long and the South Loop trail is just over 8 miles long.

While trail markers are placed throughout each trail, kayakers should include a waterproof map of the area and a compass as part of the equipment they take while working these trails. Many modern maps also offer GPS coordinates for these trails.

MULE SLOUGH

Many shallow grass flats and guts make this an ideal area for the kayaker. Due to the thick mud wading can be tough but there are also plenty of easily wadeable areas, so this is an area where the flyfisher can really do some stalking.

Work the area slowly, like a great blue heron. Try to make as little noise as possible and watch your wake when wading. There are numerous cuts, ridges, and grassy shorelines to fish. Work right up into the grass and into the creeks.

A shrimp or crab pattern with a weedguard is a good choice for the flyfisher. Light-tackle users can try a weedless gold spoon, jighead with soft plastic tail, DOA shrimp, or Topdog.

Mitchell's Cut is a good place to catch big black drum in the spring.

BIG POCKET

Big Pocket is just what it sounds like: a big pocket of water. The entire area is wadeable, with areas of hard oyster shell and also plenty of soft muddy areas. This is a great place to bring in a kayak on a larger boat and get out and paddle. Redfish will inhabit the grassy shoreline areas and trout can be found in the deeper guts running throughout Big Pocket. Weekends will see plenty of boat traffic along the western side of Big Pocket headed to the back lakes, so pay attention where you leave your boat.

Nearby Cross Reef has destroyed many props so be careful when going through this area. If you are unfamiliar with this section of the bay it is best to watch another boat maneuver through the shallow path, or hire a guide.

Flyfishers should concentrate on working the grassy shoreline. The wading will be slow due to mud, so do a lot of watching before you cast. Redfish will be right up in the grass so accurate casts help. Move slowly and get within 30 to 40 feet of your target before you make the first cast.

LIGHTHOUSE COVE

Lighthouse Cove is named for the Matagorda Island Lighthouse. This lighthouse was bombed during the Civil War and dates back to early Texas. The lighthouse remained out of service for many years but is now functional again.

The Cove is grass lined and offers excellent fishing for redfish during the fall. There is plenty of submerged grass in the area, so fishers should attempt to fish first thing in the morning before the grass turns loose and floats to the surface. There is some real soft mud in the cuts that feed the area, so be careful when wading because you can sink well past your waist.

Work in close to the grass for redfish and out deeper and in the deep cuts for speckled trout. Flounder also hang out in the area particularly near the deeper water along the cuts.

ARMY HOLE

The Army Hole is one of the most famous spots in Espiritu Santo Bay. During World War II, the Army Air Corps used the land just south of the Army Hole for bombing practice. Army Hole was created by dredging out the area so supply ships could dock and deliver their goods to the base.

For anglers, Army Hole offers deeper water surrounded by shallow flats. When there is a strong cold front, fish seek out the protected depths of Army Hole. This is a good place to fish in winter, and in the winter when you find one speckled trout, you'll find several, so make repeated casts.

During the warmer summer months fish seek out the cooler depths of the Army Hole, but fishing in the area really slows down after mid-morning in the summer. Redfish, speckled trout, and flounder all use Army Hole as a winter haven.

Flyfishers should use sink tip or full-sinking lines when working the deeper part of Army Hole and floating lines when working nearer the grass shoreline. Light-tackle fishers should use jigheads, spoons, and shrimp under popping corks. Try to cast parallel to the shoreline where possible.

BLACKBERRY ISLAND

Blackberry Island runs parallel to the Intracoastal Waterway from the Fisherman's Cut at Port O'Connor to the Government Cut. This shoreline has both hard-packed sand and muddy areas.

This is an excellent stretch for kayakers to concentrate on. Put in at the Fishing Center and quickly paddle across the Intracoastal Waterway into Fisherman's Cut. Kayakers should use caution when venturing across the canal as there is always plenty of boat traffic in the area. Kayakers should be especially careful in the early morning hours when most boats are launching and during low-light periods. A warning flag like the ones found on kid's bikes attached to a kayak makes it much more visible.

Once across from the Fishing Center turn west through Barroom Bay and you're on Blackberry Island. The island offers a straight paddle for several miles, definitely more than most kayakers can do in a day. This is prime territory for redfish and trout. Don't be surprised by a school of jacks cruising the area in the fall.

BILL DAY'S REEF

Bill Day's Reef is a U-shaped oyster-shell reef just south of Blackberry Island. This is a fairly large reef that usually holds fish during the early morning hours. The reef is made of layer after layer of oyster shells. There are deep guts running to and through the reef that offer quick access to the deeper water most fish prefer. Small prey fish, shrimp, worms, and crabs all inhabit this reef making it an ideal feeding station.

For kayakers, a short paddle from Blackberry is all it takes to fish Bill Day's Reef. If the reef already has a couple of boats on it by the time you reach the area, you'll be better served staying along Blackberry Island and fishing the reef when you can be one of the first anglers there.

Poppers and suspending flies on floating line work best. You may also want to use flies with weedguards to prevent the fly from hanging up on an oyster shell. Be prepared to lose a few flies when fishing this reef. Thoroughly work any depression or hole with deeper water.

Light-tackle casters should use soft plastics with 1/16- or 1/8-ounce jigheads and weedless gold or copper spoons. Be sure to work all sides of the reef.

DEWBERRY ISLAND

Dewberry Island is the continuation of Blackberry Island past the Government or Army Cut. The Army Cut was made to allow ships access to travel to the Army Air Base across the bay. Fishers can fish the grassy areas around the cut but there is always plenty of boat action going through, so pay attention to the waves and traffic. Dolphins also roam the cut early in the morning.

Dewberry Island goes all the way down to Fulghum's Cut, several miles down the coastline. The island has both hard-packed sandy areas and soft muddy areas. Kayakers can paddle down the island to their hearts content, just don't forget to allow yourself plenty of time to paddle back in the evening.

Dewberry Island is hard hit when the wind blows out of the south often turning the water sandy brown.

SHOALWATER LAGOON

Shoalwater Lagoon is the area between Dewberry Island and the Intracoastal Waterway. This is a very shallow and muddy area. At low tide a large portion of the lagoon will be out of the water. Redfish like to work the grassy shorelines on both sides of the lagoon. This is a great place for kayakers because very few boats run shallow enough to get through the lagoon.

Gold spoon flies and lures are the ticket for redfish in the lagoon. Use a floating fly line and 9-foot leader with a weedless gold spoon fly. Light tackle anglers are best served using reels with a fast retrieve so they can keep the spoon above the oysters, grass, and muddy bottom.

An early morning trip to Lighthouse Cove is sometimes met with calm waters.

Pay attention to the tides when in the lagoon. More than one boat has been caught going into the lagoon during high tide only to become stranded when the tide goes out. This area can be very muddy and difficult to wade so knowing when the tide is going to turn around and go out is important.

BAYUCOS ISLAND

Bayucos Island is the first of a series of islands that run in the middle of Espiritu Santo Bay. The island is made up of oyster shell and grass surrounded by shallow flats, deeper-water, and cuts. The north side of the island drops off into water 5 to 6 feet deep. The south side of the island is very shallow with water only a couple of feet deep. There is a deeper channel running between Bayucos Island and Grass Island that is used by boats going through the bay.

Bayucos is an early morning area. Redfish, speckled trout, and flounder are all found in the shallow water around the island. Keep moving until you find the fish. Be sure to work shallow for reds and out deeper for trout.

Flyfishers should use a fly with a weedguard when fishing around Bayucos due to the numerous oyster shells in the area. Light-tackle anglers can use weedless gold spoons and soft plastic tails with jigheads.

Jacks regularly visit the waters around Bill Day's Reef.

GRASS ISLAND

Grass Island is the second and largest of the islands in Espiritu Santo Bay. The island is surrounded by slightly deeper water with some areas running from 8 to 10 feet. The south side of the island is typical of Texas islands in that the hardest sand drops out nearest the deeper water and lighter sand and mud washes farther towards the shoreline.

Redfish are often found in the shallow waters around Grass Island.

Wading the drop-off ridge is not bad but the closer you get to land, the harder the wading gets. The area within 50 yards of the grass shoreline is very difficult to wade, with those adventurous enough to try ending up with mud up to their waist. Fish these areas out of a kayak to avoid getting stuck in the soft mud.

Schools of redfish like this area and can be seen tailing, looking for crabs and other food. Try for trout in the deeper water on the south side of the island. You can also drift fish the deeper water using light tackle including 1/4- to 1/2-ounce jigheads with soft plastic tails. Anglers using shrimp can use a popping cork while drifting. Make just enough noise to attract the fish. A pop of the cork every two or three minutes is probably enough. Set the bait at least 3 feet under the popping cork. A long casting or spinning rod of 8.5 or 9 feet long will help when casting the deeper set rig.

There is also a large lake on the south end of Grass Island that is mostly overlooked by anglers. This lake is an ideal location for fishing out of a kayak. The lake is very shallow, muddy, and scattered with oyster shells making wading difficult. Try fishing the lake during a high tide or you may have trouble getting through some of the shallower areas.

FARWELL ISLAND

Farwell Island is the last and smallest island in the chain. The area between Grass Island and Farwell Island is often used for drift fishing. Speckled trout prefer the slightly deeper water during the heat of the day. Anglers may also see birds chasing shrimp driven to the surface by predator fish in this area. Most of the time the fish will be small trout or gafftopsail catfish, but it is a good idea to make a few casts to any bird activity to determine what type of fish is after the bait.

OIL RIGS AND SEPARATORS IN ESPIRITU SANTO BAY

These rigs are just off Grass Island and stretch across the bay. Fish are sometimes located around the rigs and even more often around the shell pads put down during the construction of the rigs. The water is not deep around these rigs, averaging less than 10 feet. Give the rigs a shot, but don't spend too much time in non-productive water.

Heavy sinking flies, like a well-weighted Clouser, work best. Light-tackle casters should use heavy, 1/2-ounce jigheads and soft plastic tails to get down through the water column quickly.

PRINGLE LAKE

Pringle Lake is the first in a series of lakes that dot the south shoreline of Espiritu Santo and San Antonio Bays. The lake is relatively shallow with most areas less than 6 feet deep. The mouth of the lake is a little tricky to enter, requiring a couple of near 90-degree turns to successfully maneuver. Those new to the area, may want to watch other boats entering the lake or hire a guide the first time you fish here.

The areas on both sides of the mouth of the lake are also good fishing areas. Look for small patches of grass isolated from the main grass shoreline.

Pringle is a good place to use a popping cork or Mansfield Mauler rig with a soft plastic tail. Use the wind to drift across the middle section of the lake. Fly casters will have greater success by staying in the boat and casting to shallow areas along the grass circling the lake.

Contee Lake

Contee Lake is similar to Pringle, just not as large. This is a good kayak area, but watch for super-shallow-running flats boats and airboats crossing through the back lake area.

SOUTH PASS LAKE

South Pass Lake is a long way from anywhere. Whether you travel from Charlie's Bait Camp, Port O'Connor, or upper San Antonio Bay, South Pass Lake is a good boat ride away. Famed Texas coastal angler Rudy "Plugger" Grigar made this area legendary years ago.

The chain of islands just north of the lake divides Espiritu Santo Bay from San Antonio Bay. Boaters should travel through this area with caution because there are many oyster reefs just under the surface of the water. If you're unfamiliar with the area go with a guide.

FULGHUM'S CUT

Fulghum's Cut is accessed by turning on Lane Road about half way between Seadrift and Port O' Connor on Highway 185. The ramp at Charlie's is good but the parking lot gets very muddy after a strong rain. There is a fee to launch.

Somewhat like the cut across from the Fishing Center in Port O'Connor, Fulghum's Cut offers kayakers easy access to Shoalwater Lagoon after crossing the Intracoastal Waterway. There is always plenty of barge traffic in the area so kayakers need to get across the canal quickly. Another area made for kayakers is the Welder Flats area just a little farther down the Intracoastal Waterway. Most people going to Charlie's use the cut to get to the south shoreline of Espiritu Santo and San Antonio Bays.

A great place to take the kids is the fish cleaning tables at Charlie's. Any bait cast into the area under the tables is quickly devoured by a catfish. The fishing will be fast and fun. Fish for an hour or so and then move on to something different like wading the front beach at Port O'Connor to keep the kids enthusiastic about the outing.

Boat Ramps

Charlie's Bait Camp, Lane Road, 361-785-3023, Seadrift

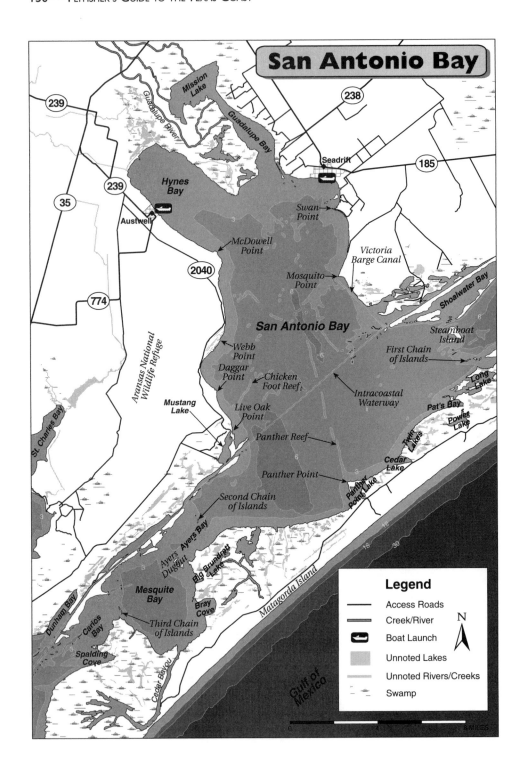

San Antonio Bay

Mission Lake

239

Guadalupe River

Guadalupe Bay

238

Seadrift

185

239

Hynes Bay

35

Austwell

Swan Point

McDowell Point

Victoria Barge Canal

2040

Mosquito Point

Shoalwater Bay

774

San Antonio Bay

Steamboat Island

Aransas National Wildlife Refuge

Webb Point

First Chain of Islands

Daggar Point

Chicken Foot Reef

Long Lake

Intracoastal Waterway

Pat's Bay

Mustang Lake

Live Oak Point

Powet Lake

Panther Reef

Twin Lakes

Cedar Lake

St. Charles Bay

Panther Point

Panther Point Lake

Second Chain of Islands

Ayers Bay

Ayers Dugout

Big Brundret Lake

Matagorda Island

Mesquite Bay

Bray Cove

Dunham Bay

Carlos Bay

Third Chain of Islands

Spalding Cove

Cedar Bayou

Gulf of Mexico

Legend

——	Access Roads
══	Creek/River
🛶	Boat Launch
▨	Unnoted Lakes
══	Unnoted Rivers/Creeks
‑ ‑	Swamp

N

0   4   8 MILES

San Antonio Bay

San Antonio Bay is somewhat overlooked but growing in popularity. The bay is west of Espiritu Santo Bay where the San Antonio and Guadalupe Rivers feed freshwater into the bay. San Antonio Bay is bordered by the Aransas National Wildlife Reserve and includes Blackjack Island. This is the area where whooping cranes winter in Texas. San Antonio Bay runs north and south and is adversely affected by strong winds.

On the northwest side of the bay is the small town of Seadrift. Take Highway 185 south out of Victoria. There are two boat ramps in Seadrift: one just south of the main part of the town and the other at Swan Point. Parking is very limited at these boat ramps and there may be a small launch fee. Follow the crab traps for an idea of boat lanes throughout the bay.

There are plenty of shell reefs in the bay. Speckled trout cruise these reefs almost year round. There is also heavy crabbing and shrimping traffic in San Antonio Bay. While the town of Seadrift is larger than Port O'Connor, more people fish the Port O'Connor area.

Use a stripping basket to help control your fly line.

In the spring freshwater running into San Antonio Bay can play a big role in the fishing. Every strong thunderstorm in the hill country of Texas is followed by an influx of fresh water into San Antonio Bay. Spring storms and their freshwater are vital parts of the coastal environment. Without the freshwater inflows, many of the juvenile shrimp, crabs, and fin fish would not have a chance to mature before heading into the more treacherous bay waters.

The fresh water inflows insure that the brackish water estuaries that provide nurseries for the immature prey species have enough freshwater to support the beginning of their life. Without freshwater many of the prey species eaten by trout, redfish, and flounder would not be able to survive.

Although the freshwater from the Guadalupe and San Antonio Rivers are vital to San Antonio Bay, if there is a big storm system that dumps a lot of fresh water into the rivers and then the bays, the fishing may be off for a few days to several weeks. But the fresh water helps ensure the salt in the bays remains at levels best for fish and their food. Without the freshwater inflows, the bay becomes too salty and fishing really slows.

San Antonio Bay has one group of islands on the eastern perimeter called the First Chain of Islands and has another group of islands on the western perimeter called

Many boat ramps charge a ramp fee.

the Second Chain of Islands. Both of these groups of islands hold many hazards for boats and anglers. I strongly suggest hiring a guide to fish this area for the first several times.

The Second Chain is a long way from any access to help. When you fish this area, make sure someone knows where you're going.

San Antonio Bay also has several reefs located just north of the Intracoastal Waterway that divide the bay north and south. Reefs like Chicken Foot Reef on the west side of the bay offer good trout fishing. There are enough reefs in the area for any serious trout angler to spend a lifetime without working them all. There are many boating hazards in San Antonio Bay so anglers should consider hiring a guide until they know the area.

Anglers may find it easier to use the Victoria Barge Canal when traveling north or south in San Antonio Bay. The canal runs along the eastern edge of the bay and has a steady stream of large vessels using the canal. The canal intersects the Intracoastal Waterway just south of Mosquito Point.

Boat Ramps

Miller's Dock & Dockside Marina & RV Park, 100 Bay Avenue, Seadrift
Swan Point Park End of Swan Point Road, Seadrift
Austwell Boat Ramp

Guides

Captain Lynn Smith Back Bay Guide Service/ 361-935-6833

LONG LAKE

Long Lake is the continuation of the lake chain that starts with Pringle Lake south of Port O'Connor. Long Lake is on the far south side of San Antonio Bay and just west of the First Chain of Islands. This lake has a soft grass bottom but is wadeable for those willing to put up with some tough wading. The shorelines are firmer with patches of sand.

Work a suspending lure like a Corky over the grassy areas for trout. Try a gold weedless spoon in the shallows for redfish.

PAT'S BAY

Pat's Bay is very remote and a long ride from any of the boat ramps in the area. If you've made the long ride, you will often be rewarded with good catches of speckled trout and redfish. This is not a place to have boat problems. Make sure someone knows where you're going when you go to Pat's Bay.

Wade the sides and work the many sand pockets in the area. There are several guts running out of the surrounding areas that provide good fishing on an outgoing tide. Waders need to be prepared to work through soft areas that may make wading tough.

Power Lake

Power Lake is actually south of Pat's Bay. This area is very shallow and most boats will have difficulty getting to Power Lake. Anglers need to pay particular attention to the tides when they're in this area. Access at high tide may mean being stuck when the tide drops out.

Twin Lakes

Twin Lakes is at the far south end of San Antonio Bay. There are shell areas at the front of the lakes offering good fishing on an outgoing tide. The lakes are wadeable but the bottom will be soft in areas.

CEDAR LAKE

Cedar Lake is actually an open cove instead of a lake. This is a long boat ride from anywhere and a real commitment for the anglers that decide to fish the lake. There is a deep cut that runs through the middle of the lake with grass around the shoreline. The wading can be tough in the back part of the lake due to a thick, muddy bottom. The west shoreline has a little more shell than the east shoreline, making it a little easier to wade.

The area outside the eastern mouth of the lake often holds nice redfish. Flounder can be found almost anywhere in this lake.

PANTHER REEF (INCLUDING PANTHER POINT LAKE AND PANTHER POINT)

Panther Reef is an oyster-shell reef in the middle of San Antonio Bay. This is not an easy place to get to. If you fish Panther Reef, you've pretty much decided it is the only place you will fish that day. There is deep water surrounding the reef and this is usually where the fish will be. This is a speckled trout haven.

The best way to work the reef is to start on one side and wade slowly around the entire reef. Thoroughly cover the complete reef because you've already made the commitment to fish it and it's a long trip back to the boat ramp no matter where you put in.

Be sure you take extra jigheads, lures, and flies with you when you leave the boat. You will lose several to the very sharp oyster shells of the reef.

Panther Reef is one spot where you can expect to catch trout in the colder winter months. Be sure to bundle up for the boat ride, and wearing insulated waders is a big plus when fishing this hard-to-reach reef.

GUADALUPE BAY

The Guadalupe River enters Guadalupe Bay at the northwest side. It is joined by the San Antonio River just west of Green Lake. Just south of Green Lake is the Guadalupe Delta Wildlife Management Area. Fresh water inflows affect Guadalupe Bay in the spring and fall.

Anglers can fish this area for redfish in the fall with gold or copper weedless spoons or spoon flies. Look for tailing redfish along the grassy shoreline.

HYNES BAY

Hynes Bay is at the far north end of San Antonio Bay. This area is impacted by springtime thunderstorms and freshwater inflows from the rivers farther inshore. Fishing may be difficult during springtime flooding.

Look to Hynes Bay when the consistent fall weather arrives. Captain Lynn Smith of Back Bay Guide Services mentioned that Hynes Bay has a steady population of alligators, so waders should be cautious when in the area.

MUSTANG LAKE

Mustang Lake is a very shallow-water area. Only anglers with extremely shallow-running boats should attempt to fish this area. Redfish often lay up in the shallows until something disturbs them, so approach this area like a stalking heron would.

A weedless spoon will catch fish anywhere along the Texas coast.

AYERS BAY

Long time coastal guide Captain Lynn Smith fishes Ayers and Mesquite Bays early in the year. Launch at Charlie's Bait Camp on the Intracoastal Waterway when fishing the south part of the San Antonio Bay system.

Smith has a flyfishing background but most of his clients use casting or spinning tackle. He particularly likes to throw large suspending lures like a Corky after big trout.

He normally starts fishing these bays after March 1, when the waters are just starting to warm.

Ayers's Dugout connects Ayers Bay to Mesquite Bay.

MESQUITE BAY

It's best to fish Mesquite Bay during tide movement. Spoil areas run through the middle of Mesquite Bay and often hold good numbers of redfish. Mesquite Bay Reef is just to the east of these spoil areas. Close-by Cedar Bayou opens into the gulf and provides access for incoming saltwater.

CARLOS BAY

Carlos Bay is the far western bay just to the west of Mesquite Bay. The water between the Intracoastal Waterway to the north and Ballou Island to the south averages about 3 feet deep. This area offers good springtime fishing for trout and reds. There are very shallow areas at both the east and west ends of Carlos Bay so be careful when boating in the area.

CEDAR BAYOU

This is the last of the three natural passes left on the Texas coast. Cedar Bayou is a narrow pass that can almost be cast across. Fish use the pass to reenter the Gulf of Mexico. This is not an easy pass to reach because it requires a long boat ride from Goose Island State Park.

Speckled trout, redfish, and flounder are all found in the pass. The mouth entering the Gulf of Mexico also often contains fish.

For those wanting to night fish, Cedar Bayou is a good spot. It also has one of the densest populations of mosquitoes found on the coast. If you fish this area at night, take at least two containers of bug spray with you and reapply a couple of times during the night.

Long sleeve shirts and caps help some with the mosquitoes. But only those die hard anglers that really want to fish this area at night will be able to tolerate a full night's worth of bombardment. Hope for a light breeze instead of a calm night.

Both feral hogs and alligators populate this area so be aware.

The currents usually determine fishing. Slack tide is not a time to be at Cedar Bayou. Anglers will do themselves a favor by checking the tide charts and timing their trips when there is the most tidal movement.

Flycasters can work the Bayou with a sinking line and a big Clouser or Half and Half. Cast the fly out and let the current move it. Light-tackle casters should try jigheads with soft plastics.

THE SURF FROM PASS CAVALLO TO CEDAR BAYOU

Surf fishing along the gulf side of Matagorda Island can be excellent depending on the weather. During late July and all of August, anglers have a chance to experience the gulf shoreline when it is calm enough to fish.

Calm surf conditions are most often associated with the hottest days. Anglers want to see the water along the gulf shoreline "green to the beach", as the old-timers called it. Unfortunately, the number of days when the wind is calm enough are very few and some years, non-existent.

Boat traffic is not allowed through Cedar Bayou so any angler wishing to fish the Matagorda Island surf must enter the gulf through Pass Cavallo or the Matagorda Ship Channel Jetties.

Travel west along the surf looking for visible fish action including fish and birds chasing prey along the surface. Be careful when anchoring along the gulf shoreline.

Surf fish will hit almost any fly or lure. These fish pull hard so be prepared to lose a few flies or lures.

Flycasters can try any baitfish or shrimp imitation. Light-tackle casters should try hard-bodied lures like Top Dogs, Catch 2000, Catch 5, Super Spooks, and Jumping Minnows.

If you're lucky enough to catch the surf calm along Matagorda Island, consider yourself blessed. It doesn't happen often.

Shallow-running boats are a must for many bay areas.

San Antonio Bay Hub Cities

AUSTIN
Population: 681,437
County: Travis

ACCOMMODATIONS

La Quinta Airport, 7625 Ben White Blvd / 512-386-6800 / 142 rooms / $109-$129 / www.lq.com

Comfort Suites, 7501 E Ben White Blvd / 512-386-6630 / 82 rooms / $89-$129

Days Inn, 4220 S IH 35 / 512-441-9242 / 62 rooms/ $50-120 / www.daysinn.com

Best Western Airport, 2751 E Hwy 71/ 512-385-1000 / 112 rooms / $89-$149 / www.bestwesterntexas.com

Courtyard By Marriott, 7809 E Ben White Blvd / 512-386-7464 / 150 rooms / $99-$149 / www.courtyard.com

Hampton Inn & Suites, 7712 E Riverside Dr / 512-389-1616 / 102 rooms / $149-$179 / www.hamptoninn.com

Holiday Inn Express, 7601 E Ben White Blvd/ 512-386-7600 / 80 rooms / $99-$139 / www.holidayinn.com

CAMPGROUNDS

Midtown RV Park, 720 Airport Blvd / 512-385-2885

Oak Forest RV Park, 8207 Canoga Ave / 800-478-7275 / www.oakforest-rvpark.com

LaHacienda RV Park, 5320 Hudson Bend Rd / 512-266-8001 / www.lahaciendarvpark.com

Hudson Bend RV Park, 5104 Beacon Dr / 512-266-8300 / www.hbrv.com

Austin Lone Star RV, 7009 I-35 S / 800-284-0206 / www.austinlonestar.com

RESTAURANTS

Salt Lick Three-Sixty, 3801 N Capital of Texas Hwy/ 512-328-4957

Matt's El Rancho, 2613 S Lamar Blvd / 512-462-9333 / www.mattselrancho.com

The Original Hoffbrau, 613 W Sixth St / 512-472-0822 / www.originalhoffbrausteaks.com

Threadgills, 6416 N Lamar Blvd / 512-451-5440 / www.threadgills.com

Z'Tejas Southwestern Grill, 1110 W Sixth St / 512-478-5355 / www.ztejas.com

SPORTING GOODS

Academy Sports / www.academy.com
12250 Research Blvd / 512-506-6000
5400 Brodie Lane / 512-891-4240
7513 North IH-35 / 512-407-6310
801 E William Cannon Dr / 512-486-6000

Cabelas, 15570 IH 35, Buda / 512-295-1100 / www.cabelas.com
McBrides, 2915 San Gabriel St / 512-472-3532 / www.mcbridesguns.com
Sportsman's Finest, 12434 FM 2244, Bee Cave / 512-263-1888 /
www.sportsmansfinest.com

Airports

Austin-Bergstrom International Airport/American Airlines 800-433-7300
/ Continental Airlines 800-525-0280 / Mexicana Airlines 800-531-7921 /
Southwest Airlines 800-435-9792 / United Airlines 800-241-6522

For more Information

Austin Convention & Visitors Bureau
209 E 6th St
512-474-5171
www.austintexas.org

PORT O'CONNOR
Population: 2,300
County: Calhoun

ACCOMMODATIONS

The Inn at Clark's, 101 7th Street / 361-983-2300 / 21 rooms / $120-$220 / www.theinnatclarks.com

Captain's Quarters, Byers Rd & Harrison St / 361-983-4982 / 28 rooms / $85-$95 / www.captainsquartershotel.com

Sand Dollar Motel, Olive & 15th / 361-983-2342 / 14 rooms / $59-$75

Tarpon Inn, Maple between 13th & 14th / 361-983-2606 / 52 rooms/ $69-$140

Poco Loco Lodge, Hwy 185 / 361-983-0300 / www.thepocolocolodge.com

CAMPGROUNDS

Gulf RV Park, Maple & 15th /361-218-1523

Beacon, 44 RV Park, 1982 W. Harrison / 361-983-4247

LaSalle's Landing RV Park, 2699 W Adams / 361-983-4854

Texas Coast RV Resorts, 140 S Byers Dr / 361-983-2326 / www.texascoastrv.com

RESTAURANTS

Clark's, 7th St / 361-983-4388

Josie's Mexican Food, 7th and Adams / 361-983-4720

Cathy's, Byers Rd & Adams Ave / 361-983-2880

The Spot, Jefferson between 13th & 14th / 361-983-2775

Toasties Subs, Hwy 185 / 361-983-2070

SPORTING GOODS

Captain Marty's, Byers & Adams / 361-983-3474 / www.captainmarty.itgo.com

Speedy Stop, 16th & Adams 361-983-4411 / www.speedystop.com

POC Hardware, Hwy 185 / 361-983-2708

FOR MORE INFORMATION

Port O'Connor Chamber of Commerce
P.O. Box 701
Port O'Connor 77982
www.portoconnor.com

SAN ANTONIO
Population: 1,144,646
County: Bexar

ACCOMMODATIONS

Hilton Palacios Del Rio, 200S Alamo St / 800-Hiltons/481 rooms/ $149 / www.hilton.com

Marriott Riverwalk, 711 E Riverwalk / 800-648-4462 / 511 rooms/ $149 / www.marriott.com

Best Western Casa Linda, 8818 Jones Maltsberger Rd / 210-366-1800 / 119 rooms/ $69-99 / www.bestwesterntexas.com

Comfort Inn & Suites, Airport 8640 Crownhill Blvd / 210-249-2000 / 100 rooms / $69-159

Doubletree Hotel, 37 NE Loop 410 / 210-366-2424 / 290 rooms / $109-299 / www.doubletree.com

Econo Lodge Airport, 2635 NE Loop 410 / 210-247-4774 / 59 rooms / $55-90 / www.econolodge.com

Holiday Inn Select, 77 NE Loop 410 / 210-349-9900 / 397 rooms / $99-169 / www.holidayinn.com

Quality Inn, 542 NE Loop 410 / 210-903-3300 / 49 rooms / $60-199 / www.qualityinn.com

La Quinta Airport, 850 Halm Blvd / 210-342-3738 / 276 rooms / $119-265 / www.lq.com

Amerisuites Airport, 7615 Jones Maltsberger Rd / 210-930-2333 / 128 rooms / $99-$149 / www.amerisuites.com

CAMPGROUNDS

San Antonio KOA, 602 Gembler Rd / 210-224-5430

Dixie Kampground, 1011 Gembler Rd / 210-337-6501 / www.dixiecampground.com

Tejas Valley, RV Park 13080, Potranco Rd / 210-679-7715 / www.tejasvalleyrvpark.com

Travelers World RV, 2617 Roosevelt Ave / 210-532-8310

Admiralty RV, 1485 E Ellison Dr / 210-647-7878 / www.admiraltyrvresort.com

RESTAURANTS

Saltgrass Steakhouse, 16910 Hwy 281 N / 210-402-6621 / www.saltgrass.com

Texas Land & Cattle Steakhouse, 60 NE Loop 410 / 210-342-4477 / www.texaslandandcattle.com

Pappadeaux Seafood Kitchen, 76 NE Loop 410 / 210-340-7143 / www.pappas.com

Sea Island Shrimp House, 4323 Amerisuites / 210-558-8989 / www.seaislandshrimp.com

County Line Smokehouse, 111W Crockett / 210-229-1941 / www.countyline.com

The Barbecue Station, 1610 NE Loop 410 / 210-824-9191 /
wwwbarbecuestation.com

Fuddruckers, 8602 Botts Lane / 210-824-6703 / www.fuddruckers.com

Jason's Deli, 25 NE Loop 410 / 210-524-9288 / www.jasonsdeli.com

SPORTING GOODS

Academy Sports / www.academy.com
4071 North Loop 1604 West / 210-408-5400
2024 N Loop 1604 E (at 281) / 210-507-4001
7555 Northwest Loop 410 (at Military Dr) / 210-257-4850
2727 NE Loop 410 (at Perrin-Beitel) / 210-871-2630
165 SW Military Dr (at S Flores) / 210-334-6740
15350 IH 35 (at Olympia Pkwy), Selma / 210-637-2600
2643 NW Loop 410 (at Vance Jackson) / 210-321-4600

Bass Pro Shops, 17907 IH 10 W / 210-253-8800 / www.basspro.com

Sportsman's Warehouse, 1911 N Loop 1604 E / 210-494-5505 /
www.sportsmanswarehouse.com

Sports Authority, 125 N.W. Loop 410, Suite 240 / 210-341-1244 /
www.sportsauthority.com

Rodmakers, 1727 Eagle Meadow / 210-479-3477

Tacklebox Outfitters, 6330 N, New Braunfels / 210-821-5806 /
www.tackleboxoutfitters.com

AIRPORTS

San Antonio International Airport 210-207-3450 / American Airlines
800-433-7300 / Continental Airlines 800-525-0280 / Mexicana Airlines
800-531-7921 / Southwest Airlines 800-435-9792 / United Airlines 800-241-6522

FOR MORE INFORMATION

San Antonio Convention and Visitors Bureau
P.O. Box 2277
San Antonio, TX 78298
210-207-6748
www.sanantoniovisit.com

SEADRIFT
Population: 300
County: Calhoun

ACCOMMODATIONS

Captain's Quarters, 201 Hwy 185 / 361-785-4982
Seadrifter Inn, 106 W Bay Ave / 361-785-2031 / www.seadrifter.com
Falcon Point Lodge, Right on Dierlam Rd / 877-375-4868 /
    www.falconpointranch.com
Bay Motel, 322 N Broadway Ave / 361-785-2226

CAMPGROUNDS

Beacon, 7 RV 1500 W Bay Ave/ 361-785-2717 / www.beacon7rvpark.com
Almost Paradise RV Park / 361-550-5584 / www.almostparadiservpark.com
Sunrise RV Park, Hwy 185 / 361-935-5414

RESTAURANTS

Barkett's, Hwy 185 / 361-785-2441
El Comal, 222 Mains St / 361-785-5083
Harbor Inn Seafood, 702 Broadway / 361-785-2397
The Pizza Place, Hwy 185 / 361-785-7100
Dockside Café, Main & Bay St / 361-785-7755

SPORTING GOODS

Bayside Express, 201 W. Broadway, 24 hour / 361-785-7002
Pic-Pac Food Store, 202 W Broadway Hwy 185 / 361-785-3391
Charlies Bait Camp, Lane Road / 361-785-3023 / www.charliesbait.com

FOR MORE INFORMATION

Seadrift Chamber of Commerce
    P.O. Box 3
    Seadrift
    361-785-2218
    www.seadriftchamber@tisd.net

VICTORIA
Population: 61,055
County: Victoria

ACCOMMODATIONS

Best Western Victoria, 8106 NE Zac Lentz Pkwy / 361-485-2300 / 54 rooms/ $80-$159 / www.bestwesterntexas.com

Comfort Inn, 1906 Houston Hwy / 361-574-9393 / 50 rooms / $50-$150

Hampton Inn, 7006 N Navarro / 361-573-9911 / 68 rooms / $80-$149 / www.hamptoninn.com

La Quinta Victoria, 7603 N Navarro / 361-572-3585 / 130 rooms/ $69-$109 / www.lq.com

Quality Inn, 3112 Houston Hwy / 361-578-2030 / 101 Rooms / $72-$85 / www.qualityinn.com

CAMPGROUNDS

Dad's RV Park, 203 Hopkins St / 361-573-1231

Gateway to the Gulf RV Park and Campground, 9809 Hwy 59 N / 361-570-7080

Lazy Longhorn RV Park, 1402 S Laurent St / 361-485-1598

RESTAURANTS

Jason's Deli, 5301 N Navarro St / 361-575-3354 / www.jasonsdeli.com

Carino's Italian Restaurant, 4904 N Navarro St / 361-485-9816 / www.carinos.com

Montana Mikes, 6409 N Navarro St / 361-576-0333

Tejas Café, 2902 N Navarro St / 361-572-9433

Texas Roadhouse, 4908 N Navarro St / 361-570-7427 / www.texasroadhouse.com

Siesta Restaurant, 2505 Houston Hwy / 361-573-6364

Pelican's Wharf, 2912 Houston Hwy / 361-578-5253

SPORTING GOODS

Victoria All Sports, 1902 Houston Hwy / 361-573-5481 / www.victoriaallsports.com

Academy Sports, 8903 N Navarro / 361-582-5200 / www.academy.com

Tackle Box, 3305 N Ben Jordan St / 361-575-8700

HOSPITALS

Citizens Medical Center, 2701 Hospital Dr / 361-573-9181 / www.citizensmedicalcenter.org

DeTar Hospital, 506 E San Antonio St / 361-575-7441 / www.detar.com

FOR MORE INFORMATION

Victoria Convention & Visitors Bureau
700 Mina Center Suite 101
Victoria, TX 77902
800-926-5774
www.visitvictoria.org

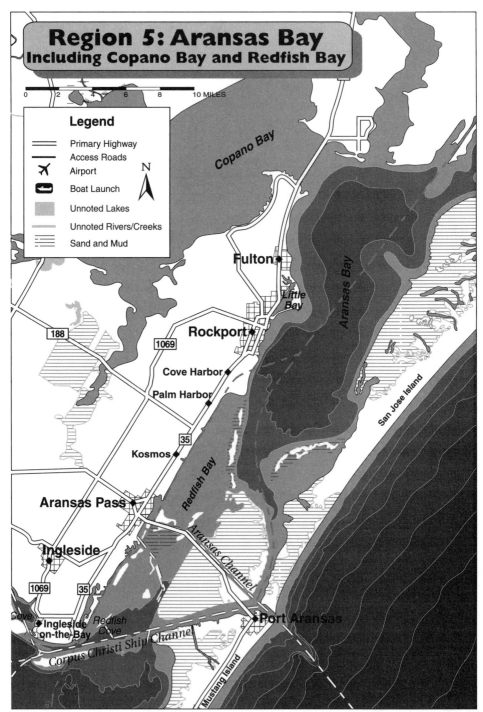

Region 5: Aransas Bay
Including Copano Bay and Redfish Bay

0   2   4   6   8   10 MILES

Legend

Primary Highway
Access Roads
✈ Airport   N
🛥 Boat Launch   ↑
Unnoted Lakes
Unnoted Rivers/Creeks
Sand and Mud

Copano Bay

Fulton

Little Bay

Aransas Bay

188

Rockport

1069

Cove Harbor

Palm Harbor

35

Kosmos

Redfish Bay

San Jose Island

Aransas Pass

Aransas Channel

Ingleside

1069   35

Cove

Ingleside
on-the-Bay

Redfish
Cove

Port Aransas

Corpus Christi Ship Channel

Mustang Island

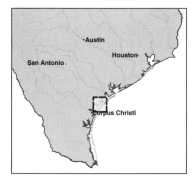

Region 5: Aransas Bay

Aransas Bay is a shallow-water angler's dream. There are vast areas with clear water less than 3 feet deep and plenty of fish. This bay system is where saltwater light-tackle fishing and flyfishing started on the Texas coast.

Aransas Bay is at the south end of three areas designated as wildlife refuges. Just north of Cedar Bayou is Matagorda Island National Wildlife Refuge (NWR), just west of there is Aransas National Wildlife Refuge on Blackjack Peninsula, and just west of there is St. Charles Bay and Goose Island State Park.

The isolated environment of these areas provides an ideal habitat for the few surviving whooping cranes that make this area their annual winter home. If you're ever lucky enough to wade the same shoreline as a whooping crane you will not forget the experience. This big crane, standing 6 feet tall, likes to look for small fish and crabs in very shallow water.

This area is also where Aransas Bay starts and the famed Coastal Bend finishes its turn south. Here, the bottom changes to mainly firm sand, and sea grasses become a predominant feature in the bays.

Two underwater creatures — stingrays and blue crabs — are found in most of the waters in the Aransas Bay region. Stingrays don't necessarily mean bad fishing

Seasonal Fishing Chart - Region 5: Aransas Bay

	Jan	Feb	Mar	Apr	May	Jun	Jul	Aug	Sep	Oct	Nov	Dec
Redfish	++	+++	+++	+++	+++	+++	+++	+++	+++	+++	+++	+++
Spotted Seatrout	++	+++	+++	+++	+++	+++	+++	+++	+++	+++	+++	++
Flounder			++	+++	+++	+++	+++	+++	+++	+++	+++	
Black Drum	++	+++	+++	+++	+++	+++	+++	+++	+++	+++	++	+
Sheepshead	++	+++	+++	+++	+++	+++	+++	+++	+++	+++	++	+
Crevalle Jack					++	+++	+++	+++	+++			
Spanish Mackerel					++	+++	+++	+++	+++			
Gray Snapper						+++	+++	+++				
Tarpon					+	+	+	+	+			
Pompano				+	+	+	+	+				
Snook						+	+	+				

+++ = Exceptional, ++ = Very Good, + = Available

locations for anglers. Redfish often patrol with a stingray. The redfish will glide along with the stingray, often beating the ray to any spooked prey. The presence of stingrays means there is plenty of food for predator fish. Anglers need to do the stingray shuffle and keep their feet on the bottom.

Blue crabs are found in most of the shallow waters in these bays. Almost everything, including redfish and anglers, likes to eat blue crabs. If you find water with a lot of blue crabs you can expect to find redfish patrolling near by. A healthy blue crab population means a healthy redfish population.

During recent years, Aransas Bay has also been THE spot on the Texas coast for kayakers. The numerous shallow water areas are perfect for the kayaker. Just take your kayak and a good map for some great fishing. There are also several guides in the area that specialize in kayak fishing. Some have kayaks for rent by the day. This is a great way to try out several different kayaks before you decide which one to purchase.

The Aransas Bay System has something for everyone. Whatever type of fishing you like to do, you can find a place in this system to do it. Many of the areas in this region can be accessed without a large boat. That means more people fishing here, especially on weekends and holidays. But with the numerous small bays, coves, cuts, and flats you'll find a spot with plenty of fish.

Everything likes blue crab.

Cavasso Creek

Cavasso Creek crosses under Highway 35 north of the LBJ Causeway. Small boats and kayaks can launch at the dirt ramp. Parking is very limited and the area where the creek intersects the road is often crowded with fishermen.

Cavasso Creek flows east into St. Charles Bay. Both shorelines where the creek enters the bay offer good wade fishing. This is an excellent area for someone new to kayaking to learn his or her paddling skills.

Cavasso Creek is isolated and most anglers willing to go to the trouble to explore this area will be by themselves. Work close to the grass and into any deeper holes you run across.

GOOSE ISLAND STATE PARK

Goose Island State Park provides access to St. Charles Bay and other areas on the north end of Aransas Bay. Enter the park on Park Road 13 heading east off Hwy 35 just before the Lyndon B Johnson (LBJ) Causeway on Lamar Peninsula.

Entrance into the park requires a fee. Goose Island State Park has several RV pads, a good paved boat ramp, parking area, and fish-cleaning station along with a fishing pier. Boaters should pay attention to marked boat lanes and watch for reefs in the area. Many reefs are marked by fishermen with a piece of white PVC pipe. For those unfamiliar with the area, watch other boats as they navigate the area or hire a guide.

There are hard-shell areas around the island where fishers can wade. St. Charles Reef protects the mouth of St. Charles Bay.

The famed Big Tree is located just north of the park. The large live oak dominates a group of several trees in the area. The Big Tree is over 1,000 years old and surrounded by a protective fence. Visitors should be aware that during most months the tree is engulfed by millions of mosquitoes. Visit with plenty of bug spray or during the less-wet winter months.

Boat Ramp

Goose Island State Park, 202 South Palmetto Ave / 361-729-2858

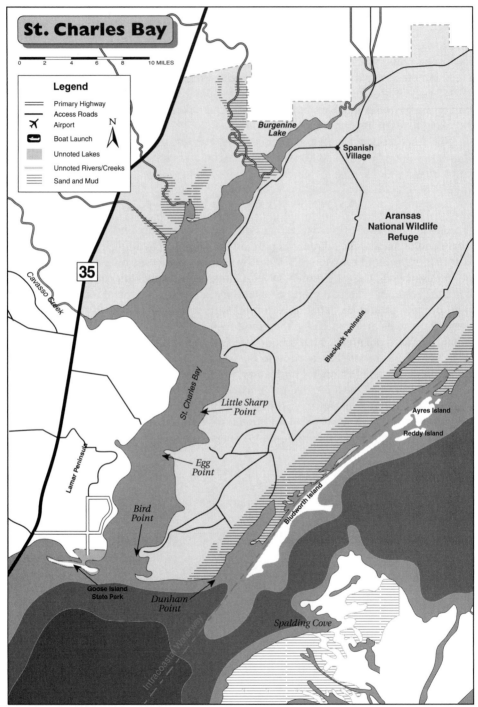

St. Charles Bay

0   2   4   6   8   10 MILES

Legend
- Primary Highway
- Access Roads
- ✈ Airport
- Boat Launch
- Unnoted Lakes
- Unnoted Rivers/Creeks
- Sand and Mud

N

Burgenine Lake

Spanish Village

Aransas National Wildlife Refuge

Cavasso Creek

35

Blackjack Peninsula

St. Charles Bay

Little Sharp Point

Ayres Island

Reddy Island

Egg Point

Lamar Peninsula

Bird Point

Bludworth Island

Goose Island State Park

Dunham Point

Spalding Cove

Intracoastal Waterway

© 2009 Wilderness Adventures Press, Inc.

St. Charles Bay

St. Charles Bay is at the far north end of the Aransas Bay system. It is one area of the Texas coast where anglers have a chance to encounter alligators. St. Charles Bay has always had a healthy population of alligators, which gives anglers something else to be concerned about.

The alligators are mostly cautious creatures and prefer to avoid humans. If a persistent gator happens to get into the area, leave. They're more interested in your catch than you, but it's always best to be safe.

The mouth of St. Charles Bay has Hail Point to the west and Bird Point to the east. The area between these two points is very shallow. Once inside the mouth of the bay, the water deepens to over 4 feet.

There are wadeable areas along both the east and west shorelines of St. Charles Bay. Reefs are scattered throughout the middle of the bay offering good fishing from a boat. Several spoil areas with shallow waters surrounded by deeper water offer good places to fish.

Blackjack Peninsula runs along the east side of St. Charles Bay. This is the area the famed whooping cranes use as a winter home. The shoreline along Blackjack Point has good wade fishing.

St. Charles Bay is somewhat protected from the wind and is easily accessed from Goose Island State Park or the public ramp at the end of 4th Street. To get to the public ramp, go north on Palmetto to 4th Street. Head east on 4th Street until it dead-ends. The boat ramp and parking area are just south, on the bay side. The ramp is paved but parking is limited. Waders and kayakers can also use this area to access St. Charles Bay.

Boat Ramp

St. Charles Bay Boat Launch, 175 Lamar Beach Rd / 361-729-1171
Goose Island State Park, 202 South Palmetto Street / 361-729-2858

COPANO BAY FISHING PIER

The Copano Bay Fishing Pier runs parallel to the LBJ Causeway along Highway 5. The fishing pier is actually the old bridge that was replaced by the new, higher causeway that opened in 1967.

The fishing pier has parking at each end. Waders and kayakers can also access Copano Bay from the parking areas. There is a per-person fee to use the fishing pier based on number of people and number of rods, with a limit of three rods per person.

Permits and bait are available in the offices on each end of the pier. Bait fishing with shrimp, crab, mullet, or cut bait is a favorite way to fish from the pier.

The fishing pier has lights placed along its entire length, but it is not possible to walk the entire length of the pier because the center section has been removed. Anglers must enter from one end or the other. The north side of the bridge is 2,500 feet long and the south side of the bridge is 6,190 feet long.

Anglers fishing the pier will need to have either long-handled nets or a drop net to help control their catch.

The pier crosses over the intersection of Copano Bay and Aransas Bay and fishing is best when the tide is moving. Pier activity picks up when a school of redfish or speckled trout cruises through. The action can be fast and hectic.

Summer months find anglers fishing in the evening when it is cooler. The lights along the pier help attract small bait, which attracts larger prey fish. Night fishing is a summertime ritual for many anglers in the area, and the pier is also a favorite of winter Texans.

Many pier fishermen use small wagons or fishing carts to transport their tack. Some are rigged to carry several rods and an ice cooler.

Boat Ramp

Copano Causeway, North Hwy 35 / 361-425-8325
Copano Causeway, South Hwy 35 / 361-425-8326

There is a $2-per-rod fee for fishing on the Copano Bay Fishing Pier.

Copano Bay

Copano Bay is to the west of Aransas Bay and west of the LBJ Causeway. The causeway connects Lamar Peninsula to the north with Fulton and Rockport to the south. It is fed by two rivers — the Mission River and Aransas River — and several creeks.

Copano Bay is an open bay that can be adversely affected by the wind. There are numerous locations around the bay ideal for wading. Waders are often seen from the causeway fishing within a short distance of the bridge. The water on both sides of the bridge is shallow enough for wading.

The north part of Copano Bay includes Turtle Pen Point and Copano Creek. Consider drift fishing this area. Also try fishing the drop-off along the shoreline using sinking lures or flies.

The mouth of Copano Bay is flanked by Redfish Point to the south and Newcomb Point to the north. There are several reefs in Copano Bay anglers should be aware of. Lap Reef, Copano Reef, and Smith Reef, to name a few, are obstacles boaters should use caution around. The water over most of these reefs is too shallow to boat through except at extreme high tide. If you are unfamiliar with this area, hire a guide.

Copano Reef stretches a long way into the bay and offers good wade fishing on both sides of the reef. Cast parallel to the reef, working the lure from the deeper surrounding water up onto the reef. Shellbank Reef, farther to the south, can be fished the same way.

Some of the reefs will be just under the surface while others will be several feet deep. These reefs offer fish a chance to patrol shallower water and have the safety of deep water close by. Boaters should use caution when going through the area. If you are unfamiliar with these reefs, it may be best to hire a guide for your first fishing trip to the area.

The far west side of Copano Bay can be accessed from Highway 136 at Black Point. This is where the Aransas River enters Copano Bay. There is a small ramp with limited parking on the south side of the road at Egery Island Marina, and a $5 ramp fee. Across the bridge at Black Point, there is a dual-lane boat ramp and limited parking. Kayakers can launch from here to fish the western shoreline.

Anglers need to be aware of freshwater inflows to this section of Copano Bay. Heavy springtime rains may make this water too fresh for successful fishing.

The west side of Copano Bay can also be accessed from Bayside. Driscoll Rooke Covenant Park is located along the bay's shoreline in Bayside and has a lighted fishing pier. There is a small parking area for park users.

Supplies can be bought at Bayside Grocery on Highway 136 on the west side of Bayside. Crofutt's Sandwich Shop is located across the street and is a good place to warm up in the wintertime.

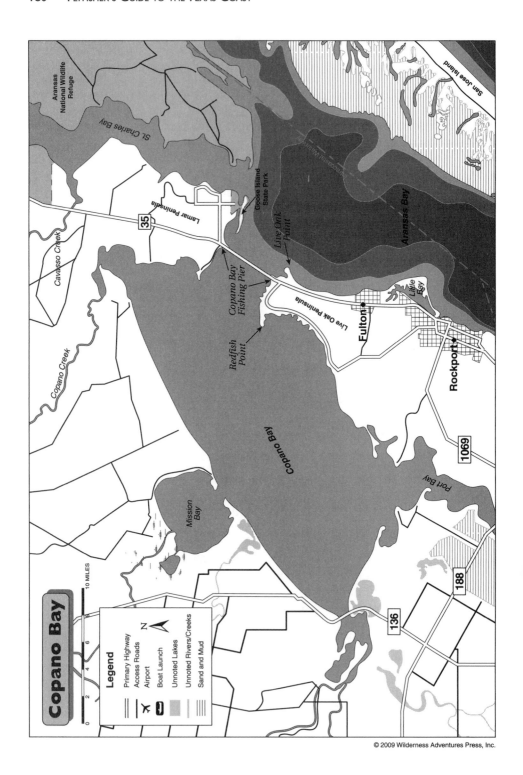

Amenities

Bayside Grocery, 1599 FM 136, Bayside / 361-529-6401
Corfutt's Sandwich Shop, 1610 FM 136 / 361-529-6663

Boat Ramps

Egery Island Marina, Hwy 136

LIVE OAK POINT

On the east side of Highway 35 at the south end of the LBJ Causeway is Live Oak Point. Fishermen can park and wade or kayak into Aransas Bay from this area. If you want to wade this area, you need to arrive early because there is almost always someone wading here. It's a beautiful spot and a great place to be fishing when the sun breaks the horizon over Aransas Bay. The shrimp boats will most likely be after their morning catch in the distance.

The area is mostly hard-packed sand and easy to wade. Early in the morning, try fishing with topwater lures like a Zara Spook or TopDog. Fly casters can use a white popper or large white Lefty's Deceiver. As the morning progresses, change to soft plastics on jigheads for light-tackle casters or Clouser Minnows for the flyfishers.

LIVE OAK PENINSULA

On the southeast side of Copano Bay is Live Oak Peninsula. Just as you cross over the LBJ Causeway on the south side, Farm Road (FR) 1781 turns back to the west. This road leads around the southeast side of Copano Bay. Anglers can park at the Copano Bay Fishing Pier parking lot on the south side and wade around Live Oak Peninsula.

Redfish Point extends into Copano Bay from the shoreline just southwest of the Causeway. The areas around Redfish Point are muddy and best fished from a boat or kayak. There are several reefs just off Redfish Point that frequently hold fish.

Continue following FR 1781 around the southeast part of Copano Bay to the Aransas County Airport Park. This little park has parking for about a dozen cars and offers quick access to this part of Copano Bay. Look for the sign marking the entrance to the parking lot.

Waders or kayakers can enter the bay from the shore. On both sides of the parking and launch area are numerous private fishing piers along the shoreline. The water drops off away from the shoreline into areas with 6-feet-deep water. Fishers can work from Redfish Point south to Hannibal Point, from this area. The area is protected from the predominantly southeast wind and is a good place for new kayakers to learn about fishing out of a kayak.

Follow FR 1781 around until you find Rattlesnake Point Road. This road leads to the Aransas County Navigation District Number 1 Rattlesnake Point where you'll find waterfront access and a kayak launch site parking lot. Kayakers and small boats can use the ramp to fish around Rattlesnake Point. Redfish Lodge is located at the end of Rattlesnake Point.

Anglers can fish the waters around Rattlesnake Point or go inside the mouth of Port Bay. Waders will find areas of mud interspersed with firmer wading areas. Redfish will hide out in the grassy shallow areas around the point.

PORT BAY

Port Bay is the small bay at the south end of Copano Bay. Turn right off FR 1781 to FR 1069. From 1069 turn right onto Port Bay Club Road. This road is paved only part of the way. The unpaved section can get messy after a hard rain. Drive slowly through the area because the road has plenty of potholes.

Port Bay is a good place for beginning kayakers to get acquainted with their boat. It is small and protected from most of the southeast wind. Shoreline areas are muddy and farther out there are patches of oyster shell.

Good wade fishing can be found around the mouth of the bay and along both sides of the bay. There are numerous shallow-water areas from Rattlesnake Point through Swan Lake. Work the drop-off, especially near the channel leading into the Port Bay area.

Fish Port Bay before and after duck season. There are numerous duck blinds, so it is best to wait until mid-morning during duck season before launching or starting a fishing trip here.

Port Bay waters run shallow, so once the waters start to heat up, fish here early in the morning for best results.

Topwater lures and flies work well in Port Bay. Shallow-running lures like a Tidewater Waker, saltwater spinnerbait, or weedless spoon also work well.

Port Bay can also be reached from Highway 188 at the Port Bay Redfish Camp. There is limited parking and a small boat ramp with a $5 fee to launch.

Boat Ramp

Redfish Camp, 5220 FM 881

MISSION BAY

Mission Bay, located to the northwest of Copano Bay, is fed by the Mission River to the west. The bay is very shallow with most areas 2-feet-or-less deep. The mouth of Mission Bay, called North Pass, offers slightly deeper water that often holds speckled trout. Reefs run throughout the bay and also hold fish.

Mission Bay is shallow and best fished during cool months or early in the day during warmer months.

Floating fly lines and flies work for flyfishers. Conventional tackle casters should use shallow running lures or soft plastics with an unweighted hook.

Aransas Bay

Aransas Bay stretches from Lamar Peninsula to the north to Harbor Island and Redfish Bay to the south. Aransas Bay is the destination many people think of when they think of fishing the Texas coast.

The bay is surrounded by many shallow water areas and has water over 10 feet deep in its center. There are numerous mid-bay reefs running from just southeast of the LBJ Causeway, all the way to San Jose Island. The water around these reefs is dangerous. If you are unfamiliar with the area, hire a knowledgeable guide.

Reefs, like Scotch Tom, Halfmoon, Mack, and Deadman are made out of oyster shell and hold speckled trout throughout the year except for the coldest months of winter. Anglers should try floating lures like a TopDog or Super Spook early in the morning. Fly anglers can try large poppers or Lefty's Deceivers.

As the day progresses, switch to sinking lures like soft plastics on jigheads, Catch 2000, or Catch 5s. Fly anglers can try Clouser Minnows, Half and Halfs, or weighted Bend Backs.

The open part of the bay is home to several bay shrimpers that regularly work the area. Anglers and boaters should use caution in this area and hire a guide if you're new to this bay system.

Kayakers can launch in Rockport at the parking lot outside the entrance to the Rockport Beach Park. A small fee is required to enter the park. There is another small parking area at the southwest end of Little Bay where kayakers can launch.

A public ramp with limited parking is located in Rockport Harbor. Cove Harbor, farther down Highway 35, has a good paved ramp and parking. A large parking area is located at the Fulton Convention Center where kayakers can launch and fish the western shoreline of Aransas Bay. There is also a long fishing pier located at the center. Anglers must pay a fee per rod when using the pier. Many fishers use natural or cut bait when fishing the pier.

Boat Ramps

Rockport Harbor, 911 Navigation Circle / 361-729-6661
Cove Harbor Marina, 161 N. Cove Harbor Dr / 361-729-6151
Beacon Bait Stand, 302 S. Fulton Beach Rd / 361-729-2284
Rockport Beach Park, 210 Sea Breeze Dr / 361-729-9392
Sand Dollar Bait House, 918 N Fulton Beach Rd / 361-790-5113

Little Bay

Little Bay is the area just east of Business Highway 35 in Rockport. It has a small parking area where Highway 35 intersects with Broadway Street. This is a good place to launch a kayak or wade.

Little Bay has numerous private fishing piers that extend from Broadway Street into the bay. Most of the motels and rentals have their own private piers. During warm months these piers are lighted at night and loaded with anglers fishing for speckled trout. Little Bay often shows slicks made by trout when the water is calm. Most of the trout will be small, but the fishing can be fast. Live shrimp or small white flies often work best at night around the piers.

Watch your prop in the Redfish Bay Scientific Area.

REDFISH BAY

Redfish Bay is east of Aransas Pass. Steadman Island is just south of State Highway 361 and Hog Island is to the north. Work drop-offs around the islands in the area. Corpus Christi Bayou, the channel around the eastern edge of Hog Island, has deep water. California Hole and Hog Island Hole have water over 4 feet deep. These deeper areas provide fish with deep-water safety close to shallow-water feeding areas.

Estes Flats, bordered by Traylor and Talley Islands, is a shallow-water area in the northern part of the bay. Most of the water throughout Estes Flats is less than 2 feet deep and a good area for kayakers. There are several cuts running through the surrounding islands that offer good fishing.

Wade fish along the islands and spoil areas around the Alternate Intracoastal Waterway just to the east. The deeper water of the Intracoastal Waterway and Alternate offer good wintertime fishing. There are several harbors along the Intracoastal Waterway that are fished by winter Texans and natives alike.

Kayakers can access Redfish Bay at several locations. The Aransas Pass Community Park on Johnson Avenue is a good place to launch, but there is a fee to enter the park. The Ransom Channel Boat Ramp and Hampton's Landing are located at the end of Ransom Road. Both have good boat ramps and paved parking areas. Parking is limited and full on the busiest days. There is a fee to use the Hampton's Landing ramp and parking.

There is also a fishing pier at the Ransom Channel Boat Ramp where anglers can fish the channel.

Flyfishers should use a floating line and Lefty's Deceivers, lightweight Clouser Minnows, and Half and Halfs. Also try shrimp and crab patterns near the grass.

Conventional tackle anglers can use light-weighted jigheads with soft plastics, weedless spoons, and Corkies.

Boat Ramps

San Patricio Navigation District Number 1 / 361-758-1890
Palm Harbor Marina, 151 Port Ave / 361-729-8540
Hampton's Landing, 430 Ransom Island Dr / 361-758-1562

SOUTH BAY

South Bay is the area just west of Harbor Island and the Lighthouse Lakes. This little bay has shallow-water flats and many guts. The mangroves just to the east protect South Bay from strong southeast winds making it an ideal location for shallow-water anglers.

Fish South Bay during the spring and summer months before the water gets too hot. The drop-offs surrounding the area are ideal habitat for trout and redfish. You'll also find fish warming on the clear-water flats during cold days.

Fly casters can try Lefty's Deceivers and lightweight Clouser Minnows. Lure casters can use topwater lures, saltwater spinnerbaits, and gold spoons.

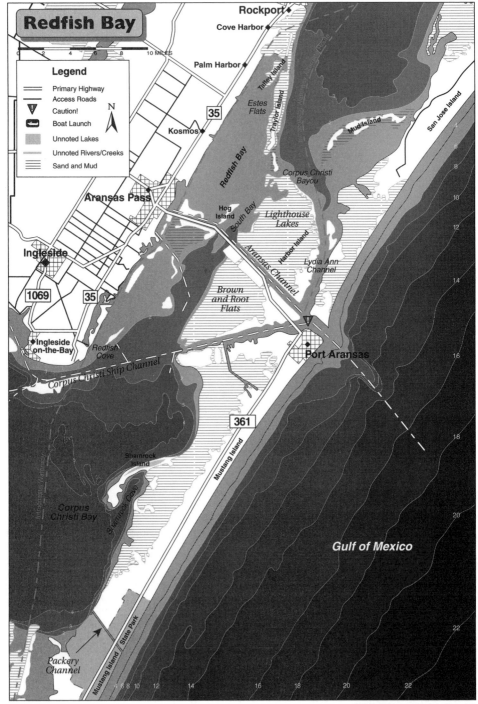

Redfish Bay

Rockport
Cove Harbor
Palm Harbor

Legend

- Primary Highway
- Access Roads
- Caution!
- Boat Launch
- Unnoted Lakes
- Unnoted Rivers/Creeks
- Sand and Mud

N

0 2 4 6 8 10 MILES

Talley Island
Estes Flats
Traylor Island
Mud Island
San Jose Island

35

Kosmos

Redfish Bay

Corpus Christi Bayou

Aransas Pass

Hog Island
South Bay
Lighthouse Lakes
Harbor Island
Lydia Ann Channel

Ingleside

Aransas Channel

1069   35

Brown and Root Flats

Ingleside on-the-Bay
Redfish Cove

Port Aransas

Corpus Christi Ship Channel

361

Shamrock Island

Mustang Island

Corpus Christi Bay

Shamrock Cove

Gulf of Mexico

Packery Channel

Mustang Island State Park

4 6 8 10   12   14   16   18   20   22

HARBOR ISLAND

Harbor Island is the triangle-shaped island inside Aransas Bay. The island is divided into two parts: Lighthouse Lakes to the north and Brown and Root Flats to the south.

The Corpus Christi Channel and Lydia Ann Channel border the east side of the island. The community of Port Aransas is just across the Corpus Christi Channel.

The water intersection of the Corpus Christi Channel, Lydia Ann Channel, and the jettied opening to the gulf can cause rapidly moving and rough water. Boaters need to use caution when traveling through this area.

LIGHTHOUSE LAKES

Lighthouse Lakes is where kayaking started on the Texas coast. The lakes are accessed from the nearby Aransas Channel. Kayakers only have to paddle across the deep channel to get into the lakes.

The lakes get their name from the nearby lighthouse, which is always a good landmark for kayakers and fishers alike. They are divided by grass and mangroves. There is an almost endless number of fishing locations here.

Texas Parks and Wildlife first started their paddling trails here. There are four trails for kayakers in the area, and each offers a different route through the lakes with each one a different distance in length.

The longest trail — the Redfish Loop — is 6.8 miles. Redfish Loop begins at the Aransas Channel across from the Lighthouse Lakes shelter and proceeds east to the eastern edge of Harbor Island. The trail comes close to the lighthouse and then turns north along the Lydia Ann Channel.

Redfish Loop continues and crosses the South Bay Loop at the northwest corner. It then heads south and rejoins near the original starting location. There are a wide variety of fishing locations along this trail. It crosses a deep channel and goes through several of the area's lakes. An interesting side trip would be to take one of the cuts that feed from the lakes to the Lydia Ann Channel. Fish where the water drops off into deeper depths.

The second longest trail is the South Bay Loop, which starts out at the Aransas Channel, which runs parallel to Texas State Highway 361. It then makes a large loop around the north part of the island close to the Quarantine Shoreline and then along Corpus Christi Bayou. The loop completes an easterly run across South Bay and back to the start at the Aransas Channel. South Bay Loop is about 6.7 miles and plenty for a full day of paddling.

The next longest trail is Cutters Loop, approximately 5 miles long. Cutters Loop starts halfway between Redfish and South Bay Loops on the Aransas Channel. It crosses Redfish Loop following the inside shoreline of many of the same lakes that line Redfish Loop. As Cutters Loop heads back south it crosses both of the two longer loops and then heads back east.

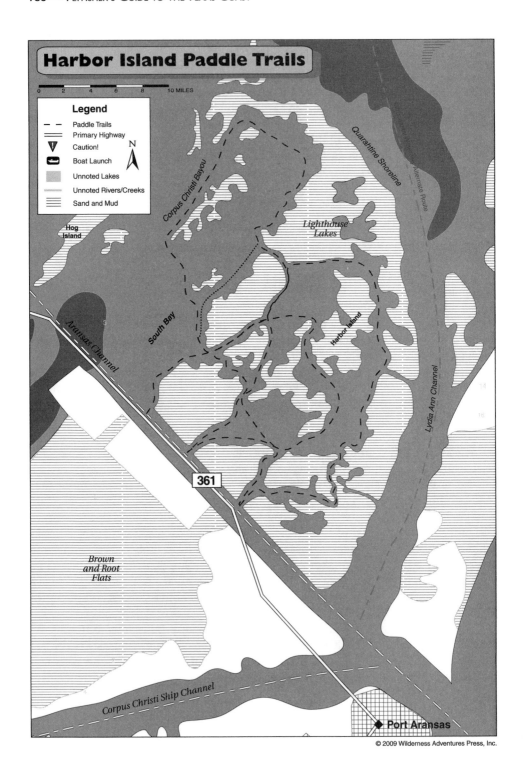

Harbor Island Paddle Trails

0 2 4 6 8 10 MILES

Legend

- – – Paddle Trails
- ═══ Primary Highway
- ▼ Caution!
- ◤ Boat Launch
- ▓ Unnoted Lakes
- ═══ Unnoted Rivers/Creeks
- ═══ Sand and Mud

N

Corpus Christi Bayou

Quarantine Shoreline

Alternate Route

Hog Island

Lighthouse Lakes

Aransas Channel

South Bay

Harbor Island

Lydia Ann Channel

14

16

361

Brown and Root Flats

Corpus Christi Ship Channel

◆ Port Aransas

Electric Lake Loop is the shortest of the trails at only 1.25 miles long. This loop is a good place for beginning kayakers to hone their skills. Electric Loop branches off of Redfish Loop and then circles a small lake.

There are also several shortcuts and connecting trails through the lakes giving kayakers an almost endless variety of paddling areas. It's easy to lose track of the direction when kayaking through the lakes so take along a compass, a good map, and a GPS if you have one.

Watch for the paddle-trail markers located throughout the lakes. If you get lost, look for the lighthouse or highway to get your bearings. Don't forget to take along plenty of water to drink.

This is a no-prop-damage zone. Anglers using a regular motorboat are not to leave behind any prop damage when boating through the area.

This is also a very popular duck hunting area. Anglers may want to start later in the morning when fishing during duck hunting season.

It's also a good idea to attach a flag to your kayak for easy identification by hunters. If you hear a boat, wave your paddle up high to let the boater know you're in the area. Wave the paddle several times until you're sure the boater is aware of your location.

Kayakers can either fish from their rig or tie it to the back of their belt and wade. Most of the water is shallow, so floating lures or flies often work best. Lightweight lures such as soft plastics on 1/8-ounce jigheads or Clouser Minnows work in deeper areas.

Lighthouse Lakes is a great place to fish if you have just one day in the area. The lakes are easy to access and there are numerous secluded areas to fish.

BROWN & ROOT FLATS

Brown & Root Flats is the south side of Harbor Island. This side has large shallow-water flats to the west and an industrial area to the east. There are numerous deep holes on the flats that provide excellent speckled trout fishing.

Brown & Root Flats is surrounded by the Corpus Christi Channel, Sail Boat Channel, and Morris and Cummings Cut to the west. There are also several deep cuts running from the deep-water channels into the interior of the island. Approach these deeper holes quietly and make as long a cast as possible. Let any lure or fly sink into the deep water. Trout will often be right at the bottom.

Don't forget to work the outside edge around the flats where deeper water intersects the shallow-water flats. This is a big-fish area where large predators can ambush unsuspecting prey in the shallows.

The far south tip of the flats past the spoil islands offers a unique wade-fishing opportunity for those willing to paddle to the area or for those with larger boats.

Brown & Root Flats is more open than the Lighthouse Lakes but still has plenty of features to attract fish. Work the flats slowly and quietly to keep from spooking redfish and trout.

Lydia Ann Channel and Corpus Christi Channel

Lydia Ann Channel and Corpus Christi Channel form the eastern part of the Intracoastal Waterway. The Intracoastal Waterway splits north of Harbor Island just to the east of Rockport. These channels offer bay access to large ships coming into Corpus Christi.

The channels have much deeper water than the surrounding bays. The Highway 361 ferryboats cross the channel numerous times during the day and recreational boat traffic is heavy. The combined boat traffic along with changing, strong tides makes waters in this area continuously rough. Boaters should be aware of their surroundings and use caution when traveling through this area.

Anglers can try working the drop-offs along the channels. It is not unusual to see dolphin within only a few feet of dry land running along the channels. Fly casters can use a sinking fly on sinking line to work the drop-off. Work parallel to the land for best results.

Conventional tackle anglers will want to use lures heavy enough to quickly sink into the deep water. Use soft plastics with 1/4-ounce-or-heavier jigheads. Bait casters can fish with shrimp or cut bait weighted with several split shot to get the bait down deep. Work from the shallow water out into the deeper channel.

Redfish Bay State Scientific Area

On May 1, 2006 the Redfish Bay Scientific Area was established in response to the scarring of native seagrasses. Inside the area boaters are restricted from uprooting or digging out rooted seagrasses by submerged propellers.

There are no closed zones to fishing in this area nor is it a violation to anchor or use electric trolling motors. Boaters are encouraged to use the existing man-made cuts to access shallow areas.

The Scientific Area runs from just north of Cove Harbor in Rockport, south along the Intracoastal Waterway to just south of Dagger Island near Port Ingleside, then east along the Corpus Christi Ship Channel and back west along the Lydia Ann Channel to Rockport.

Scientific area maps are located at area boat ramps. The maps also show the existing cuts that boaters are encouraged to use.

Coastal seagrasses often take decades to reestablish. The Scientific Area gives boaters in the area a chance to enjoy the fishing habitat while protecting the native seagrasses. Please observe the restrictions when inside this area.

Mud Island

Mud Island is a long island in the eastern part of Aransas Bay. Blind Pass is at the far-east end of Mud Island, separating the island from San Jose Island. Blind Pass is deeper than the surrounding waters and offers fish quick access to deep water. Many boats use Blind Pass to get to the eastern shoreline area of Aransas Bay, so be aware when fishing the area.

Waders can fish both the north and south sides of Mud Island working the drop-off. Most areas on the north side are hard sand and shell, making for easy wading. There are grassy areas on the south side of the island.

Anglers can work close in to the island for redfish and at the deeper water break for trout. Use weedless spoons in the grass for redfish, and Topdogs, Mirrolures, and Corkies farther out for trout.

Captain Sally Ann Moffett with a nice back lake redfish.

EAST SHORELINE AND LAKES

The east shoreline of Aransas Bay has many shallow-water cuts and lakes along San Jose Island. Areas like Vinson Slough, Fence Lake, South Lake, and Allyn's Bight all offer good shallow-water fishing. Parts of these areas may be completely out of water during the lowest tides of the year.

The shoreline along the eastern edge of Aransas Bay just to the west of the back lakes also offers good wade fishing. The passes leading into the back lakes often hold fish. This area is protected from the predominantly southeast wind.

A very shallow-running boat is required to fish most of this area. Anglers with deeper draft boats can anchor on the outside shoreline and wade or use a kayak to fish the shallow waters. The lakes are ideal for kayakers, but are a long way from the nearest access point. Anglers with a boat can transport a kayak, park their boat on the outside, and fish the lakes from their kayak.

There are several shuttle services in the area that will take you and your kayak to the area and return for you at the end of the day. This is a great way to explore some less crowded water by yourself.

Look for redfish and trout in these shallow areas. Pay close attention to the surface action and to any birds in the area. Birds will often gather in locations where predator fish drive prey fish and shrimp to the surface.

A wader or kayaker can effectively work these waters, being cautious of the many stingrays in the area. Redfish will often hover over or near stringrays while gulping down any bait spooked by the ray. Stingrays can range in color from a very light tan

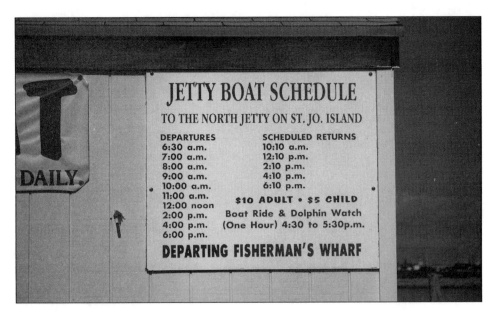

Shuttles carry anglers to the Port Aransas North Jetty. Don't miss the last boat!

to almost black, allowing them to blend in with the bottom color. Wade using the stingray shuffle or stay in your kayak or boat.

Be sure someone knows where you are when fishing this area. You're a long paddle back to any dock and an unexpected wind may make the trip back even more difficult.

Flies to use include the Foxy Clouser, Clouser Deep Minnow, Spoons, Lefty's Deceiver, Red and White Hackle Fly, and shrimp and crab patterns.

Casting lures include Zara Spooks and Topdogs, gold and copper weedless spoons, soft plastics with lightweight jigheads, and suspending or shallow running lures like saltwater spinnerbaits and Mann's Tidewater Waker. Carry heavier lures and flies to work the outside shoreline.

PORT ARANSAS JETTIES AND MUSTANG ISLAND

Port Aransas is across from Harbor Island. Texas Highway 361 leads to the Port Aransas Ferry. The ferry service is open 24 hours a day. There are posted signs in the area showing the number of ferryboats working on any particular day. The ferry system, run by the Texas Department of Transportation, does a good job of shuttling visitors across to Mustang Island.

Visitors can expect delays on the busiest days, weekends and holidays. Consider this additional traveling time when making your plans to fish the area.

Once on Mustang Island and into Port Aransas, anglers enter island time. During the winter the island has many visitors from northern states trying to escape cold weather. Springtime finds spring breakers lining the streets. Spring break occurs in March in Texas, bringing some of the largest crowds of the year to the island.

When driving on the island, slow down and use caution. There is plenty of pedestrian traffic as well as many small rented golf cart style buggies on the streets. Port Aransas is just like any other island town with plenty of tourist.

To the immediate left after leaving the ferry is Dennis Dreyer Municipal Harbor. Auto traffic can be crowded in this area, so go slow and watch the signs. The harbor has a large paved parking lot and modern boat ramp. Pay attention to street signs when leaving the parking area. There is also a small pier to the south of the ferry area.

The Ancel Brundrett Fishing Pier is located along Aransas Channel at the north end of the island. The water around the pier is constantly moving due to both the currents and boat traffic in the area. It can accommodate several anglers at one time.

Most fishers use casting or spinning tackle with either lures or natural bait when fishing from the pier. A popping cork used with natural bait works well. Fly casting from the pier is difficult due to the high handrail surrounding the pier.

Upon exiting the ferry, go straight on Cotter Street until reaching the I.B. Magee Beach Park and the south Port Aransas Jetty. No parking permit is required when parking in the I.B. Magee Beach Park, but be aware that a parking permit is required to park anywhere on the beach along Mustang Island. Parking permits can be purchased at any of the convenience stores on the island. The permit is valid for parking along the entire island regardless of whether you're in the Port Aransas or Corpus Christi city limits.

There is a large parking area in the south jetty. Anglers frequently use bait to fish from the jetties. Regular jetty fishers will have numerous rods and maybe a jetty cart. Anglers can back their vehicle right up to the jetty.

The south Port Aransas jetty is topped by a concrete walkway for part of its distance, which allows easy walking access. Farther out towards the gulf the pavement stops and the jetty is made of stacked granite rocks. Use caution when moving along the rocks. The constant wave action keeps the rocks wet, slick, and algae covered.

Fly anglers can also fish the jetties. Use a sinking line and cast parallel to the jetties. A sinking fly like a chartreuse-and-white Clouser works well. Be sure to consider your back cast when fishing the jetties with fly tackle, as they are often crowded with other anglers.

The north jetty can be accessed via a shuttle. Jetty shuttle service is offered from the Fisherman's Wharf located on Tarpon Street. The shuttle makes 10 trips daily to the north jetty with the last shuttle at 6:30pm. If you miss this shuttle you're stuck on the north side overnight.

Watch for the Tarpon Inn on the right hand side on Cotter Street when in Port Aransas. Tarpon Street turns north directly across from the inn. Fisherman's Wharf is located at the end of Tarpon Street. Jetty departure and arrival times are posted on the building, and there is a $10 fee for the shuttle. Parking around the Fisherman's

Port Aransas Jetties are a great place for land-locked anglers.

Wharf is limited and often full with vehicles belonging to anglers fishing on one of the offshore party boats. North jetty fishers need to be aware that San Jose Island is privately owned and anglers are restricted to the beach and jetty area.

Be sure to take along anything you're going to need when you go to the North Jetty. One bottle of water and a T-shirt is not enough. Take along at least a small cooler with several bottles of water, extra sun block, and a long-sleeve shirt. A lightweight rain jacket will not only keep off the rain but will also help cut down the effects of an unexpected cold wind.

All jetty fishers should be aware that the jetty rocks can get very slick with algae. Use caution when you move along the rocks; wear shoes with good traction and don't get too close to the water. A large ship can produce an unexpected wave that may come well up on the rocks. Pay attention when rock hopping and take your time.

Any visitor to Port Aransas should take a few minutes and stop at the Tarpon Inn, a famous hotel with a great history. Port Aransas was actually known as Tarpon, Texas, at one time. The wall on the inside of the office is covered with large tarpon scales from fish caught throughout the last 100 years. Historical photos line another wall. The old inn itself is part of history and the outside reminds anglers of another time.

One of the most famous visitors to Port Aransas was President Franklin D. Roosevelt, who visited the island and caught a tarpon on May 8, 1937. His tarpon scale is shown as well as thousands of others. The size of these scales attests to the large tarpon once caught in the area. Although current Texas fishing regulations require the release of almost all tarpon, several are caught in the area each year.

Mustang Island is about 18 miles long. The northern part of the island is in the city of Port Aransas and the southern part is in Corpus Christi. The island offers beach and surf access, and many winter Texans use the beach to camp. Camping regulations are posted on signs along the beach. The speed limit on the beach is 15 miles per hour and regular traffic laws apply. The surf can be accessed from five access roads, each of which is clearly marked along Highway 361.

Anglers can also fish the surf along Mustang Island. The Horace Caldwell Pier is located on the beach. The pier is over 1,200 feet long and extends well into the gulf, allowing anglers a chance to cast into calmer water. Fees to use the pier are $1 per person and $1 per rod with a three-rod limit. Tackle can also be rented on the pier.

Gulf Beach Access Road 1A is just south of town on Highway 361 after leaving the ferry. The beach access roads are paved to the beach. Once on the beach, drivers are best served to pay attention to the beach condition signs posted at each access point. Drive in the tracks made by other vehicles. The sand along the beach is fine grain and vehicles can easily become stuck. Freeing a stuck vehicle can be a long and costly process, so drive carefully. Remember, do not drive on the dunes.

Spinning and casting anglers often use a piece of PVC pipe as a sand spike to hold their fishing rod while fishing the surf. A heavyweight and circle or Kahle hook with shrimp, crab, or cut bait often produces fish.

Some of the best fishing is close in to the shoreline. Look for areas where the water is darker. Fish will often come right into these deeper areas to feed. Anglers can also try casting lures and soft plastics on jigheads. Fly casters can use Lefty's Deceivers,

Clouser Minnows, and other sinking flies. Along with redfish and trout, anglers can find crevalle jack and whiting in the surf. Sheepshead are caught in the late winter and early spring along the jetties and channels. Pompano are also found in the surf during the early part of the year.

Again, this area is very crowded during the spring break season and best avoided by serious anglers at that time.

There is a small airport on Mustang Island across from Gulf Beach Access Road 1A. There are several beach condos along the beach. Each has its own access to the beach but remember these are private access points.

Mustang Island State Park is located on Highway 361.There is a fee to enter the park. The park has a small grocery and souvenir store. There are also primitive camping and RV sites within the park. Showers are available at several locations along the beach.

Boat Ramp

Dennis Dreyer Municipal Harbor
Fisherman's Wharf, Tarpon Street / 361-749-5448
Horace Caldwell Pier / 361-749-2828

Redfish hit flies in the shallow water of East Flats.

CORPUS CHRISTI SPOIL ISLANDS AND PELICAN ISLAND

Pelican Island is just south of the Corpus Christi Ship Channel. Two other spoil islands are located to the west of Pelican Island. Numerous large ships travel along the north side of these islands each day, causing large fluctuations in the water level.

There are areas on the north side of the islands that anglers can wade, but be sure to pay attention to the movements of the ships in the channel. The constant rise and fall created by the ships creates water movements similar to those made by the changing tides. Baitfish and prey species are moved with the water change and predator fish know this. Just don't get caught off guard by a large ship-created wave.

There is also good wading on the south side of Pelican Island and the spoil islands. Ship-created waves are not as drastic on the south side but still have an impact. Work the drop-off farther out for speckled trout and the grassy areas closer in for redfish. Flounder are also found in this area.

EAST FLATS AND LITTLE FLATS

East Flats and Little Flats are tucked in the corner created by the Corpus Christi Ship Channel and Mustang Island. This area is protected from the wind and is an excellent location for beginning kayakers to learn about shallow-water fishing.

Most of the area is less than 2 feet deep, and includes areas of both hard sand and soft mud throughout the flats. A very shallow draft boat poled through the area or a kayak, are both excellent ways to fish these flats.

Redfish regularly patrol this area and can often be seen tailing. Cast slightly in front of the lead fish to avoid spooking any school of redfish. Large speckled trout will also inhabit these flats but are easily spooked by any noise or movement.

If the fish get spooked, rest the area to give them a chance to re-form. Wade, pole, or paddle slowly through the area to avoid spooking the fish.

Flies like Trimble's Foxy Chicken, red and white Seaducers, lightly weighted chartreuse-and-white Clouser Minnows, and spoon flies work well. Light-tackle casters can use 1/8-ounce copper or gold weedless spoons, very lightly weighted jigheads with soft plastics, or Super Spook Juniors.

WILSON'S CUT

Wilson's Cut is on the west side of Highway 361 across from the Sea Gull and Sand Piper Condos property. The parking area is on private property but is used by anglers to park and launch kayaks. It can get rough and muddy when it rains, so go slow and avoid the muddiest areas. Larger boats can be launched with four-wheel drive vehicles, because the ramp is not paved and gets muddy during wet months.

Be a good steward for this area and take out everything you take in.

Fish Pass

Fish Pass is on the west side across Highway 361 from Mustang Island State Park. The parking area is part of the state park. Go slow after turning off Highway 361 as the road is rough and can be muddy. Drive in tracks made by other vehicles.

Kayakers can launch from this area to access the eastern part of Corpus Christi Bay and Mustang Island Flats.

East of the highway on the gulf side, anglers can use the Fish Pass jetties by entering at Beach Access Road 2 or Mustang Island State Park. The jetties give anglers a chance at calmer water east of the surf along the island.

Corpus Christi Pass

Across from Gulf Beach Access Road 3 is a small parking area with water access. The parking area is rough and gets muddy when wet. Go slow when driving off the road. Corpus Christi Pass goes west to a good fishing area at Kate's Hole. Kayakers can access the eastern shoreline and fish along the grassy areas.

Newport Pass

Newport Pass is across from the Newport Pass Beach Access Road. There is an unpaved parking area near the water on the Corpus Christi Bay side at the Mollie Beattie Habitat site. The area can get muddy after a rain and there are plenty of potholes so go slow.

Newport Pass leads west to Deadman's Hole. This is a good fishing area protected from strong southeast winds.

Mustang Island Paddling Trails

The Mustang Island Paddling Trails are located on the west side of the island, and include three trails. The North Trail is just over 8 miles long. The Shamrock Loop Trail is just over 5 miles long and the Ashum Trail is 6.8 miles long.

The Ashum Trail starts at the Fish Pass parking area and goes west straight through Fish Pass until reaching Corpus Christi Bay, and continues until reaching Wilson's Cut. The shoreline between Fish Pass and Wilson's Cut is firm sand and offers excellent wade fishing.

Work the shallow areas for redfish and the drop-off for speckled trout. The area east of Marker 4 is very shallow and covered with grassy patches. Fish around the islands.

Anglers with two vehicles can park one at Fish Pass, park the other at Wilson's Cut and work from one end to the other.

The Shamrock Loop Trail is accessed from Wilson's Cut. Markers 7 and 8 follow the east shoreline. Markers 9 through 12 follow a deeper cut west. The loop then completes by heading south along the east shoreline of Corpus Christi Bay.

There are several islands and numerous grassy shorelines inside Shamrock Loop. Work the drop-offs along the deeper cuts for speckled trout. Work the shallow grassy areas for redfish.

The North Trail starts at Marker 11 and makes a loop around Green Shack Cove. The trail then goes north along the eastern shoreline of Corpus Christi Bay to Little Flats, past Coyote Island, and finishes at Island Mooring Marina. This is a diverse area with a variety of islands, grassy flats, and deep cuts.

Island Moorings Marina allows kayakers to use their parking lot and access to the water. Kayakers need to consider the marina's needs and follow all management requests.

These trails offer excellent fishing for both waders and kayakers. This is a perfect place to flyfish for redfish in shallow water. It is also a great place to stretch your paddling muscles and learn to kayak the coastal waters.

SHAMROCK ISLAND AND SHAMROCK COVE

Shamrock Island is just off the eastern shoreline of Corpus Christi Bay. This area offers shallow water near deep bay waters. Just east of the island, Shamrock Cove is protected from the strong southeast wind. Shamrock Island itself is a bird sanctuary and fishers need to stay off dry land on the island (stay in the water).

Kayakers can work the many small coves throughout the island. Also work the shallow water between Shamrock Island and the eastern shoreline. Waders will find sand on the east side of the island. Work the drop-off for speckled trout.

Shrimp are one of the natural prey in Aransas Bay.

PACKERY CHANNEL

The Packery Channel is at the southernmost end of Mustang Island. It gets its name from the numerous meat packeries once located in the area. Recently, the Packery Channel has been dredged and larger boats can now access the Gulf of Mexico through the channel. It is now lined with brick-covered jetties out to the gulf.

There is a paved boat ramp and sand parking area at the channel. Anglers can fish from the brick jetties and the shore on the north side of the bridge. Boaters and kayakers can use the channel to fish the area or go out into the surf. This area is a favorite for winter Texans.

Just north of the Packery Channel is Zahn Road and J.P. Luby Park, where the beach and surf can be accessed. All beach rules apply including the parking permit.

In recent years, a number of snook have been caught in the Packery Channel. Snook are making a comeback in Texas in general and the opening of the Packery Channel seems to have helped their population in this part of the coast. Texas anglers are best served by releasing all snook and letting this rebounding species continue to grow.

Cast baited hooks with a popping float from the jetties, or try heavy silver spoons for Spanish mackerel. Use a metal leader and expect to lose several spoons to sharp-toothed fish. Fly casters can work parallel to the jetties with a sinking line and fly. For best results, try to plan your trip to the channel when the current is moving.

Boat Ramp

Packery Channel Boat Ramp

The Packery Channel allows both fish and anglers access to the gulf waters.

Aransas Bay Hub Cities

ARANSAS PASS
Population: 8,138
County: Nueces

ACCOMMODATIONS

Days Inn, 410 Goodnight Ave / 361-758-7375 / 32 rooms / $76-$99 /
www.daysinn.com

Hawthorne Suites, 501 E Goodnight Ave / 361-758-1774 / 86 rooms / $69-$129 /
www.hawthorne.com

Microtel Inn, 401 Goodnight Ave / 361-758-8000 / 60 rooms / $55-$104 /
www.microtelinn.com

Travelodge, 545 N Commercial / 361-758-5305 / 46 rooms / $35-$98 /
www.travelodge.com

Super 8 Motel, 500 E Goodnight / 361-758-7888 / 49 rooms / $50-$99 /
www.super8.com

CAMPGROUNDS

Don-Ell RV Park, 128 E Myrtle / 361-758-5218

Fin & Feather Marina & RV Park, 100 Steadman Island / 361-758-7414

Hummer Haven RV Park, 1708 S Commercial St / 361-758-5602

ICW RV Park, 427 E Ransom / 361-758-1044

Mobil Village RV Park, 164 Stane / 361-758-8367

Portobelo Village RV, 2009 West Wheeler / 361-758-3378

Ransom Road RV Park, 240 Ransom / 361-758-2715 /
www.ransomroadrvparkinc.com

RESTAURANTS

Bakery Café, 434 S Commercial St / 361-758-3511

Captain Billy's Lighthouse, 2130 Hwy 35 / 361-758-6795

Church's Fried Chicken, 1901 West Wheeler Ave / 361-758-7166 /
www.churchs.com

Dairy Queen, 535 Cleveland Blvd / 361-758-5341 / www.dairyqueen.com

Ice Wagon BBQ, 1041 N Commercial St / 361-758-4689

Mac's Barbecue, 1933 West Wheeler / 361-758-0641

Pepitos Mexican Restaurant, 1212 Hwy 35 N / 361-758-5562

Pizza Hut, 1119 West Wheeler Ave / 361-758-2813 / www.pizzahut.com

Whataburger, 936 West Wheeler Ave / 361-758-8700 / www.whataburger.com

SPORTING GOODS

Offshore Adventures & Crab Man, Marina Hwy / 361 361-758-6900

Outdoor Texas, 259 S Commercial / 361-758-1560
Port A Kayak, 888-396-2382 / www.portakayak.com
Slow Ride Kayak Rentals, 361-758-0463 / www.slowrideguide.com

PORT ARANSAS
Population: 3,370
County: Nueces

ACCOMMODATIONS

America's Best Value Inn, 306 S Alister / 361-749-5450 / 25 rooms / $79-$129 / www.bestvalueinn.com
Beach Comber Motel, 539 12th St / 361-749-6191 / 12 rooms / $75-$265
Best Western, 400 E Ave G / 361-749-3010 / 48 rooms / $59-$189 / www.bestwesterntexas.com
Captain's Quarters Motel, 235 W. Cotter / 888-272-6727 / 42 rooms / $59-$149
Days Inn & Suites, 3995 Highway 361 / 361-749-2324 / 48 rooms / $79-$199 / www.daysinn.com
Holiday Inn Express, 727 S 11th Street / 361-749-5222 / 74 rooms / $79-$189 / www.holidayinn.com
Sea Breeze Suites Hotel, 407 Beach St 888-545-1422 / 24 rooms / $59-$119 / www.seabreezeporta.com
Tarpon Inn, 200 E Cotter / 800-365-6784 / 24 rooms / $89-$225 / www.thetarponinn.com
Travelodge, 300 W Ave G / 361-749-6427 / 56 rooms / $54-$100 / www.travelodge.com

CAMPGROUNDS

Beachway, RV 237 N Station / 361-749-6351
Funtime RV Park, 400 W Ave C / 361-749-5811
Gulf Breeze, 413 Trojan / 361-749-5691
Gulf Waters RV Resort, 5601 Highway / 361 361-749-8888 / www.gulfrv.com
I.B. Magee Beach Park, End of Cotter St / 361-749-6117
Island RV Resort, 700 6th St / 361-749-5600 / www.islandrvresort.com
Marina Beach & RV Resort, 241 W. Cotter / 361-749-7823 / www.mbrvresort.com
Mustang Island State Park, Highway 361 / 361-749-5246
Mustang RV Park, 300 E Cotter / 361-749-5343
Oceanside RV Resort, 701 Oceanside Dr / 361-749-5052
On The Beach RV Park, 907 Access Road 1A / 361-749-4909 / www.onthebeachrvpark.com
Pioneer Beach Resort RV, 120 Gulfwind Dr / 888-480-3246 / www.pioneerresorts.com
Surfside RV, 1820 11th St / 361-749-6128 / www.surfsiderv.com
Tropic Island RV Park, 315 Cut-Off Rd / 361-749-6128 / www.tropicislandresort.com

RESTAURANTS

Dairy Queen, 307 W Cotter Ave / 361-749-5283 / www.dairyqueen.com
Fin's Grill, 420 W Cotter / 361-749-8646 / www.finsgrillandicehouse.com
The Wharf, 500 Cutoff Road / 361-790-0075
La Playa Mexican Grill, 222 Beach Street / 361-749-0022
Little Joe's Smokin Grill, 200 W Ave G / 361-749-2333
Pelican's Landing Restaurant, 337 Alister / 361-749-6405 /
   www.pelicanslanding.com
Trout Street Bar & Grill, 104 West Cotter / 361-749-7800 / www.tsbag.com
Whataburger, 305 W Cotter / 361-749-5400 / www.whataburger.com

SPORTING GOODS

Port A Outfitters, 126 W Cotter / 361-749-3474 / www.islandtackle.com
Woody's Sports Center, 136 West Cotter / 361-749-6969 / www.woodysonline.com
Island Tackle, 207 West Avenue G / 361-749-1744
Bilmore & Son Hardware & Tackle, 115 N. Alister / 361-749-5880 /
   www.bilmore.doitbest.com
Port Aransas Ace Hardware, 1115 Highway 361 / 361-749-2004 /
   www.acehardware.com

AIRPORT

Mustang Beach Airport, Highway 361 / 361/749-4111

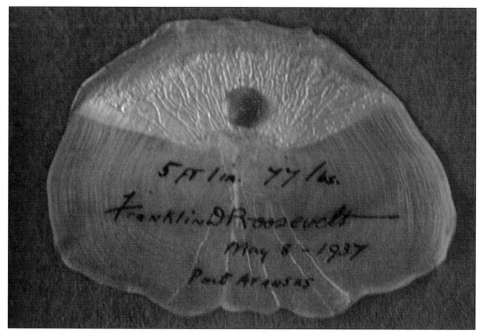

Large tarpon scales line the wall of the Tarpon Inn.

ROCKPORT/FULTON
Population: 8,938
County: Aransas

ACCOMMODATIONS

Best Western, Hwy 35 N / 361-729-8351 / 73 rooms / $93-$144 / www.bestwesterntexas.com

Days Inn, 1212 Laurel @ Hwy 35 / 361-729-6379 / 29 rooms / $56-$150 / www.daysinn.com

Hampton Inn, 3677 Hwy 35N / 361-727-2228 / 64 rooms / $89-$159 / www.hamptoninn.com

Holiday Inn Express, 901 Hwy 35 N / 361-727-0283 / 50 rooms / $81-$85 / www.hiexpress.com

Laguna Reef Hotel Suites, 1021 Water St / 361-729-1742 / 68 rooms / $95-$250 / www.lagunareef.com

Lighthouse Inn, 200 S Fulton Beach Road / 361-790-8439 / 78 rooms / $119-$189 / www.lighthousetexas.com

Pelican Bay Resort, 4206 Hwy 35 N / 361-729-7177 / 20 rooms / $89-$175 / www.pelicanbayresort.com

CAMPGROUNDS

Aransas Bay Mobile Resort, 1907 FM 3036 / 361-727-0761 / www.mhvillage.com

Blue Heron RV Park / 1136 Heron Lane / 361-727-1136

Coastal Oaks RV Resort / 1031 N Hood / 361-729-5633 / www.coastaloaksrvresort.com

Copano Hideaway RV Park, 3966 FM 1781 / 361-729-9292

Big D RV Resort, 3101 FM 1781 / 361-727-1339 / www.bigdrvrockport.com

Goose Island State Park, 202 S Palmetto Street / 361-729-2858

Raintree RV Park, 1924 W Terrace / 361-729-7005

Sandollar Resort & RV Park, 4022 Hwy 35 N / 361-729-2381 / www.sandollar-resort.com

Taylor Oaks RV Park, 707 S Pearl / 361-729-5187

RESTAURANTS

Alice Fayes Rocky Hill, 910 N Fulton Beach Road / 361-729-6708 / www.alice-fayes.com

The Big Fisherman, Hwy 188 @ Walker Rd / 361-729-1997 / www.bigfishermanrestaurant.com

Boiling Pot, Fulton Beach Road / 361-729-6972 / www.theboilingpotonline.com

Charlotte Plumber Seafare Restaurant, 202 N Fulton Beach Road / 361-729-1185

Dairy Queen, 1729 Hwy 35 N / 361-729-3198 / www.dairyqueen.com

Fry BayBy's, 201 B South Hwy 35 / 361-790-5886

Mac's Barbecue, 815 Market / 361-729-9388

Cheryl's By The Bay, 112 S Fulton Beach / 361-790-9626
Hemingway's Bar & Grill, North Magnolia Street / 361-729-7555 /
    www.hemingwaysrockport.com
Jalisco Restaurant, 1701 Hwy 35 N / 361-727-0555
Whataburger, Hwy 35 N / 361-729-3022 / www.whataburger.com

SPORTING GOODS

Pelican Bait, 412 Navigation Circle / 361-729-8448
Rockport Tackletown, 3010 Hwy 35 N / 361-729-1841 /
    www.rockporttackletown.com

The Lighhouse Lakes Paddling Trail starts just across the channel.

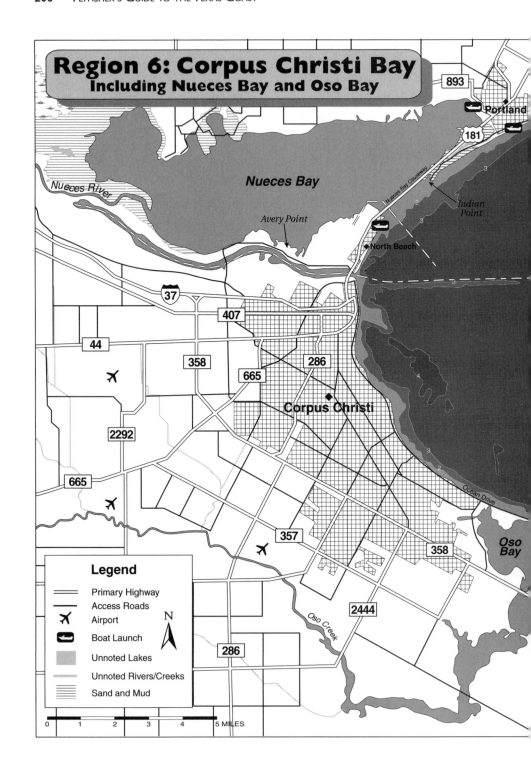

Region 6: Corpus Christi Bay
Including Nueces Bay and Oso Bay

893

Portland

181

Nueces River

Nueces Bay

Avery Point

Indian
Point

North Beach

37

407

44

358

665

286

2292

Corpus Christi

665

Ocean Drive

357

358

Oso
Bay

2444

286

Oso Creek

Legend

Primary Highway
Access Roads
Airport
Boat Launch
Unnoted Lakes
Unnoted Rivers/Creeks
Sand and Mud

N

0   1   2   3   4   5 MILES

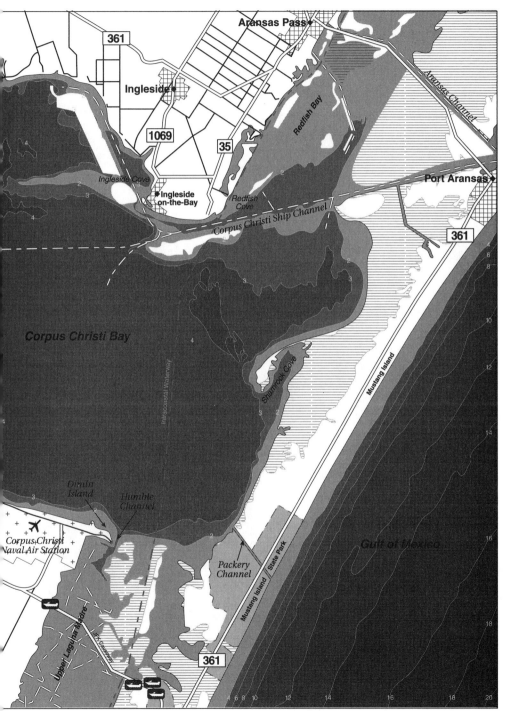

Region 6: Corpus Christi Bay

Corpus Christi Bay is a large bay with areas of deep water. Large ships regularly enter as they cross from the Aransas Channel, through the Corpus Christi Ship Channel to the industrial area near the Nueces Bay Causeway. Bay waters are often roiled by the ship traffic and predominant southeast winds. Corpus Christi Bay is often too rough for most anglers but there are surrounding locations that can be fished even on very windy days.

Corpus Christi has an extensive petro-chemical industry, so oil tankers and refining facilities are sites anglers will see when they come to this large bay. The deep Corpus Christi Channel that enters the bay system at Port Aransas allows deep vessels access to the bay. The deep waters of the channel also provide water circulation needed for a healthy bay.

Wind plays a big role in this bay. Many wind surfers choose Corpus Christi as home because they know there will be some wind on most days. The wind that makes their hobby possible also affects those wishing to fish the area. Calm days are rare.

Downtown Corpus Christi faces the bay. The drive down Shoreline Boulevard provides a great view of it. This is one of the most populated areas on the Texas coast and also a favorite with visitors from across the country. Plan your fishing trip for mid-week to avoid the largest crowds.

Seasonal Fishing Chart - Region 6: Corpus Christi Bay

	Jan	Feb	Mar	Apr	May	Jun	Jul	Aug	Sep	Oct	Nov	Dec
Redfish	++	+++	+++	+++	+++	+++	+++	+++	+++	+++	+++	+++
Spotted Seatrout	++	+++	+++	+++	+++	+++	+++	+++	+++	+++	+++	+
Flounder				++	+++	+++	+++	+++	+++	+++	+++	+
Black Drum	++	+++	+++	+++	+++	+++	+++	+++	+++	+++	++	+
Sheepshead	++	+++	+++	+++	+++	+++	+++	+++	+++	++	++	+
Crevalle Jack					++	+++	+++	+++	+++			
Spanish Mackerel					++	+++	+++	+++	+++			
Gray Snapper					++	+++	+++	+++				
Tarpon						+	+	+				
Pompano				+	+	+	+	+				
Snook						+	+	+				

+++ = Exceptional, ++ = Very Good, + = Available

Nueces Bay

Nueces Bay is a small bay on the southwestern end of Corpus Christi Bay. The Nueces River enters Nueces Bay at the southeast end. The river brings freshwater into the Bay and ultimately into Corpus Christi Bay.

The freshwater inflows ensure a healthy blue crab population and provide nursery grounds for many different prey fish and shrimp. Freshwater inflows are critical to the survival of these immature creatures.

During heavy rains — the heaviest of which come in the spring — the Nueces River will make Nueces Bay too fresh for most saltwater fish. Anglers should learn about local rains before planning a trip here. After heavy rains, the bay may remain fresh for several months. Anglers should target Nueces Bay during the dryer months in the fall and winter.

Nueces Bay is littered with numerous oyster shell reefs. Many of these reefs will be just under the water's surface, except at extreme low tide in winter. The reefs make traveling with a motorboat through Nueces Bay very dangerous.

Anglers should travel this bay under extreme caution. A few guides regularly fish Nueces Bay and it is definitely recommended to hire one on your first trip. Learn the waters before venturing out on your own.

Kayakers and waders have several options for fishing this bay. The predominant southeast wind does not affect Nueces Bay as much as it does Corpus Christi Bay. Overall Nueces Bay is shallow, which does not let the wind build up large rolling waves like in Corpus Christi Bay.

Anglers can enter the bay from the Indian Point side in Portland or from the Corpus Christi side. Take along a GPS when wading or using your kayak and record the locations of reefs you run across for future reference.

Nueces Bay often has a good population of redfish, speckled trout, and flounder. Since most boaters cannot travel through this shallow bay, you'll have plenty of room to explore. Be sure to fish around the many oil rigs scattered throughout the bay. The surrounding waters will be slightly deeper and older rigs were built on a base of oyster shell. The oyster shells attract small prey creatures like shrimp and crabs that in turn attract predator fish.

Anglers can access Nueces Bay from the Portland side by using Indian Point Park. West of the park, Nueces Bay has very shallow water and there are numerous reefs and oil wells in the area. This area is protected from a southeast wind and can be fished by waders and kayakers.

To access Nueces Bay from the Corpus Christi side take the Beach Avenue exit. If you're going south on Highway 181 from Portland take the Beach Avenue exit and turn back under the bridge, then back north and under the bridge again. There is a boat ramp and limited unpaved parking at the Nueces Bay Bait and Tackle just west of the Nueces Bay Causeway.

The Nueces River can be accessed by taking IH 37 to Carbon Plant Road along the river. Pay attention to the signs and fish back to the west as the sign directs. Kayakers can use this spot to access Nueces Bay, but it will be a pretty good paddle back east to the bay.

Pay attention to the many Private Property and No Trespassing signs in the area. There is also heavy truck traffic along the road.

Nueces Bay is often overlooked by anglers but deserves more attention. Just use caution when working through the bay and around the numerous reefs.

Fly casters can use Lefty's Deceivers, small crab patterns, and poppers. Lure casters can use lightweight jigheads with soft plastics, saltwater spinnerbaits, or topwater lures like Zara Spooks, Corkies, or TopDogs. Baitcasters can try free shrimp or shrimp under a popping cork.

Boat Ramp

Nueces Bay Bait & Tackle, 5151 E Causeway Blvd / 361-882-6420

Corpus Christi Bay

Corpus Christi Bay is a large, deep-water bay whose waters are often very rough. The predominant southeast winds run across the greatest part of the bay. The deepest water in the bay is over 12 feet deep and high winds help create large rolling waves. Anglers should be aware of the wind and avoid fishing the middle of the bay during very windy days.

At the south end of Corpus Christi Bay, Billings Bait Camp is located on the north side of the JFK Causeway. There is a boat ramp right next to Billings. The ramp itself is paved but the parking area is dirt and gets muddy when wet. Nearby is Clem's Marina. There is a fee pier located next to Clem's.

Across the street and under the bridge are Marker 37, Snoopy's and Doc's. Marker 37 has a paved four-lane boat ramp. The parking area, however, is not paved. There is a fee to use the ramp and park. Red Dot and Cosway bait camps are also located on the south side of the JFK Causeway.

The Packery Channel Park is part of the Nueces County Parks & Recreation Department. This park is located near the west side of the Packery Channel Bridge. The road into the parking lot is paved but very rough, so go slow. There is limited parking in the area. Kayakers can launch from the parking area and fish the channel and surrounding flats. The channel goes all the way to the Intracoastal Waterway.

The Humble Channel runs along the west shoreline from the JFK Causeway to Dimitt Island. The channel is deeper than the surrounding waters and attracts fish to the area.

The Philip Dimitt Municipal Fishing Pier offers anglers access to fish the channel, but the parking area is very limited. There are numerous shallow areas and islands nearby. Take Waldron off Highway 361, and turn east on Skipper Lane to get to the pier. You cannot drive through the Corpus Christi Naval Air Station.

Around the south side of Corpus Christi Bay are a number of city parks. Anglers can fish from the naval air station all the way around to the Nueces Bay Causeway. Corpus Christi Bay Trail connects the bay front from the Art Museum of Texas to just in front of Texas A & M – Corpus Christi. The trail is paved and designed for bikes as well as walkers. Palmetto Park has very limited parking. Next in line traveling west is Swatner Park with plenty of parking. Dodridge and Ropes Parks have very limited parking.

Cole Park is divided into several different sections connected by the bike-walk path. The area at Oleander Point has more parking. There is a pier located in the park as well as a shorter handicap pier. Cole Park has many different features and attracts lots of visitors. On weekends and holidays, the park gets crowded and is not the best place for fishing solitude.

When the wind is out of the southeast, the area along these parks is protected. A north wind will blow waves right into the park areas. Anglers can wade all along the south shoreline of Corpus Christi Bay.

The Philip Dimitt Pier provides anglers access to deeper channel waters.

The L-Head near downtown has a paved parking area and multi-lane boat ramp for launching into Corpus Christi Bay. Turn off Shoreline Boulevard onto Cooper's Alley. There is also a small fishing pier.

In the middle of Corpus Christi Bay, there are several oil rigs that regularly attract fish. Attempt to fish these rigs only when the wind is light and predicted to stay that way. These rigs are too far for kayakers to safely venture to.

The older rigs were placed on pads of oyster shells. The shells create an environment for prey species that attract larger predator fish. When fishing these deeper waters, light-tackle anglers should use heavy jigheads with soft plastics, spec rigs, or heavy lures like a Mirrolure 52M.

For anglers using natural bait, work the shell pads around the oil rigs with both free shrimp without a weight and shrimp weighted under a popping float.

Also, watch for any diving bird activity in Corpus Christi Bay. The birds may only be hovering over hardhead catfish, but will also fly over schools of speckled trout. Set up your drift to intercept the school. Don't run into the middle of the school with your boat to maximize casting chances without scaring the fish.

On the north side of Corpus Christi Bay along Highway 181, anglers can access the beach area in several locations and also at the Corpus Christi North Beach Access site. Kayakers and waders can also use this area to access the bay, but there is limited parking. Some of the roads are not paved and become very muddy when wet.

Across the Nueces Bay Causeway anglers can access the bay at the Indian Point Park and Pier just off Highway 181 near Portland. The park has limited parking. In Portland anglers can access the bay by taking the Moore Street exit to Sunset Drive off Highway 181 to Sunset Lake Park. The park has a paved parking area, but parking is limited. There are also a couple of pull-off spots along the road where waders and kayakers can access the bay. There is a $1-per-person and $1-per-rod (limit 3 rods) fee for fishing on Indian Point Pier. Anglers can also rent tackle at the pier.

A strong southeast wind will blow right into this area so anglers may want to fish here when the wind is out of the north.

Corpus Christi has a large windsurfing population. During the spring and summer, most parks will be full with people swimming, wind surfing, or just enjoying the water. Anglers need to consider the multiple uses Corpus Christi Bay provides and plan accordingly.

Boat Ramps

Clem's Marina, 13304 S Padre Island Dr / 361-949-8445
Billings Bait Camp / 361-949-8692
Indian Point Pier, Hwy 181 N / 361-643-5483
Jane's L-Head Coopers Alley / 361-882-2248

INGLESIDE ON THE BAY

Ingleside is at the northern end of Corpus Christi Bay. Ingleside Cove has a boat ramp, paved parking area, and kayak rentals. The La Quinta Channel, Corpus Christi Channel, and Intracoastal Waterway all intersect just southeast of Ingleside. Watch for larger boat traffic while in this area.

There are numerous spoil islands in the area that help protect Ingleside Cove. This small cove is not as affected by the predominantly southeast wind as other areas and is a good place to avoid a strong wind, making it ideal for kayakers and flyfishers. Fishers can work the shallow areas around the spoil islands and the drop-off into the deep channels.

Linda's Bait Camp, across the street from the Ingleside Cove Boat Ramp, has gas, supplies, and bait.

Amenities

Kayak Rentals / 361-778-2887
Bahia Marina, 145 Live Oak / 361-776-7295
Linda's Bait Stand, FM 1069 / 361-776-3360

MUSTANG ISLAND

Mustang Island is at the eastern edge of Corpus Christi Bay. The island runs from the Port Aransas Channel on the north end to the Packery Channel on the south end. The island has numerous hotels and condos along the surf side.

Anglers can reach the surf along the Gulf of Mexico from several locations along the island. Travel by automobile is allowed along the beach. A parking pass is required for all vehicles parking on the beach.

The surf along Mustang Island offers excellent fishing within easy reach for anglers. Look for areas where deeper water comes closer to the beach. Deeper water is often seen as more green water. Look for jumping prey fish.

There are also several access points to the Corpus Christi Bay side of the island. Small boats or kayaks can be launched from these access points. The bay side of the island offers many shallow-water spots that regularly hold redfish, trout, and flounder.

The bay side of the island is also an excellent place to get out of the predominant southeast wind.

Review the Mustang Island section of Port Aransas for more details.

OSO BAY

Oso Bay is located on the south side of Corpus Christi Bay. Oso Bay is a shallow-water area anglers often think of in the winter for its protected waters. Corpus Christi Power and Light has a power plant located near the bay. When the plant is in operation, bay waters are used to cool heated pipes which then wamr the surrounding waters. Fish find the warm water in cool months irresistible.

Oso Bay has a gut running into its mouth from Corpus Christi Bay. This is the area just west of the naval air station. Most of Oso Bay can be waded although some areas are muddy.

From the east, anglers can access Oso Bay from the Oso Bay Turnaround but there is no paved parking. This part of Oso Bay has numerous small islands and areas protected from the wind, making it ideal for kayakers.

Anglers can also access Oso Bay from a couple of locations on the west side. Take Ennis Joslin Road Exit off Highway 358 to Hans & Pat Suter Park. Waders and kayakers can access the water from the park, but it is a pretty good hike. Parking is limited to about 25 spaces.

Farther down, Ennis Joslin Road leads to Ocean Drive. Ocean Drive runs in front of Texas A & M University - Corpus Christi and to the Corpus Christi Naval Air Station. Oso Bay is just to the west of the Naval Air Station gates.

Anglers can park their vehicle across from the bay along Ocean Drive and walk across to Oso Bay or go to the north to Corpus Christi Bay. There are several small oil rigs in Oso Bay that offer some structure for predator fish. Most of these rigs are on shell bases.

Oso Bay is also a perfect place for beginning kayakers to learn how their crafts work. The narrowness of Oso Bay helps prevent the water from becoming too rough from the strong winds.

Corpus Christi Bay Hub Cities

CORPUS CHRISTI
Population: 380,783
County: Nueces

ACCOMMODATIONS

America's Best Value Inn & Suites, 133 US Hwy 181 / 361-643-4300 / 55 rooms / $45-$149 / www.bestvalueinn.com

Bay Front Plaza Hotel, 601 N Water St / 800-688-0334 / 200 rooms / $60-$109 / www.bayfrontplazahotelcc.com

Best Western Marina Grand Hotel, 300 N Shoreline Blvd / 361-883-5111 / 171 rooms / $79-$149 / www.bestwesterntexas.com

Best Western Navigation Inn, 902 N Navigation Blvd / 361-888-8333 / 49 rooms / $69-$139 / www.bestwesterntexas.com

Comfort Inn, 722 N Port Ave / 800-424-6423 / 44 rooms / $80-$130

Days Inn Corpus Christi Beach, 4302 Surfside Blvd / 361-882-3297 / 56 rooms / $60-$150 / www.daysinn.com

Holiday Inn Airport Hotel, 5549 Leopard St / 800-HOLIDAY / 249 rooms / $89-$129 / www.holidayinn.com

La Quinta Corpus Christi South, 6225 South Padre Island Dr / 361-991-5730 / 129 rooms / $85-$145 / www.lq.com

Quality Inn, 3202 Surfside Blvd / 361-883-7456 / 119 rooms / $79-$209 / www.qualityinn.com

CAMPGROUNDS

Greyhound RV Park, 5402 Leopard St / 361-289-2076

Gulfway RV Park, 7436 S Padre Island Dr / 361-991-0106

Gulley's RV Park, 822 S Padre Island Dr / 361-241-4122

Hatch RV, 3101 Up River Rd / 361-883-9781 / www.hatchrv.com

Laguna Shore Village, 3828 Laguna Shore Rd / 361-937-6035 / www.lagunashorevillage.com

Padre Palms RV, 131 Skipper Ln / 361-937-2125

Puerto Del Sol Park, 5100 Timon Blvd / 361-882-5373

Shady Grove RV, 2919 Waldron Rd / 361-937-1314

RESTAURANTS

Black Diamond Oyster House, 7202 S Padre Island Dr / 361-992-2432

Johnny Carino's, 1652 S Padre Island Dr / 361-854-7373

Cracker Barrel, 4229 S Padre Island Dr / 361-855-1778 / www.crackerbarrel.com

Jason's Deli, 1416 Airline Rd / 361-992-4649 / www.jasonsdeli.com

IHOP, 5202 S Padre Island Dr / 361-993-5535 / www.ihop.com

Landry's Seafood House, 600 N Shoreline Blvd / 361-882-6666
Outback Steakhouse, 4221 S Padre Island Dr / 361-814-6283 / www.outback.com
Rudy's Country Store & Bar-B-Q, 6101 S Padre Island Dr / 361-906-0327 /
   www.rudys.com
Snoopy's Pier, 13313 S Padre Island Dr / 361-949-8815
Texas Roadhouse, 2029 S Padre Island Dr / 361-854-9505 /
   www.texasroadhouse.com
Whataburger, 14301 S Padre Island Dr / 361-949-7777 / www.whataburger.com

SPORTING GOODS

Academy Sports, 5001 S Padre Island Dr / 361-986-7200
Gulf Sporting Goods, 3900 Leopard St / 361-882-6461
Roy's Bait & Tackle, 7613 S Padre Island Dr / 361-992-2960 /
   www.roysbait-tackle.com

AIRPORT

Corpus Christi International Airport / 361-289-0171

FOR MORE INFORMATION

Corpus Christi Convention and Visitors Bureau
   1823 N Chaparral St
   800-766-2322
   www.corpuschrisitcvb.com

INGLESIDE
Population: 9,388
County: San Patricio

ACCOMMODATIONS

Best Western Naval Station Inn, 2025 State Highway 361 / 361-776-2767 / 37
rooms / $75-$150 / www.bestwesterntexas.com
Comfort Inn, 2800 Hwy 361 / 361-775-2700 / 40 rooms / $69-$129
Mainstay Suites, 2787 Hwy 361 / 361-775-2000 / 54 rooms / $79-$85 /
www.mainstay.com
Our Place on the Bay, 1233Bayshore Dr / 361-776-6484/ 6 rooms / $99-$129 /
www.ourplaceonthebay.net

RESTAURANTS

Blackbeards Too, 2753 W Main / 361-776-0393
Dairy Queen, 2611 Hwy 361 / 361-776-2506 / www.dairyqueen.com
Floyd's Ranch House, 2144 Hwy 361 / 361-776-3511
Subway, 2450 Hwy 361 / 361-776-0588 / www.subway.com
Twin Pizza, 2819 S Main / 361-776-3487
Whataburger, 309 Hwy 361 / 361-776-3281 / www.whataburger.com

PORTLAND
Population: 14,827
County: San Patricio

ACCOMMODATIONS

Best Western, 1707 Hwy 181 / 361-777-3100 / 40 rooms / $98-$109 /
www.bestwesterntexas.com
Comfort Inn, 1703 Hwy 181 / 361-643-2222/ 40 rooms / $76-$115
Hampton Inn, 1705 N Hwy 181 / 361-777-1500 / 54 rooms / $99-$129 /
www.hamptoninn.com

CAMPGROUNDS

Sea Breeze RV Park, 1026 Sea Breeze Lane / 361-643-0744

RESTAURANTS

Bad Brad's Bar-B-Que Joint, 1807 Hwy 181 / 361-643-5000
Chili's Grill & Bar, 2010 Hwy 181 / 361-777-0100 / www.chilis.com
Dairy Queen, 911 Dallas St / 361-643-5222 / www.dairyqueen.com
Sonic Drive In, 106 Lang Rd / 361-643-0982 / www.sonicdrivein.com
Taqueria El Tapatio, 922 Railroad Dr / 361-643-0737
Whataburger, 1010 Wildcat Dr / 361-643-2563 / www.whataburger.com

FOR MORE INFORMATION

Portland Chamber of Commerce, 361-643-2475

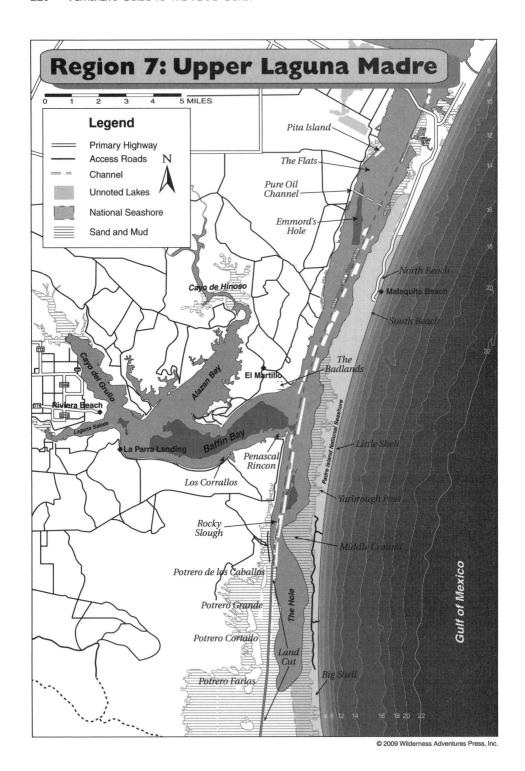

Region 7: Upper Laguna Madre

0 1 2 3 4 5 MILES

Legend

Primary Highway
Access Roads
Channel
Unnoted Lakes
National Seashore
Sand and Mud

N

Pita Island

The Flats

Pure Oil Channel

Emmord's Hole

Cayo de Hinoso

North Beach

Malaquite Beach

South Beach

Cayo del Grullo

Alazan Bay

El Martillo

The Badlands

Riviera Beach

Laguna Salada

La Parra Landing

Baffin Bay

Penascal Rincon

Little Shell

Los Corrallos

Yarbrough Pass

Rocky Slough

Middle Ground

Potrero de los Caballos

Potrero Grande

The Hole

Potrero Cortado

Land Cut

Potrero Farias

Big Shell

Padre Island National Seashore

Gulf of Mexico

© 2009 Wilderness Adventures Press, Inc.

Region 7: Upper Laguna Madre

The Upper Laguna Madre of Texas is the most isolated region of the state, made up of parts of three counties: Kleberg, Kenedy, and Nueces. This area is sparsely populated with one of the counties holding less than 1,000 people. Most of the land in two of these counties is privately owned with very limited land access to the coastal areas.

The Laguna Madre is the only hypersaline lagoon in North America and one of only five in the world. There are vast shallow-water flats and areas of tidal mud flats.

The Upper Laguna Madre Region offers two diverse areas for fishing. The inshore area is dominated by the Laguna Madre and vast holdings of private lands. The gulf side of the region is dominated by a national park and long beaches open to the public. Padre Island National Seashore, or PINS, is directly across from the vast King and Kenedy Ranches. Padre Island National Seashore offers great surf fishing for those properly equipped. Padre Island is the longest barrier island in the world.

The Intracoastal Waterway was dredged across an area now known as the Land Cut. This is where the canal was actually cut through land that was dry at least part of the time. The Land Cut now connects water areas allowing some circulation of bay waters.

Seasonal Fishing Chart - Region 7: Upper Laguna Madre

	Jan	Feb	Mar	Apr	May	Jun	Jul	Aug	Sep	Oct	Nov	Dec
Redfish	++	+++	+++	+++	+++	+++	+++	+++	+++	+++	+++	+
Spotted Seatrout	++	+++	+++	+++	+++	+++	+++	+++	+++	+++	+++	+
Flounder			++	+++	+++	+++	+++	+++	+++	+++	+++	+
Black Drum	++	+++	+++	+++	+++	+++	+++	+++	+++	+++	+++	+
Sheepshead	++	+++	+++	+++	+++	+++	+++	+++	+++	++	+	+
Crevalle Jack					++	+++	+++	+++	+++	+		
Spanish Mackerel						++	+++	+++	+++	+		
Gray Snapper						++	+++	+++	+++			
Tarpon						+	+	+	+			
Pompano				+	+	+	+	+				
Snook						+	+	+				

+++ = Exceptional, ++ = Very Good, + = Available

In the past, the dividing line between the Upper and Lower Laguna Madre was always difficult to pin down. The Texas Parks and Wildlife Department changed that in 2007, when it enacted the first special fishing regulation for a saltwater region. Until then, all saltwater regulations were consistent statewide. The new regulation limits the daily take of speckled trout to five fish in the Lower Laguna Madre. Texas Parks & Wildlife defined the boundary line between Upper and Lower Laguna Madre as marker 21 in the Land Cut.

Marker 21 is in the south end of the Land Cut between Southeast Point and Rincon de San Jose. This spot has a channel running east out of the Intracoastal Waterway making it an easily recognizable landmark. The special regulation is for inshore water only and does not include the gulf waters.

There are vast areas of seagrass, predominantly shoalgrass, in the Upper Laguna Madre. Average water depth of the Upper Laguna Madre is just over 3 feet.

There are four natural islands in the Upper Laguna Madre and many man-made dredge islands were created when digging the Intracoastal Waterway. All of these islands offer good fishing by providing a depth change, which predator fish use to assist them in corralling prey fish.

Another unique feature of the Laguna Madre is that it has no river runoff to help replenish it. All other bay systems in Texas have several rivers bringing freshwater inflows to the bay. The Laguna Madre relies on a meager flow from the Gulf of Mexico and the Intracoastal Waterway for inflows. Salinities can get very high in the Laguna Madre. Years go by without significant rainfall in the area and salinities rise. The rainfall is highest from May through June and August through October.

Big trout are at home in the waters of the Upper Laguna Madre.

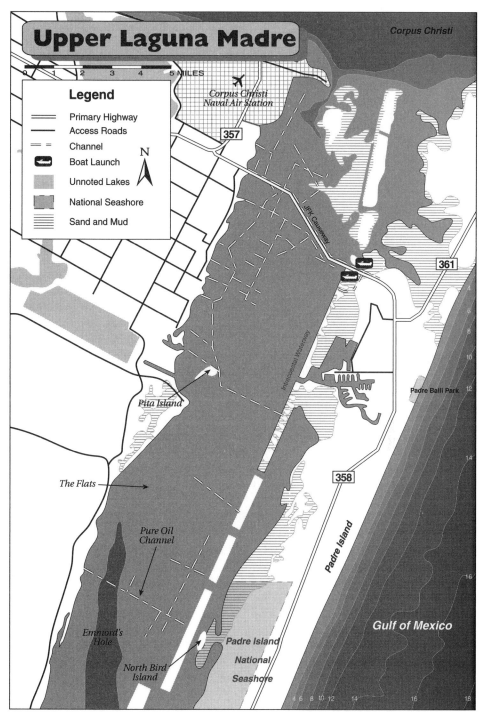

Upper Laguna Madre

0 1 2 3 4 5 MILES

Legend

——— Primary Highway
——— Access Roads
— — Channel
Boat Launch
Unnoted Lakes
National Seashore
Sand and Mud

N

Corpus Christi

Corpus Christi
Naval Air Station

357

JFK Causeway

361

Intracoastal Waterway

Padre Balli Park

Pita Island

The Flats

Pure Oil
Channel

358

Padre Island

Emmord's
Hole

North Bird
Island

Padre Island

National

Seashore

Gulf of Mexico

© 2009 Wilderness Adventures Press, Inc.

Hurricanes play a role in the life of the Laguna Madre. This area has been hit by hurricanes going back as far as there are records. A hurricane can open many passes to the Gulf of Mexico, which often stay open less than a year, at which point the Laguna returns to a normal situation with low circulation.

But even a pass open for a short duration provides a great service to the Laguna Madre. Rich nutrients enter the system and all living organisms benefit. These infrequent events cause a big increase in the fish population living inside the Laguna.

Part of the Upper Laguna Madre Region includes Baffin Bay. For anyone living on or regularly visiting the Texas coast, Baffin Bay holds a special attraction because is not easily accessed. The isolation helps protect a fish population highly valued by Texas coastal anglers.

Even though Baffin Bay is known as a big trout destination it also has a large black drum population. Black drum are often found with their tail or part of their backs out of the water just like redfish. The fins of a black drum are almost clear, somewhat similar to mullet fins.

Schools of black drum numbering in the hundreds can be seen rooting in the soft sand and mud looking for a meal. Once the school moves on the area appears pock marked, like the surface of the moon. Each black drum makes a circular crater using its mouth and gills, which signify good fishing to the angler able to recognize them.

Black drum are an excellent target for the fly caster. They are not picky about the fly but they can be picky about the way it is presented. Often the best presentation is to simply place the fly where it will intersect the path of the black drum and let it sit. A simple black fly like Cory's Little Black Fly works great.

Once you find a school of black drum, you can often catch several fish from the same school. They put up a strong fight, just like their cousin the redfish; and for those anglers wishing to keep a fish to eat, a small black drum offers excellent table fare.

The fillet is white and tastes great grilled. Most stories of black drum being undesirable for eating come from people that caught very large black drum.

Large black drum are often plagued by worms. A black drum that approaches the upper limit of 31 inches will have these worms along its back. The worms are not harmful to humans but most people don't like the sight of them.

Smaller black drum at the bottom of the slot limit often do not have these worms and are just right for eating. The larger fish, over 31 inches, may be decades old and are the spawners that keep the species going. Even though they are strong pullers, they should all be released.

Even though the Upper Laguna Madre is difficult to get to it is worth the effort. It is a unique habitat that all Texas coastal anglers should visit.

Boat Ramps

There are two public boat ramps near the JFK Causeway on the Padre Island side. Other boat ramps are:

Marker 37, Marina Padre Island / 361-949-8037

Clem's Marina, Padre Island / 361-949-8445

Bluff's Landing, 4242 Laguna Shores Dr / 361-937-7100 / Flour Bluff, Fee / www.bluffslanding.com

Pita Island

Pita Island is the first large island south of the JFK Causeway. It is located along the western shoreline at the end of a man-made cut running west from the Intracoastal Waterway. The cut provides water up to 5 feet deep running through an area with mostly shallow water less than 2 feet deep. This area is across from the Padre Balli Park.

The Flats

The Flats is a large area south of Pita Island running to the Pure Oil Channel. The water in this area is very shallow, usually running less than 2 feet deep.

Pure Oil Channel

The Pure Oil Channel is a manmade cut, running west between the Intracoastal Waterway and the King Ranch shoreline. The channel is privately maintained and runs about 3.5 feet deep. There are several spoil islands in the area. Anglers should work around the spoil islands and the edges of the channel for redfish and speckled trout.

EMMORD'S HOLE

Emmord's Hole runs parallel to the Intracoastal Waterway and is just south of the Pure Oil Channel. This area is deeper than the surrounding area, running 4 to 5 feet deep in some places. The northeast end of Emmord's Hole cuts across the western end of Pure Oil Channel. There are several islands on the east side of the hole. The west side of the area is part of the massive King Ranch.

King Ranch employees regularly patrol the western shoreline, so be sure to stay in the water and off private lands. The western shoreline between Emmord's Hole and the King Ranch shoreline offers good shallow-water fishing. Several windmills are located on the King Ranch shoreline and can be used as landmarks for those fishing the area.

The deeper water drop-off that makes up Emmord's Hole is a good speckled trout area. Trout prefer the deeper water and cooler temperatures it provides. Fish the surrounding shallow areas on both sides of the Intracoastal Waterway for redfish and flounder.

There are several spoil islands just south of Emmord's Hole. The water to the east and south of these islands is deeper than the surrounding shallow-water flats. Some of this area is 4 feet deep and offers cooler water temperatures to fish living in the area.

This slightly deeper water runs close to the western shore of Padre Island and offers a quick drop-off providing game fish with a chance to dart into shallow water when seeking a meal and before returning to the comforts of the deeper water.

Some of the flats are tidal flats and very shallow. Anyone boating in the area for the first time should proceed with caution. For anglers unfamiliar with the area it is suggested you hire a guide.

COMPUERTA PASS AND POINT OF ROCKS

Compuerta Pass leads to the famous Baffin Bay. This is the area along the western shoreline right where Baffin Bay joins the shallower Intracoastal Waterway area. The big island just east of Compuerta Pass is Palms West Two. There are rocks in the area that boaters should be cautious of. Anglers unfamiliar with the area are best served using the Intracoastal Waterway to enter Baffin Bay, thus avoiding the Compuerta Pass/Point of Rocks area.

Baffin Bay

For most Texas saltwater anglers, Baffin Bay is a special place. When anglers think of Baffin Bay, they usually think of two things: large speckled trout and rocks.

Baffin has long had a reputation for big speckled trout and continues to do so today. In the early spring, anglers from all over come to Baffin to try for the trout of a lifetime. Guides that normally work other bay systems go to Baffin in the early spring seeking large speckled trout. Double-digit trout are taken from Baffin Bay each year. It is a very fertile bay system and the relative isolation helps insure its protection.

Baffin Bay is also home to a large number of rocks located either right at the surface or just below the surface. These rocks are actually skeletal remains of ancient worms. Serpulid worms formed reefs in Baffin Bay and the fossilized worm skeletons are what's left today. These rocks have been responsible for many lost lower motor units and broken props. Anglers unfamiliar with these rocks are encouraged to hire a guide until they feel comfortable boating through this large bay.

There are markers throughout the middle of the bay. Boaters can stay near the markers for safe passage through the area.

Most of the land surrounding Baffin Bay is privately owned which limits access to boaters and fishers. It can be approached from three different directions. Most boaters go south out of Corpus Christi to reach Baffin Bay. Boat ramps at Bluff's Landing, public ramps on Padre Island, and the ramp inside Padre Island National Seashore Park at Bird Island Basin can be used by boaters. The ramp at Bird Island Basin is 12 miles south of the JFK Bridge. The small fee at the Padre Island National Seashore Park will be more than offset by the cost of gas boating south from the bridge area.

Anglers can also approach from Port Mansfield to the south, but it is a much longer boat ride. The third entrance into Baffin Bay is from the west part of the bay at Loyola Beach and Riviera Beach. Boat ramps at Williamson's Boat Works and Kaufer Hubert Memorial Park provide access to western Baffin Bay.

Flies used include Dahlberg Divers, Snook-A-Roo, large foam poppers, Lefty's Deceivers, and Clouser Minnows.

Casting lures for speckled trout for all of Baffin Bay include the Catch 2000 and Catch 5, Bomber Long A, Topdog, and soft plastics used with a jighead.

Baffin Bay is very large. Boaters need to start their fishing day with a full tank of gas because there are no on-the-water gas stations. For those entering from the west, fuel may be purchased at Brown's Convenience Store near Loyola Beach.

Baffin Bay is not the place to run out of gas and expect to find help. Make sure you have a marine radio and, if possible, a cell phone when fishing this large bay. Make a trip plan and give it to someone that can help you if you run into trouble. Also take extra water, food, and a change of clothes when fishing Baffin Bay in case of boating problems.

The Badlands

The Badlands is a very shallow area with plenty of rocks, especially at the south end. Boaters should go past the area using the Intracoastal Waterway and turn at the markers in the middle of the bay, then turn back once past Marker #4 to get close to the Badlands.

Tide Gauge Bar

This is a long sand bar that parallels the eastern shoreline of Baffin Bay that is made of hard-packed sand. Inshore from the bar, the bottom gets softer the farther in you go. There is good wade fishing in this area. Cast parallel on each side of the bar for speckled trout. Fish for redfish inside the bar.

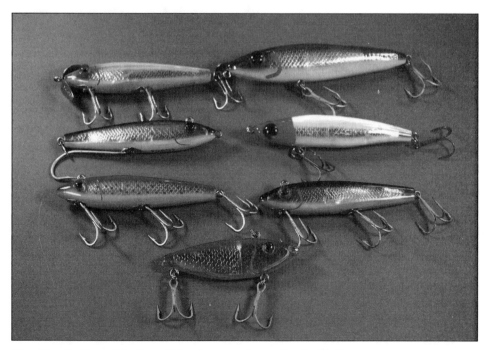

Hard-bodied lures like these Mirrolures work great in Baffin Bay.

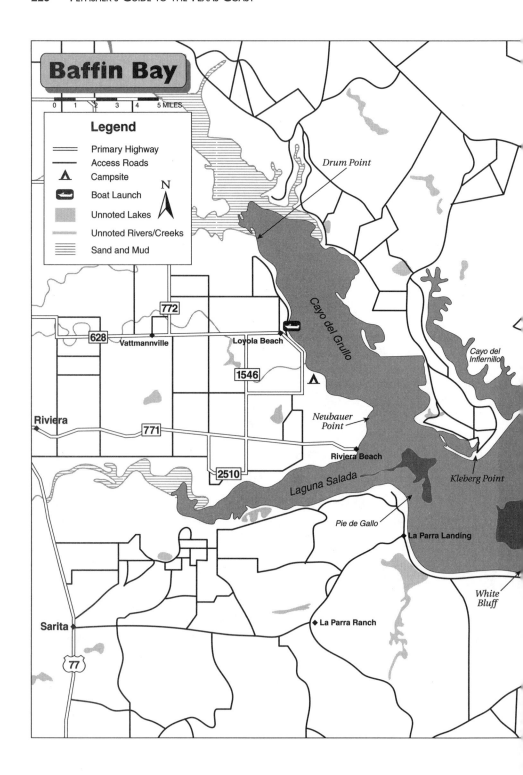

Baffin Bay

0 1 2 3 4 5 MILES

Legend

Primary Highway
Access Roads
▲ Campsite
Boat Launch
Unnoted Lakes
Unnoted Rivers/Creeks
Sand and Mud

N

Drum Point

Cayo del Grullo

Cayo del Inflernillo

772

628 Vattmannville

Loyola Beach

1546

▲

Riviera

771

Neubauer Point

2510

Riviera Beach

Laguna Salada

Kleberg Point

Pie de Gallo

La Parra Landing

White Bluff

Sarita

77

La Parra Ranch

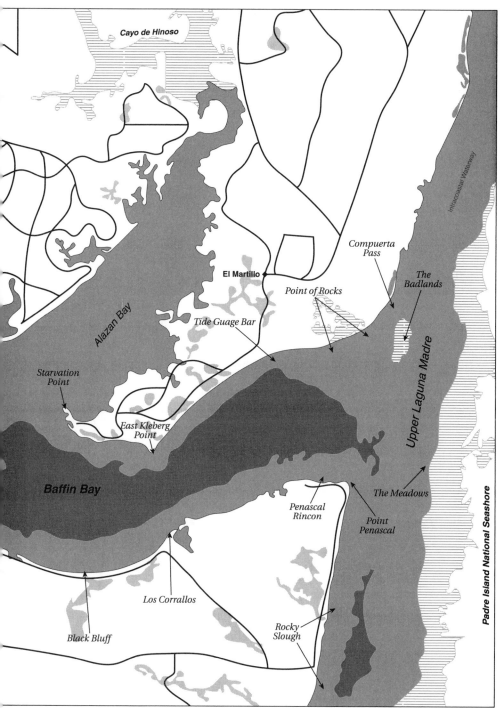

Cayo de Hinoso

El Martillo

Compuerta Pass

Point of Rocks

The Badlands

Tide Guage Bar

Alazan Bay

Starvation Point

Upper Laguna Madre

Intracoastal Waterway

East Kleberg Point

Baffin Bay

The Meadows

Penascal Rincon

Point Penascal

Padre Island National Seashore

Los Corrallos

Black Bluff

Rocky Slough

EAST KLEBERG POINT

East Kleberg Point has numerous rocks just off the point. Anglers are best served staying in their boat and fishing the deeper side of the rocks for speckled trout. Throw large topwater lures and poppers early in the morning around the rocks. Once the sun gets up switch to jigheads and soft plastics. An electric trolling motor will make for a quiet approach to the rocks. If the water is clear enough, anglers may be able to target specific fish.

Use 1/8- or 1/16-ounce jigheads to avoid hooking into the rocks. If you continue to hook the rocks use a Mansfield Mauler or topwater lure with the soft plastics on a jighead underneath to avoid hanging the rocks.

Fly casters should use a large popper early and switch to large Clouser Minnows or Lefty's Deceivers as the sun rises.

Starvation Point

Starvation Point is the end of the shoreline before entering Alazan Bay. Anglers can wade fish both sides of Starvation Point. Look for redfish in the shallow water and speckled trout at the drop-off.

ALAZAN BAY

Alazan Bay is the long bay branching north off of Baffin Bay. Alazan Bay is surrounded by private land and there is no road access. The mouth of Alazan Bay is not deep, with most areas less than 4 feet.

Shallow-running boats are a must when fishing Alazan Bay. The best fishing is along the north shoreline and around the rocks close to the mouth of the bay. The water on the south side of the bay is very shallow.

The north shoreline offers a good drop-off into 4 feet of water. Fish for speckled trout along the drop-off.

The back of the bay is soft and best fished from a shallow-running boat. Look for black drum and redfish cruising in the shallow water.

Kleberg Point

Kleberg Point is directly across from Starvation Point and is on the other side of the mouth of Alazan Bay. Anglers can wade fish the area from Kleberg Point to the Sandy Hook area.

CAYO DEL GRULLO

Cayo Del Grullo is the far western part of Baffin Bay and is easily reached from the boat ramp at Kaufer Hubert Memorial Park, which offers multiple lanes and a large parking area.

This area is also a good place to launch a small watercraft like a kayak or canoe. The shoreline along the Loyola Beach area offers good shallow-water fishing. Be sure to test the bottom with a paddle or rod tip before abandoning your boat because there are areas of hard bottom and areas of soft mud. The Cayo can be slick calm at times making for an easy paddle, but it can also get very windy so don't overestimate the area you want to try to cover.

The far west end of the Cayo is called Drum Point and there are often plenty of the namesake fish to cast to. Tailing black drum can be more difficult to catch than tailing redfish as they are easily spooked by loud noises. Approach the area quietly for best results.

Try small black flies like Capt. Corey Rich's Little Black Fly when pursuing black drum.

Black drum will also hit both live and dead shrimp for the casting anglers. Use a Kahle hook and a single split shot, and a strong leader is a good idea. Don't be surprised by the strong pull of the black drum. They are worthy adversaries on any tackle.

Work the drop-offs in the area for speckled trout.

Get quick access to Cayo Del Grullo and western Baffin Bay from Kaufer-Hubert Memorial Park.

NEUBAUER POINT

Neubauer Point is across from Sandy Hook, just west of Kleberg Point. This area is easily accessed from Kraatz Bait Camp. There is a small café and bait camp with tackle at Kraatz's. It's a good place to take a break from paddling and get out of the summer heat for awhile.

Laguna Salada

Laguna Salada is in the far southwest corner of Baffin Bay. This area offers both large and small boating areas. Boats can launch from Williamson's boat ramp off County Road 1546 for a small launch fee.

Kayakers can launch directly from the road, but there is very little parking. This is a good place for a beginning kayaker to learn how their boat works without having to worry about lots of boat traffic or strong winds.

There are soft mud areas in the Laguna so test the bottom before leaving your boat.

Pie De Gallo

Pie De Gallo is the point of land at the mouth of Laguna Salada. Off the point, between Sandy Hook and Pie De Gallo, is a deeper hole of water with depths to 7 feet. This is the area between Markers 38 and 40.

Anglers can fish the deeper water for speckled trout.

White Bluff, Black Bluff and Rocks

White Bluff and Black Bluff areas make up a large part of the south shoreline of Baffin Bay. Work the shoreline for redfish and the drop-offs for speckled trout. There are several rocks along the shoreline so boat carefully.

In the center of Baffin Bay just north of the marker lane between Markers 26 and 34 are two larger groups of rocks. Using an electric trolling motor, work these rocks from the boat for speckled trout.

Los Corrallos

Los Corrallos, farther east from Black Bluff, also has a group of rocks that regularly holds fish. Work these rocks from the boat as the bottom can be muddy. Use Clouser Minnows and Lefty's Deceivers, or lighter jigheads with soft plastic to avoid hanging up in the rocks.

Penascal Rincon and Point Penascal

The areas along the south shoreline of Baffin Bay nearest the mouth of the bay are Penascal Rincon and Point Penascal. There are many rocks in the area so it is recommended that you fish with experienced anglers or a guide.

Cast around the rocks either while drifting or using an electric trolling motor. Avoid bumping into the rocks and quietly fish the area for the best results. Point Penascal is the south side of the mouth of Baffin Bay directly across from The Badlands and Compuerta Pass.

Anglers can wade fish between the rocks and the shoreline. Remember the land bordering this area is all private. Cast to redfish in the shallow waters and speckled trout farther out at the drop-off and around the rocks.

The Meadows

The Meadows is a shallow-water area across from the mouth of Baffin Bay between the Intracoastal Waterway and Padre Island. It has grass that often holds redfish. The water is less than 3 feet deep and can be successfully waded using flies or gold spoons with casting tackle.

Fly anglers should have spoon flies, crab and shrimp patterns, Rattle Rousers, orange and red Lefty's Deceivers, and Clouser Minnows in chartreuse and white.

Casting and spinning fishers should have copper and gold spoons in 1/8- and 1/4-ounce sizes, and pumpkinseed chartreuse, red-head white-tail, firetiger and red-flash shad colored soft plastics on jigheads in 1/8- and 1/16-ounce sizes.

Redfish often patrol around and through the grass, so anglers can stand in one location and cast to cruising fish. Avoid making a big wake with your legs when wading through the area.

ROCKY SLOUGH AND YARBROUGH PASS

Rocky Slough is to the west of the Intracoastal Waterway. To the east of the Intracoastal Waterway is the Yarbrough Pass area. This is directly across Padre Island from the Little Shell beach area.

Rocky Slough offers deeper water than the surrounding water and has numerous rocks anglers need to watch for. This area can be drifted from a boat using topwater lures and fly-rod poppers early in the day. Once the sun is up, switch to jigheads with soft plastics and Clouser Minnows.

Going east across the Intracoastal Waterway, there is a deeper pocket of water that drops to over 7 feet. This area is to the east of the spoil islands lining the Intracoastal Waterway. There are rocks in the area so be careful when boating through.

Most of the area along the east shore of Padre Island requires a shallow-running boat as the water is often less than 2 feet deep.

Drift fishing and casting under the birds is a good way to catch speckled trout. Approach any visible birds quietly and be careful not to crash through the fish. Make as long a cast as you can to avoid scaring the fish. Look for birds in the area, especially during the afternoon hours.

The east side of the spoil islands in the area is usually muddy and best fished from a boat. Also fish around the numerous cabins located in the area. Be sure to cast into any shaded area, searching for flounder and snook.

Flies such as the Tiger Rattler work well for flounder, and snook flies include the Snook-A-Roo, Dahlberg Diver, large Lefty's Deceivers, and Clouser Minnows.

Lures for flounder include the Flounder Pounder, jigheads with soft plastic tails, and live shrimp. Lures for snook include large diving lures like a Long A, Shallow Mac, and Corkies.

Speckled trout are the reason to fish Rocky Slough.

LAND CUT

The Land Cut was made when the Intracoastal Waterway was dug. The surrounding tidal mud flats are often out of water during low tide. These mud flats are subject to changes in water depth with the wind playing a significant role on how the tides affect the area.

There are numerous fishing cabins lining the Intracoastal Waterway in the Land Cut. These cabins offer structure in an otherwise structure-less area. Fishing around these cabins and the deeper water of the Intracoastal Waterway can result in good catches. The relatively deeper areas provide cooler water and the shade created by the cabins also cools the water.

There are numerous spoil islands in the area that also hold fish. Look for birds hovering over bait and game fish in the afternoons.

Barges traversing the area also act to change the water flow and can cause a flooded area to temporarily lose all of its the water. Boaters and waders need to be aware of the changes these large vessels make and be prepared to adjust their plans accordingly.

The relatively deep water also provides refuge when the occasional cold front comes through the area protecting vulnerable fish like the common snook.

The Land Cut is over 20 miles long and offers many different types of fishing opportunities.

The Hole

This is a large area offering deeper water surrounded by shallow-water flats. The area is less than 3 feet deep and best worked from a shallow-water boat.

There is a channel running east towards Padre Island between Markers #3 and #4 that has water over 4 feet deep. Look to this channel in the hot summer days and anytime a cold front blows through the area.

Marker 21

Marker 21 in the Land Cut has been designated by the Texas Parks and Wildlife Department as the boundary line for separating the Upper and Lower Laguna Madre. Marker 21 is also where the regional catch limit for speckled trout changes from ten trout per day to five trout per day.

The Texas Parks and Wildlife Coastal Fisheries Division has gathered data for over 30 years. Their database shows that large speckled trout are declining in the Lower Laguna Madre. To help counteract this decline, the first regional limit was implemented in 2007.

Anglers should consider releasing all trout that will not be immediately consumed to further help with the replenishment.

Upper Laguna Madre Hub Cities

KINGSVILLE
Population: 25,575
County: Kleberg

ACCOMMODATIONS

Best Western Kingsville Inn, 2402 E King Ave / 361-595-5656 / 50 rooms /$69-$110
/ www.bestwesterntexas.com
Budget Inn, 716 S 14th St / 361-592-4322
Comfort Inn, 505 N Hwy 77 / 361-516-1120 / 47 rooms / $60-$80
Econolodge, 221 S Hwy 77 / 361-595-7700 / 34 rooms / www.econolodge.com
Economy Inn, 1415 S 14th St / 361-592-5214
Hampton Inn, 2489 S Hwy 77 / 361-592-9800 / www.hamptoninn.com
Motel 6, 101 S Hwy 77 / 361-592-5106 / www.motel6.com
Quality Inn, 221 S Hwy 77 / 361-592-5251 / 73 rooms / $60-$70 /
www.qualityinn.com
Rodeway Inn, 3430 Hwy 77 S Bypass / 361-595-5753 / www.rodewayinn.com
Super 8, 105 S Hwy 77 / 361-592-6471 / www.super8.com
Cast 'N Stay Lodge / 361-297-5636

CAMPGROUNDS

Angle Road Mobile Home Park, 1709 Howell Dr / 361-592-6291
Bayview Campgrounds / 361-297-5720
Country Estates Mobile Ranch, South FM 1717 / 361-592-4659
Oasis Mobile Home Park, 2415 E Santa Gertrudis Ave / 361-592-0764
University Mobile Home Park, 1200 W Kennedy Ave / 361-592-3791
Village Mobile Home Park, 130 W Corral Ave / 361-595-1375
Wrights Mobile Home and RV Park, 1629 Senator Truan Blvd / 361-592-7243

RESTAURANTS

CB's BBQ, 728 N 14th St / 361-516-1688
Baffin Bay Café, E Riviera Beach / 361-297-5354
Chili's, 2727 US 77 Bypass / 361-592-3840 / www.chilis.com
King's Inn, Loyola Beach / 361-297-5265
Little Caesars Pizza, 307 S 14th St / 361-592-4338 / www.littlecaesars.com
Pizza Hut, 1310 S 14th St / 361-595-5652 / www.pizzahut.com
El Corral, 1415 N 14th St / 361-592-7622
Whataburger, 2701 S Hwy 77 / 361-221-9559 / www.whataburger.com
Subway, 2700 S Hwy 77 / 361-595-7490 / www.subway.com
Dairy Queen, 715 E King Ave / 361-592-9471 / www.dairyqueen.com
Big House Burger, 2209 S Brahma Blvd / 361-592-0222

Cactus Café, 1900 E King Ave / 361-595-7792
El Marcado, 1021 E 14th / 361-595-5332
Gem's Pancake House, 129 S Hwy 77 / 361-592-2891
Sirloin Stockade, 1500 Brahma Blvd / 361-595-1182

FOR MORE INFORMATION

Visit www.kingsvilletexas.com

RIVIERA
Population: 230
County: Kleberg

ACCOMMODATIONS

Americas Best Value Inn, 6232 Hwy 77 / 361-296-3333 / www.bestvalueinn.com
Baffin Bay Lodge, 1299E CR 2327 / 361-297-5555 / www.baffinbaylodge.com
Wild Horse Lodge / 361-584-3098 / www.wildhorselodge.com
Baffin on the Rocks / 361-592-3474 / www.baffinontherocks.com
Turcotte Cottage / 361-297-5278
Baffin Bay Inn / 361-297-5158 / www.baffinbayinn.com

CAMPGROUNDS

Sea Wind RV Park, 1066 East FM 628 / 361-297-5738 / www.klebergpark.org
Riviera Beach RV Park, 991 East FM 771 / 361-297-5254 / www.rivierabeachrv.com

RESTAURANTS

King's Inn, FM 628 / 361-297-5265
Baffin Bay Café, East End FM 771 / 361-297-5354
Route 77 Pizzeria, Hwy 77 / 361-296-3643
Kubsch's Southern Fried Chicken, Hwy 77 / 361-296-3306
Pepe's Patio Hwy, 285 / 361-296-3926
Laredo Taco Restaurant (inside Stripes), Hwy 77 / 361-296-3818
Dairy Queen, Hwy 77 / 361-296-3243 / www.dairyqueen.com
Barn Door Restaurant, Hwy 77 / 361-296-3132

SPORTING GOODS

Browns Convenience, Store FM 628 & FM 1140 / 361-297-5747
Kraatz Bait Camp, East End FM 771 / 361-297-5717
Stripes, 6240 Hwy 77 / 361-296-3818

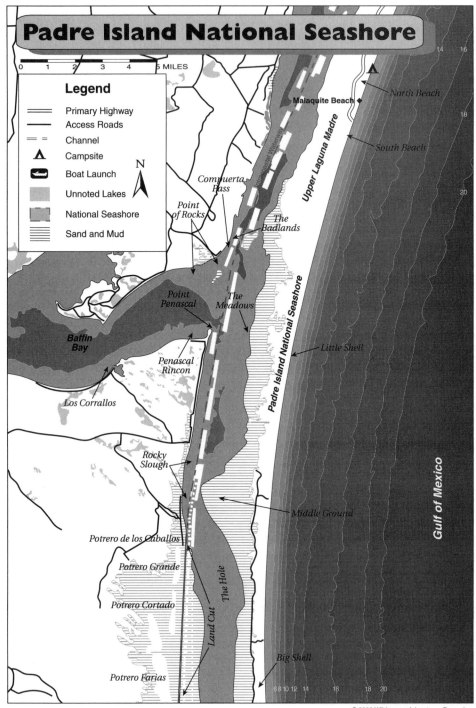

Padre Island National Seashore

0 1 2 3 4 5 MILES

Legend

Primary Highway
Access Roads
Channel
Campsite
Boat Launch
Unnoted Lakes
National Seashore
Sand and Mud

N

14 16
18
20

North Beach
Malaquite Beach
South Beach

Upper Laguna Madre

Intracoastal Waterway

Compuerta Pass
Point of Rocks
The Badlands

Point Penascal
The Meadows

Baffin Bay

Little Shell

Penascal Rincon

Padre Island National Seashore

Los Corrallos

Rocky Slough

Middle Ground

Gulf of Mexico

Potrero de los Caballos

Potrero Grande

The Hole

Potrero Cortado

Land Cut

Big Shell

Potrero Farias

6 8 10 12 14 16 18 20

© 2009 Wilderness Adventures Press, Inc.

Padre Island National Seashore

Padre Island National Seashore, first designated as a National Seashore in September 1962, is America's longest barrier island and offers the largest undeveloped wild coastal area outside of Alaska.

To get to Padre Island National Seashore, turn east on South Padre Island Drive (Highway 358) out of Corpus Christi. Cross the JFK Causeway and connect with Park Road 22. There is no bus or public transportation in the area. Pay attention to the sign stating NO GAS past this point on Highway 358/Park Road 22. Take time to fill up your gas tank before entering the park.

Padre Island National Seashore does not have any restaurants, but the park store has some picnic supplies. Camping is allowed and a free camping permit is available at the entrance station, visitor's center, or from any park ranger.

RV hookups and tent sites are available in the park. Camping is also available at Bird Island Basin, on North Beach, South Beach, and at the Yarborough Pass area.

The park allows only street legal vehicles and all ATVs are prohibited. Driving traffic is restricted to the beach area, and it's best to drive in the tracks along the beach. Your vehicle bearings will last longer if you stay out of the water as much as possible, but stay off the sand dunes. The speed limit along the beach is 25 miles per hour or less. Slow down around other anglers, cars or fishing camps. Speed limits are enforced.

Don't forget about the different tides you'll encounter. Going in on a low tide, the driving might be easy, but by the time you decide to return the tide may be in and the water may be all the way to the dunes. Plan your trip to take advantage of the lower tides.

The park has several different animals that visitors might encounter including two types of rattlesnakes. The endangered Kemp's Ridley sea turtle calls the seashore home, so be careful not to disturb any turtles in the area. Four other turtle species may also be found along the beach.

The Bird Island Basin area is on the western shore and is accessed through the Padre Island National Seashore Park. This area offers primitive camping in an isolated area and is a great place for kayakers. There is an excellent boat ramp and large parking area located at Bird Island Basin.

Anglers wishing to fish Padre Island National Seashore should consider several things before they venture down the beach. The beach can go from sand packed as hard as pavement to super soft in a very short distance. Beach conditions are posted at the entrance gate, so pay attention to them. The farther south you go the less people you will encounter.

Four-wheel drive vehicles are required just past the Malaquite visitor's center. When considering vehicles to use, a high ground clearance is more important than a vehicle high off the ground. If the transfer case or differential is low to the ground you may drag center and get stuck. Consider whether your vehicle is made for this type of trip.

The National Park office distributes a flyer with suggestions if you become stranded. One of the things they list is the fact that park employees will not rescue you unless there is imminent danger of vehicle loss. They do not want to tow your vehicle. Private towing companies are located in the area and park employees will assist you in contacting these companies. Be prepared because these towing companies are often very expensive.

The first thing most beach drivers should consider is lowering the air pressure in their tires. A slightly flat tire will get more traction than a thin, fully filled tire. Just remember to check your tire pressure once you get off the sand and outside the park.

Always take along a basic tool kit to get yourself unstuck if you get stranded on the beach. A basic tool kit should include a 30 foot length of cable, chain or towing rope strong enough to assist in removing the vehicle when stuck, several shovels, several pieces of plywood to place under tires to assist in getting traction, extra food, water, and gas. If you're not prepared with at least these basic tools and the proper vehicle, it may be best to hire one of the guides that regularly make the trip along the beach. More than one vehicle has been swamped while stuck.

The beach is crowded on holidays and most weekends but is almost deserted during the week and off-season.

Padre Island National Seashore offers a unique fishing opportunity. Go properly prepared and you'll have a great time. Don't forget to take out more trash than you take in. The beach belongs to all of us. Let's help keep it clean.

When fishing the surf along Padre Island National Seashore, it is best to have two different outfits rigged for action. Bait and spin fishers should have both light and heavy rigs ready at all times. The light rig should have 10- to 12-pound test line and the heavy rig should have 17- to 25-pound test line.

The same goes for flyfishing. Have an 8-weight rig and a 10- to 12-weight rig ready. You never know when a school of crevalle jack might cruise by. With both rigs at the ready you can cast the appropriate sized rig to the fish. This will increase the chances of landing the fish and releasing it in good condition.

Sinking lines are often the ticket to catching fish in the surf. It's best to have both floating and sinking rigs ready and let the fish determine which to use.

Many regular beach fishers even modify their vehicle for this fishing. You will see rod racks placed on the front or back of a vehicle with several outfits ready to go. The angler just has to stop the vehicle and grab the appropriate rig. You're not going to move too fast down the beach anyway and having rods out and ready saves time and missed opportunities.

Some of the best fishing areas are within the first 40 feet of the surf. Look for green water close all the way to the beach, as fish will often come right up using the deeper gut that runs along parts of the beach.

Also watch for jumping bait or diving birds, as either one signals fishing activity. Birds resting on the shoreline are a good indicator of yesterday's activity, but not necessarily today's.

Fish can often be seen in the crest of the waves chasing bait. Drive slowly and look for fish or splashes in the water. Watch the incoming waves to determine how far you should wade into the surf. The last wave to the beach may not come in as far as the next wave. Anglers should turn their bodies perpendicular to the waves if possible. This allows the waves to hit a smaller area than when an angler is facing the waves.

Anglers also need to move their feet on a regular basis. The sand under your feet is pulled out by the retreating wave, digging a hole. The longer you stand in one place the deeper the hole will become. Simply move to one side while you're fishing to avoid getting stuck in the sand.

Padre Island National Seashore is accessed from Corpus Christi. Review the Corpus Christi section for hub city information.

NORTH BEACH

North Beach is the area north of the barrier and park entrance at Malaquite Beach. Park Road 22 runs north out of the park and connects to the road at Padre Balli Park and the Bob Hall Pier. You can drive down the beach, but be cautious of loose sand.

Don't ignore this sign before venturing down the Padre Island National Seashore.

You can travel south from Padre Balli Park along the beach and re-connect with Park Road 22 without entering the Padre Island National Seashore and paying the park fee.

Fishing from North Beach is greatly affected by the wind. When the wind is calm, the water greens up to the beach. Both light casting and fly tackle can be effective under these conditions.

When the wind picks up anglers using casting or spinning tackle have an advantage. Many beach anglers use bait, both alive and dead, and heavy spinning tackle with long surf casting rods to get their offerings away from the shoreline. Bait is available at the Bob Hall Pier and there is a $1-per-angler and $1-per-rod (limit three rods) fee on the pier.

For casters wanting to try artificial lures, heavy spoons in silver and gold, large casting lures like a Bomber Long A, and soft plastics on jigheads work well. Fly casters should try baitfish patterns like Lefty's Deceivers and Clouser Minnows. Pay close attention to bait jumping in the area and cast to the disturbance.

The Bob Hall Pier has been the site of many tarpon catches over the years. The pier is still used today by bait anglers.

Amenities

Bob Hall Pier / 361-949-8558

The Bob Hall Pier is a great place for land-locked anglers.

South Beach

South Beach is the area immediately south of the barrier at the end of Malaquite Beach. A sign designating four-wheel drive vehicles past this point is posted on South Beach between the Malaquite Beach barrier and Little Shell Beach. Park rangers regularly patrol this beach.

Fishing from South Beach depends on the wind and size of the waves. On light wind days, both fly and spin casters can work the shoreline water with success. On windier days, casting tackle is required.

Malaquite Beach

Malaquite Beach is the type of beach most Texans are familiar with — brown sand with interspersed small shell fragments and brown water. The water does however green up when the winds are light. Many people come to the Malaquite Visitors Center and fish the area close to the center. For those willing to take a short hike or bicycle ride away from the visitors center, excellent fishing is available within a short distance.

The area directly in front of the visitor's center does not allow any vehicle traffic but just a short distance away from the center vehicles are allowed along the beach.

Be sure to read the posted beach conditions sign at the park entrance.

Little Shell

Little Shell Beach begins at about the 5-mile marker, where the slope of the beach starts to become steeper. Yarborough Pass is located opposite Little Shell Beach on the Laguna Madre side. This pass was dredged several times in the past, but closed up after each attempt to keep it open.

You don't have to wade out deep to successfully fish the Padre Island National Seashore.

Big Shell

Big Shell Beach begins at about the 18-mile marker and runs through mile marker 29. The slope of the beach becomes much steeper at this area, along with larger shells and coarser sand. The Big Shell area is also where gulf currents converge and hit the beach area with the most direct force.

Anglers wading along the beach need to be cautious. Large sharks regularly patrol this area and a favorite saying along the beach is "if you're in deeper than your knees, you're part of the food chain". Wade with caution.

There can be spectacular fishing along both Big Shell and Little Shell beaches. Drive down the beach until you notice prey fish or shrimp jumping, or birds diving. Quietly stop your vehicle and make casts into the disturbed area. Gold or silver treble-hooked spoons work great. For fly casters simple white or chartreuse baitfish patterns work well.

It's best to have your tackle ready with lures or flies already tied on because you'll want to be able to quickly leave your vehicle and make a cast if you see busting bait. If you take time to change flies or lures the school of fish will be farther down the beach and out of range.

It's a good idea to have several outfits rigged and ready. Having both a floating and a sinking lure or fly already rigged will allow you to quickly cast to the fish while they're near. Redfish, speckled trout, ladyfish, and crevalle jack all patrol this section of the beach.

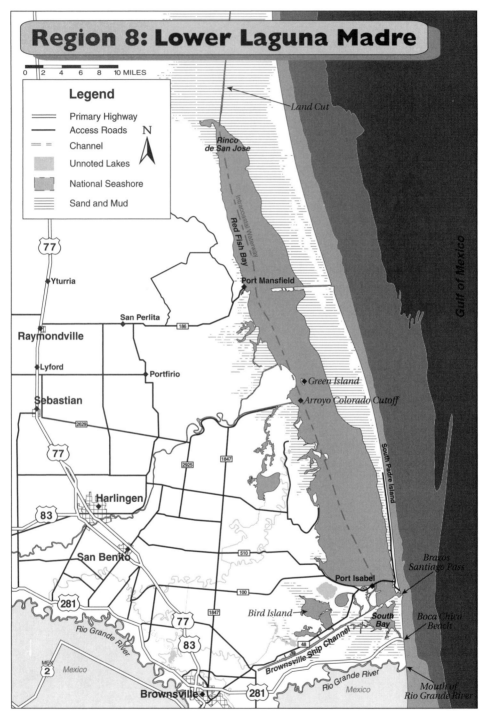

Region 8: Lower Laguna Madre

0   2   4   6   8   10 MILES

Legend

━━━ Primary Highway
─── Access Roads
══ ═ Channel
Unnoted Lakes
National Seashore
Sand and Mud

N

Land Cut

Rinco de San Jose

Intracoastal Waterway

Red Fish Bay

77

Yturria

Port Mansfield

San Perlita

186

Raymondville

Lyford

Portfirio

Green Island

Arroyo Colorado Cutoff

Sebastian

2629

77

2925

1847

South Padre Island

Gulf of Mexico

Harlingen

83

San Benito

510

Brazos Santiago Pass

Port Isabel

281

77

1847

Bird Island

100

South Bay

Boca Chica Beach

83

Rio Grande River

MEX 2

Mexico

Brownsville Ship Channel

48

Brownsville

281

Rio Grande River

Mexico

Mouth of Rio Grande River

Region 8: Lower Laguna Madre

When most people think about going to the Texas coast they think about South Padre Island, which is the most commercialized area of the coast. When out-of-state spring breakers think of the Texas coast, they usually think of the beach area of far South Padre Island.

For fishers, South Padre Island and the Lower Laguna Madre Region offer some truly unique fishing opportunities. The southern most section of the Lower Laguna Madre is more like fishing in Florida than fishing in east Texas coastal waters.

The Lower Laguna Madre offers anglers a chance at a true sub-tropical fish – snook. It also offers almost year-round fishing. The area rarely experiences a wintertime freeze. Rainfall is limited and there are no rivers to flood out a trip in the spring or fall. An angler fishing South Bay for the first time could easily be fooled into thinking they were in Florida with the vast amount of turtle grass and crystal clear water in the area.

Port Mansfield, in the northern part of the Lower Laguna Madre area, is connected to the Gulf of Mexico by East Cut (also known as the Mansfield Ship Channel). East Cut allows quick access to the Gulf of Mexico and all of the fish normally associated with gulf waters. On the gulf side of East Cut, large jetties protect the shoreline and boats using the cut.

Seasonal Fishing Chart - Region 8: Lower Laguna Madre

	Jan	Feb	Mar	Apr	May	Jun	Jul	Aug	Sep	Oct	Nov	Dec
Redfish	++	+++	+++	+++	+++	+++	+++	+++	+++	+++	+++	++
Spotted Seatrout	++	+++	+++	+++	+++	+++	+++	+++	+++	+++	+++	++
Flounder			+	++	+++	+++	+++	+++	+++	+++	+	+
Black Drum	++	+++	+++	+++	+++	+++	+++	+++	+++	+++	++	+
Sheepshead	++	+++	+++	+++	+++	+++	+++	+++	+++	++	++	+
Crevalle Jack					++	+++	+++	+++	+++			
Spanish Mackerel					++	+++	+++	+++	+++			
Gray Snapper					++	+++	+++	+++	+++			
Tarpon					+	+	+	+	+			
Pompano				+	+	+	+	+				
Snook						+	+	+	+			

+++ = Exceptional, ++ = Very Good, + = Available

Port Mansfield has an excellent harbor with two boat ramps and a marina. Both boat ramps have large parking areas close by. The marina is protected from the wind and boaters should use idle speed while going through the marina.

There are two convenience-type stores that offer basic fishing supplies and groceries. There are several motels, numerous cabins for rent, and several on-the-water places to purchase gas including one that offers 24-hour service if you have a credit card.

Most of the water east of the Intracoastal Waterway is very shallow, therefore a shallow-water boat is required. This is a large bay and there are literally miles of shallow-water flats with water less than 2 feet deep. Most of the time this water remains very clear and anglers can see fish from a long distance. The far eastern side of the Lower Laguna Madre is mostly firm sand bottom. The western side has grass-covered flats. East winds help cloud the water and cause the grasses in the area to turn loose, further clouding the water.

Port Mansfield Guide, Captain Trisha, likes to be prepared with both a floating and a sinking lure.

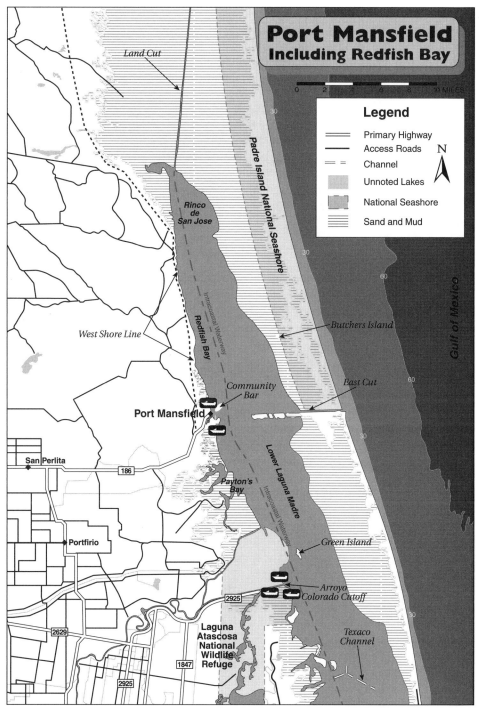

Port Mansfield
Including Redfish Bay

Land Cut

0   2   4   6   8   10 MILES

Legend

Primary Highway
Access Roads
Channel
Unnoted Lakes
National Seashore
Sand and Mud

N

Padre Island National Seashore

Rinco de San Jose

Intracoastal Waterway

Redfish Bay

West Shore Line

Butchers Island

Community Bar

East Cut

Port Mansfield

San Perlita

186

Payton's Bay

Lower Laguna Madre

Intracoastal Waterway

Gulf of Mexico

Portfirio

Green Island

2925

Arroyo Colorado Cutoff

2629

Laguna Atascosa National Wildlife Refuge

Texaco Channel

1847

2925

In the evening, visitors to Port Mansfield will see numerous deer right in town including a few that will make any hunter envious. These deer are fed by the community and caution should be used when driving through town especially at night. The deer regularly wander throughout town and can been seen in many of the yards at night. Get off the water a little early and be in place when the public supported feeders go off to see both deer and wild turkeys.

The tides in the area account for only about a half of a foot of water rise and fall. All other tidal movement is caused by the wind. Some areas will be completely out of water at low tide and other shallow areas will be completely flooded during strong winds. Know the area you're going to fish or hire a guide.

The Texas International Fishing Tournament (TIFT), held annually at the end of July is a big fishing tournament drawing thousands of people to the Lower Laguna Madre. Anglers may want to avoid the area during this time. To check on tournament dates, go to www.tift.org.

RINCON DE SAN JOSE

Rincon de San Jose is the area just south of the Land Cut on the western shoreline, and it offers good wade fishing for redfish and speckled trout year round. The backside of the island offers a protected area if the winds happen to get too high to fish other areas. Just be prepared for a long boat ride when coming from Port Mansfield because this area is over 15 miles from the marina.

WEST SHORELINE

The West Shoreline from just south of Rincon de San Jose to just north of Port Mansfield offers shallow-water wade fishing. The land inshore is all private. Any strong easterly wind will mud up this area quickly.

Landmarks in the area include Rincon de San Jose at the northern end and Big Oak Mott and Little Oak Mott (two groupings of oak trees) midway down the bay. Anglers should cast and wade parallel to the shoreline. If there is more than one angler, work different depths out from the shore.

Water depths in the Oak Mott areas drop off to over 6 feet in some places. Work the deep-water drop-off drifting in a boat.

Anglers can also drift fish this area from a boat if the wind allows. Fish the shallow water for redfish and the drop-off for speckled trout. There are grass patches in the area that attract redfish on a regular basis.

Fly anglers need spoon flies, Clouser Minnows, and Lefty's Deceivers for redfish and foam poppers and Clouser Minnows for speckled trout.

Redfish lures include soft plastic on jigheads and weedless copper and gold spoons. Speckled trout can be caught on topwater lures and soft plastics.

REDFISH BAY

Redfish Bay is the area north of East Cut (or the Mansfield Ship Channel). This is the second bay named Redfish Bay on the Texas coast. The Intracoastal Waterway runs though the middle of the bay and provides both deeper water and assists with the flushing of the entire bay system.

The western edge of Redfish Bay is part of the King Ranch. The western shoreline provides wadeable water along its length. Anglers are recommended to anchor and wade instead of fishing out of the boat. Most of the shoreline is wadeable, but you may encounter some muddy areas.

Pay attention to the wind because a strong easterly wind will make the water along the shoreline muddy in color and fishing will not be as productive.

Closer to Port Mansfield, the Community Bar offers wade fishing with quick access to deep water.

There are several islands in the bay including Butchers Island. Wade around these islands looking for tailing redfish and black drum. Move slowly so the fish can't hear you or feel your wake while wading.

When you encounter a group of fish, make a cast to the outside edge rather than directly in the middle of the group. This will give you a chance of catching more than one fish out of the school.

When the group spooks, wait several minutes to give them a chance to re-group and then cast to the group again. If you work slowly and quietly, the school may reform several times and give you several chances to catch fish from a single group.

There is a series of cuts in the bay that are over 5 feet deep. These cuts connect areas that range from a half-foot to 3 feet deep, and offer fish the protection of deeper water and easy access to prey fish in shallow water. These cuts hold fish during the hottest and coolest times of day and year.

Port Mansfield is one of the few places outside of Florida where manatee have been spotted, and therefore boat traffic in the marina is strictly idle speed. If you see a manatee please avoid getting too close to it.

Boat Ramps

Public boat ramps are located on both the north and south side of the Willacy County Navigational District marina. Port Mansfield Marina, 600 Mansfield Dr 956-944-2331 has gas on the water.

EAST CUT

The small town of Port Mansfield is directly west of East Cut (the Mansfield Ship Channel). There are numerous spoil islands on each side of East Cut that offer excellent fishing. Look for channels that lead back onto the flats around the spoil islands for the deepest water in the area.

Use soft plastics on jigheads or sinking flies like Clouser Minnows on sinking line when flyfishing for redfish and trout. Flounder will also frequent the areas with very shallow water, and anglers can work the drop-off from the shallow areas around the spoil islands into East Cut for speckled trout. Make repeated casts to the area as fish are continuously cruising along the deep-water drop-off. As you get closer to the Gulf of Mexico, you may also encounter Spanish mackerel along the drop-off.

Fish for redfish in the shallow water and try for speckled trout where the water drops off into the channel. The shallows heat up very quickly, even during winter (once the sun is up). Give the flats an hour or so to wake up and then look for fish in the warmer shallows.

Fly casters can use poppers and sinking flies like Clouser Minnows. Cast up in the water less than 2 feet deep for flounder.

Bait and spin casters can use soft plastics on jigheads, including pumpkinseed with chartreuse tail, red and white and Texas Cockroach. Anglers able to cast farther out into the cut and retrieve their lure down the drop-off line will catch the most fish.

Redfish from the second Redfish Bay.

Payton's Bay and Spoil Islands

South of Port Mansfield along the Intracoastal Waterway is another series of spoil islands. These islands offer shallow areas close to deeper waters of the Intracoastal Waterway. Anglers can work around these islands for redfish and speckled trout. Check the bottom before leaving your boat as some areas are soft. Long casts made with surface lures like a Topdog, Corky, or Super Spook Jr. often produce spectacular surface strikes. If a fish misses the lure, let it sit for a while before moving it again. The fish will often come back for a second strike thinking it has wounded the bait.

This is a distance game and the casters that can cast the farthest will catch the most fish. Make sure your reels are properly greased and working in top-notch order. It is a good idea to use a light running line with a heavier 4-foot leader to gain maximum distance. If the fish in the area repeatedly miss topwater lures, change to soft plastics on jigheads.

Payton's Bay is the shallow area west of the Intracoastal Waterway. Most of the area has a soft bottom, so wade fishers need to check before jumping out of the boat.

Green Island and Bird Island

Green Island and Bird Island at the mouth of the Arroyo Colorado Cutoff offer wadeable areas for the fisherman. That said, waders in the Bird Island area need to be careful of boats coming out of the Arroyo Colorado Cutoff.

Watch for hovering birds in the afternoon in this area. Drift into the birds instead of motoring into them. Make casts as long as possible to prevent scaring the fish under the birds.

Arroyo Colorado Cutoff

The Arroyo Colorado Cutoff is a man-made extension of the Arroyo Colorado, and offers fairly deep water with vast areas of very shallow flats. The Cutoff goes directly into the Intracoastal Waterway just south of Port Mansfield. Boaters and waders in the area need to be aware of boat traffic entering the Intracoastal Waterway from the Cutoff.

There are numerous fishing cabins along the Cutoff. Fish around the cabins, especially in the shaded areas. Old pilings and boat docks also provide excellent fish hiding locations.

Anglers should pay attention to the birds in the area. Gulls will often spot fish cruising the area pushing bait along. Always try to get in front of the birds and don't run a boat through the school of fish. Try to intercept the fish. Schools of fish disturbed by a boat running directly through them will often go down and not reform. Also remember you are in very shallow water and any noise will be transmitted to the entire area, often spooking fish.

The Arroyo Colorado Cutoff is now the major waterway for water entering the Laguna Madre from the west. The original Arroyo Colorado does not have the flow it did before the Cutoff was dredged. The Arroyo snakes and curves to the north of the Cutoff.

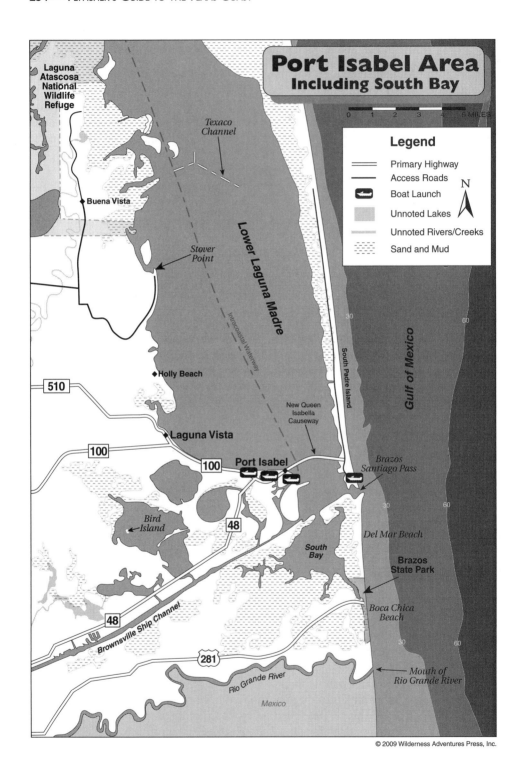

© 2009 Wilderness Adventures Press, Inc.

Boat Ramps

Adolph Thomae, Jr. County Park at the end of FM 2925, Arroyo City / 956-748-2044
Gabby's on the Arroyo, FM 2925 & FM 1847, Arroyo City
Sanchez Bait Stand, 36485 Marshall Hutts, Arroyo City

Spoil Islands in Lower Laguna Madre

There are numerous spoil islands located in the Lower Laguna Madre. The area from the Arroyo Colorado Cutoff to the Intracoastal Waterway across from Stover Point is dotted with spoil islands.

Watch for hovering birds and visible fish in these areas. Most of the water in this area outside the Intracoastal Waterway is less than 3 feet deep and best fished from a shallow-running boat.

There are several channels, including the Texaco Channel, that branch off from the Intracoastal Waterway and provide deeper water. Many of these channels are only a couple of feet deep, but in an area with little water over 2 feet deep, any deeper water is a fish magnet. Not far past Stover Point the water drops off to 4-foot depths and deeper.

The area just east of Laguna Vista is a big, wide-open bay. The predominant southeast wind will assist in making long drifts through this area. Make long casts with soft plastics or topwater lures.

The areas along the shoreline are wadeable and are ideal locations for kayak and canoe fishers. Fly anglers should concentrate on the west shoreline using floating line with a popper or Clouser Minnow.

The eastern shoreline of the Lower Laguna Madre also offers wade and drift fishing. Most of the water east of the Intracoastal Waterway is very shallow.

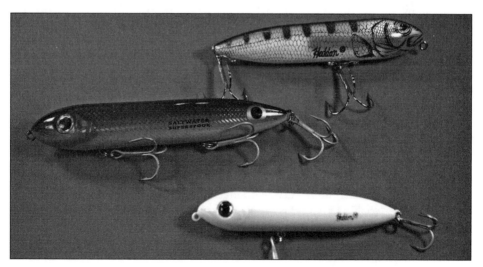

A Super Spook or Super Spook Jr. is a great Port Mansfield lure.

SOUTH PADRE ISLAND

South Padre Island is one of the few areas along the Texas coast that is commercially developed, with numerous high-rise hotels lining the beach area. For anglers wishing to get away from the crowd, the beach just a few miles north of the hotel district offers areas not nearly as crowded. Those wishing to venture up the beach should read the section on Padre Island National Seashore and pay attention to the hazards associated with traveling Texas beaches. Four-wheel drive vehicles are a must when traveling north out of South Padre Island along the beach. Go prepared or suffer the consequences.

Spring break along South Padre Island is like spring break anywhere — noisy with lots of people. If you're a serious fisherman you'll probably want to avoid South Padre Island during the spring break season, which in Texas is the month of March.

Anglers are better served fishing this area in the off-season. Hotel rates drop drastically and the crowd is gone beginning in the early fall. There are several restaurants and you can usually get served within a reasonable amount of time.

Fish the surf zone with the same tackle as listed in the Padre Island National Seashore section. Fly casters need to consider the wind and try to fish early or late in the day. A basic outfit of casting or spinning tackle will handle most situations.

For those wanting a fish dinner, several of the restaurants on the island will cook your fish. Just ask when you go in.

Boat Ramps

Anchor Marine, 40 Tarpon Ave, Port Isabel / 956-943-9323
City Park, end of Pompano, Port Isabel
Park center, 702 Champion, Port Isabel
Pirate's Fishing Pier, 204 North Garcia, Port Isabel / 956-943-7437
South Point Marina, 500 South Point Dr, Port Isabel / 956-943-7926
White Sands Motor Lodge and Marina, 418 W Highway 100, Port Isabel / 956-943-6161
Destination South Padre Island RV Park, 1 Padre Blvd, South Padre Island / 956-761-5665
Jim's Pier, 209 W Whiting South, Padre Island / 956-761-2865
Sea Ranch Marina, 1 Padre Blvd, South Padre Island / 956-761-7777
South Padre Marina, 6101 Padre Blvd, South Padre Island / 956-761-9457
Ted's Restaurant, 5717 Padre Blvd, South Padre Island / 956-761-5327

BRAZOS SANTIAGO PASS

Brazos Santiago Pass is the waterway connecting the Brownsville Ship Channel to the Gulf of Mexico. This area offers anglers a chance to catch tarpon and snook as well as the normal coastal species. The pass can be reached from either Port Isabel or South Padre Island. There are long jetties on the gulf side of the Pass to help control the waves in the area.

Tarpon and snook use the pass as a feeding station. These fish are most active during the early morning and late evening hours. The area where the pass cuts through Padre Island offers excellent fishing for most of the sport fish of Texas. Work the areas where the land drops off drastically for the best results.

BROWNSVILLE SHIP CHANNEL

The Brownsville Ship Channel is a manmade body of water that reaches inland several miles from the Gulf of Mexico. The Brownsville Ship Channel serves as a pathway for large ships and tankers to a protected inland dock. The ship channel is used by ships refueling, loading and unloading cargo, and by ship salvagers.

There is the constant sound of people working in the ship channel. Loud hammers against big metal pipes, cutting torches burning through inch-thick steel, and cranes lifting and pulling pieces of metal apart all make this a noisy environment. But even in this heavy industrial waterway, there are underwater microenvironments that encourage fish to use it as their home.

The Brownsville Ship Channel is home to a strong and growing population of common snook, large speckled trout, the largest gray snapper found in the state, and other fish.

Two of the best tools for helping find snook in the ship channel are your ears. Snook make a very distinctive pop when attacking prey. The pop sounds more like a gun shot than anything else. If you here one of these pops, stop and try to locate where the noise came from.

Large speckled trout call the Brownsville Ship Channel home.

There are several long shallow flats along the sides of the ship channel that snook regularly use to catch their prey. The relatively shallow waters allow snook and other fish to patrol the area without being too far from quick access to the deep water and the safety of the channel.

This quick access to deep water is probably the reason snook have faired so well in this otherwise unnatural location. Snook can quickly drop off into deep water anytime cold weather comes into the area (south Texas cold fronts are rare but they do occur). The deep water of the channel allows snook to feed in the warm shallows and drop down into the deeper water when needed.

Anglers seeking snook in the channel need to maneuver quietly through the area. An electric trolling motor works best but there are also areas where a push pole will work. Watch for shrimp jumping high out of the water and listen for that loud snook pop.

Fly anglers should use large Dahlberg Divers and poppers for top-water action. Like anytime an angler goes after a fish on the surface, wait to feel the fish before setting the hook. More than one snook has been missed because the angler was too anxious and pulled the fly away before the snook had the fly firmly in its mouth.

The Brownsville Ship Channel - the ugliest fishing hole in the world.

Sinking flies to try include Clouser Minnows and large Lefty's Deceivers. Solid white works well as does white with a little gold or silver flash material.

Casting tackle used for snook includes large diving lures and poppers. Soft plastic baitfish in solid white, white with gold or silver speckles, and white with chartreuse all work well.

Make sure all flies and lures have very sharp hooks because snook have tough mouths. It is also a good idea to use a strong leader on both fly and casting tackle. Snook have very sharp gill plate covers that can quickly cut lightweight lines. A 3-foot leader made of 30-pound monofilament or fluorocarbon works well.

For the best results, make long casts into shallow areas while making a quiet approach. Also look for any object in the water. Snook like to hang around old pilings, pieces of metal from salvaged ships, or anything else that might give them a little cover.

Snook have made a remarkable recovery in south Texas. Anglers are encouraged to release any snook they catch regardless of what the limit may be. With continued conservation, the snook population will continue to grow and be strong enough to outlast any severe cold front that might hit the area.

Large speckled trout also use the ship channel as a home. Speckled trout, like snook, like to be able to quickly drop off into the protective deep water at the first sign of danger. This is a hostile environment for fish and the largest trout know how to avoid potential danger.

Trout anglers should work the junctions where the ship docking channels intersect the main ship channel. Hit each side of the point with long casts while your boat is still well away from the area.

Fly anglers should use large Clouser Minnows and large Lefty's Deceivers. Solid white and variations with white work best, but don't be afraid to try darker colors.

Soft plastics on jigheads work best for the casting crowd. Topwater lures like a Super Spook or Topdog also work. Topwater lures in bone or white work well.

Another great fish found in the Brownsville Ship Channel is the gray snapper or mangrove snapper. In most parts of Texas gray snapper rarely exceed 16 inches. In the manmade world of the Brownsville Ship Channel, gray snapper reach lengths over 25 inches and offer a great sport on light tackle.

Gray snapper are usually found around some type of structure. Look for old pilings, parts of boats, and docks. Cast to anything a fish might be able to use as cover. The gray snapper found in the ship channel can grow very large, so anglers are should use a strong leader to attach their lures and flies.

Use sinking lures similar to those suggested for snook in slightly smaller sizes for gray snapper. Solid white or white with another color seem to work best. Quickly pull any fish hooked away from the structure because gray snapper will do their best to dart back into the protected area and most often cut a light line. These are fun fish to catch on light tackle.

At least one guide has reported catching gray snapper over 25 inches long, so don't be surprised by how big these far-south Texas specimens get.

SOUTH BAY

South Bay is the last bay along the Texas coast. The crystal-clear water and seagrass of South Bay look more like south Florida than Texas. Boaters need to pay particular attention to damaging the seagrasses with a boat prop and are better served poling through the area.

Redfish, speckled trout, and even snook inhabit South Bay. This is a great wintertime fishing location, which rarely sees freezing temperatures. The bay is protected by the barrier islands from strong eastern winds.

Fly, bait, and spin casters can cast to visible fish in South Bay's clear water. Most of the water in the bay is less than 2 feet deep, making it an ideal sight casting location.

Boca Chica Beach

Just south of the Brownsville Ship Channel and South Bay is Boca Chica Beach and Del Mar Beach. This is one of the most remote areas along the entire Texas coast.

Take Highway 4 east off Highway 77 to get to Boca Chica. A four-wheel drive vehicle is a must for this trip if you're going to travel along the beach. Anglers can fish the surf or South Bay. Going north takes you to the Brownsville Ship Channel. Heading south leads to the mouth of the Rio Grande River.

Go to this area prepared. Take plenty of water, a cell phone, GPS, and tools to get your vehicle unstuck.

RIO GRANDE RIVER

Hart Stilwell is considered by many to be the grandfather of Texas coastal fishing. Certainly there were earlier coastal anglers, and there have been more famous anglers. But he was definitely one of the first to bring national attention to the region. Hart Stilwell recorded accounts of catching tarpon from the shore of the Rio Grande River in his classic 1946 book Hunting and Fishing in Texas. He used heavy casting tackle and large lures to catch 40- to 60-pound tarpon from shore.

In 2001, the flow of the Rio Grande River did not reach the Gulf of Mexico. Since then, it sporadically flows into the gulf depending on how wet the year is in far west Texas.

There may not be enough water left in the Rio Grande for all of the users upstream and the tarpon. I, for one, would like the experience of hooking a tarpon from the shoreline of the river. If we all become more aware of our water resources, who knows? Maybe one day, the sound of a screaming reel and an angler running down the shore of the Rio Grande River will be heard again. It's all up to us.

Lower Laguna Madre Hub Cities

BROWNSVILLE
Population: 175,000
County: Cameron

ACCOMMODATIONS

Best Western Rose Garden, 845 N Expressway 77 / 956-546-5501 / 121 rooms / $95-$120 / www.bestwesterntexas.com

Courtyard by Marriott, 3955 N Expressway / 956-350-4600 / 90 rooms / www.courtyard.com

Days Inn, 715 N Expressway / 956-541-2201 / 124 rooms / $50-$100 / www.daysinn.com

Hawthorn Suites, 3759 n Expressway / 956-574-6900 / www.hawthorne.com

Holiday Inn Express, 1985 N Expressway / 800-465-4329 / 74 rooms / $89-$259 / www.holidayinn.com

La Quinta, 5051 North Expressway / 956-350-2118 / 62 rooms / $70-$95 / www.lq.com

Motel 6, 2255 N Expressway 77 / 956-546-4699 / www.motel6.com

Palace Inn Motel East, 7364 Padre Island Hwy / 956-832-0202 / 44 rooms /

Red Roof Inns, 2377 N Expressway 77 / 956-504-2300 / 122 rooms / www.redroof.com

Staybridge Suites, 2900 Pablo Kisel Blvd / 956-504-9500 / 99 rooms / $80-$160 / www.staybridge.com

CAMPGROUNDS

Gulf Breeze Mobile & RV Park, 1313 N Minnesota Ave / 956-831-4606 / www.gulfbreezeresort.net

Rio RV Park, 8801 Boca Chica Blvd / 866-279-1775 / www.riorvpark.com

Riverbend Resort, 4551 Hwy 281 / 956-548-0191

RESTAURANTS

Captain Bob's Seafood, 2034 E Price Rd / 956-554-3445 / www.captainbobsrestaurant.com

Carinos Italian Grill, 2600 N expressway 77 / 956-986-2550 / www.carinos.com

Chicago Deli, 1552 Palm Blvd / 956-550-9910

El Pato Mexican Food, 2425 Paredes Line Rd / 956-547-9100

Jason's Deli, 4365 S Expressway 77 / 956-350-2400 / www.jasonsdeli.com

La Mexicana, 2050 N Expressway / 956-554-3084

McDonalds, 2721 Boca Chica Blvd / 956-554-7715 / www.mcdonalds.com

Red Lobster, 1075 FM 802 / 956-544-2614 / www.redlobster.com

Rudy's Bar-B-Q, 2780 N expressway 83 / 956-542-2532 / www.rudys.com

Taco Cabana, 4250 N Expressway 77 / 956-350-0515 / www.tacocabana.com
Whataburger, 6100 FM 802 / 956-831-0761 / www.whataburger.com

SPORTING GOODS

Academy Sport, 4305 Old Highway 77 / 956-554-6900 / www.academy.com
Boaters World, 2952 Boca Chica Blvd / 956-542-0340 / www.boatersworld.com

Snook in Texas!

EDINBURG
Population: 48,465
County: Hidalgo

ACCOMMODATIONS

Best Western, 2708 S Business Hwy 281 / 956-318-0442 / 56 rooms / $70-$100 / www.bestwesterntexas.com

Comfort Inn, 4001 Closner / 956-318-1117 / 55 rooms / $60-$90

Echo Hotel, 1903 S Closner Blvd / 800-422-0336 / 102 rooms / $47-$62 / www.echohoteltx.com

CAMPGROUNDS

Cactus Garden RV Park, Rt 5 Box 44 / 956-383-5757

Gazebo RV Park, 1314 E Chapin Rd / 956-384-9283

Orange Grove RV Park, 4901 E Hwy 107 / 956-383-7931 / www.ogrvp.com

Royal Palms RV Park, 3319 W University Dr. / 956-383-8004

Valhalla MH & RV Park, 505 E Ramseyer Rd / 956-381-8220

Valley Gateway RV Park, Rt 3 Box 97P / 956-383-1883

RESTAURANTS

107 Café, 4100 W University Dr / 956-380-1107

Crusitas Kitchen, 804 S Closner Blvd / 956-287-2822

Jack in the Box, 102 E Monte Cristo Rd / 956-316-1558 / www.jackinthebox.com

McDonalds, 2120 W University Dr / 956-316-3424 / www.mcdonalds.com

Playa Azul Seafood, 2616 E University Dr / 956-381-6230

Starlite Burger, 1106 W University Dr / 956-383-8111

Taco Grill, 815 N Closner / 956-287-7750

Whataburger, 1812 W University Dr / 956-380-0373 / www.whataburger.com

FOR MORE INFORMATION

Visit www.edinburgtexas.com

HARLINGEN
Population: 57,564
County: Cameron

ACCOMMODATIONS

Best Western Casa Villa, 4317 S Expressway 83 / 956-412-1500 / 67 rooms / $70-$159 / www.bestwesterntexas.com

Comfort Inn, 406 N Expressway 77 / 956-412-5751 / 51 rooms / $50-$90

Country Inn, 3825 South Expressway 83 / 956-428-0043 / 65 rooms / $80-$120 / www.countryinns.com

Days Inn, 1901 West Tyler Ave / 956-425-7227 / 70 rooms / $42-$52 / www.daysinn.com

Econo Lodge, 1821 West Tyler / 956-425-1810 / 100 rooms / $40-$60 / www.econolodge.com

Hampton Inn, 1202 Ed Carey Dr. / 956-428-9801 / 70 rooms / $70-$119 / www.hamptoninn.com

Holiday Inn Express, 501 South P Street / 956-428-9292 / 129 rooms / $70-$100 / www.hiexpress.com

La Quinta, 1002 S Expressway 83 / 956-428-6888 / 130 rooms / $75-$109 / www.lq.com

Ramada Limited, 4401 South Expressway 83 / 800-272-6232 / 45 rooms / $60-$100 / www.ramada.com

Super 8 Motel, 1115 South Expressway 77-83 / 800-800-8000 / 59 rooms / $45-$60 / www.super8.com

CAMPGROUNDS

Carefree Valley Resort, 4506 N Business 77 / 956-425-2540

Park Place Estates RV Resort, 5401 W Business 83 / 956-428-4414 / www.parkplaceestatesharlingen.com

Posada Del Sol RV, 28513 S Palm Court Dr / 956-428-2448 / www.posadadelsoltx.com

Sunshine RV Resort, 1900 Grace Ave / 956-428-4137

RESTAURANTS

Big John's BBQ, 3806 W Business 83 / 956-423-3240 / www.bigjohnsbarbq.com

Capital City Burgers & Shakes, 501 S 77 Sunshine Strip / 956-440-9600

El Pato Mexican Food, 601 S 77 Sunshine Strip / 956-687-5227

Wendy's, 1415 Ed Carey Drive / 956-425-8465 / www.wendys.com

Dairy Queen, 1613 N && Sunshine Strip / 956-423-6600 / www.dairyqueen.com

El Rancho Mexican, 206 N 77 Sunshine Strip / 956-412-9291

Golden Corral, 1605 W Tyler Ave / 956-425-6907 / www.goldencorral.com

Jason's Deli, 2224 S 77 Sunshine Strip / 956-428-3354 / www.jasonsdeli.com

La Playa Mexican Café, 502 S 77 Sunshine Strip / 956-421-2000

Lone Star Restaurant, 4201 W Business 83 / 956-423-8002
Luby's Cafeteria, 2506 S 77 Sunshine Strip / 956-423-4812 / www.lubys.com
Oyster Bar Restaurant, 2301 S 77 Sunshine Strip / 956-425-9904
Pepe's Mexican Restaurant, 117 S 77 Sunshine Strip / 956-423-3663
Quiznos Sub, 1338 N Ed Carey Dr. / 956-412-2221 / www.quiznos.com
Rudy's Country Store & Bar-B-Q, 2780 N Expressway / 956-542-2532 /
www.rudys.com

AIRPORT

Valley International Airport, 3002 Heritage Way / 956-430-8605 /
www.flythevalley.com

FOR MORE INFORMATION

Harlingen Chamber of Commerce, 311 E Tyler 78550 / 800-531-7346 /
www.harlingen.com

McALLEN
Population: 120,000
County: Hidalgo

ACCOMMODATIONS

Aloha Motel, 301 E Business 83 / 956-682-6082 / 44 rooms / $40-$65 / www.alohamotel.net

Best Western Rose Garden Inn, 300 E Expressway 83 / 956-630-3333 / 92 rooms / $65-$80 / www.bestwesterntexas.com

Comfort Suites, 800 Expressway 83 / 956-213-0333 / 56 rooms / $80-$110

Courtyard by Marriott, 2131 S 10th St / 956-668-7800 / 110 rooms / www.courtyard.com

Days Inn, 1421 S 10th St / 956-686-1586 / 73 rooms / $60-$75 / www.daysinn.com

Drury Inn, 612 W Expressway 83 / 956-687-5100 / 89 rooms / www.druryhotels.com

Embassy Suites Hotel, 1800 S 2nd St / 956-686-3000 / 252 rooms / www.embassysuites.com

Fairfield Inn, 2117 S 10th St / 956-971-9444 / 40 rooms / www.fairfieldinn.com

Hilton Garden Inn, 617 Expressway 83 / 956-664-2900 / 104 rooms / www.hilton.com

Holiday Inn Express, 1921 S 10th St / 956-994-0505 / 108 rooms / www.holidayinn.com

La Copa Inn, 101 W Houston St / 956-683-7700 / 33 rooms / $45-$60

La Quinta Inn, 1100 S 10th St / 956-687-1101 / 120 rooms / www.lq.com

Microtel Inn, 801 E Expressway 83 / 956-630-2727 / 102 rooms / www.microtelinn.com

Ramada Limited, 1505 S 9th St / 956-686-4401 / 49 rooms / www.ramada.com

Residence Inn by Marriott, 220 W Expressway 83 / 956-994-8626 / 78 rooms / www.marriott.com

Super 8, 1420 E Jackson Ave / 956-682-1190 / 40 rooms / www.super8.com

CAMPGROUNDS

Valley Grande RV & Mobile Home Park, 4101 W Expressway 83 / 956-686-8144

RESTAURANTS

Blue Onion, 925 Dove Ave / 956-682-9884 / www.myblueonion.com

Chick-Fil-A, 1300 E Jackson Ave / 956-664-1994 / www.chick-fil-a.com

Chili's, 501 Expressway 83 / 956-971-0213 / www.chilis.com

Church's Chicken, 3817 Pecan Blvd / 956-618-4953 / www.churchs.com

Costa Messa Restaurant, 1621 N 11th St / 956-618-5449

Country Pancake House, 809 Savannah Ave / 956-686-4232

Double Dave's Pizza, 7700 N 10th St / 956-585-9274 / www.doubledave.com

El Pato Mexican Food, 2035 N 23rd / 956-618-2829

Golden Corral, 1100 E Jackson / 956-630-0982 / www.goldencorral.com
Hungry Howie's Pizza, 5000 N 23rd / 956-972-1122 / www.hungryhowies.com
Iguana's Bar & Grill, 125 W Nolana Ave / 956-631-1668
Jason's Deli, 4100 N 2nd St / 956-664-2199 / www.jasonsdeli.com
Johnny Carino's Country Italian, 421 E Nolana / 956-631-6400 / www.carinos.com
La Pampa, 3300 N McColl Rd / 956-687-5857
Luby's Cafeteria, 2200 S 10th St / 956-928-1853 / www.lubys.com
McDonald's, 2800 Nolana Ave / 956-631-2679 / www.mcdonalds.com
Morado's Restaurant, 113 S 11th St / 956-631-3112
Outback Steakhouse, 1109 E Business 83 / 956-618-0577 / www.outback.com
Pier 67, 2901 N 10th St / 956-929 5010
Pizza Hut, 404 S 10th St / 956-682-4115 / www.pizzahut.com
Ramos BBQ, 10801 N 10th St / 956-386-1818
Red Lobster, 701 Expressway 83 / 956-687-7323 / www.redlobster.com
Santa Fe Steak House, 1918 S 10th St / 956-630-2331
Subway, 3512 N 23rd St / 956-994-8710 / www.subway.com
Wendy's, 4100 N 10th St / 956-687-7228 / www.wendys.com

SPORTING GOODS

Academy Sports / www.academy.com
716 E Expressway 83 / 956-632-3000
3901 Expressway 83 / 956-217-7600

AIRPORT

McAllen- Miller International Airport, 2500 S Bicentennial Blvd / 956-682-9101 /
www.mcallenairport.com

FOR MORE INFORMATION

McAllen Convention & Visitors Bureau, P.O. Box 790 78505 / 956-682-2871 /
www.mcallenchamber.com

PORT ISABEL
Population: 4,865
County: Cameron

ACCOMMODATIONS

Casa Rosa Motel, 761 W Hwy 100 / 956-943-2052
Queen Isabel Inn, 300 Garcia St. / 956-943-1468 / www.queenisabelinn.com
Southwind Inn, 600 E Davis St / 956-943-3392 / www.southwindinn.us
White Sands Motor Lodge, 418 W Highway 100/ 956-943-2414 /
    www.the-white-sands.com
Yacht Club Hotel, 700 Yturria St / 956-943-1301

CAMPGROUNDS

Anchor Marina RV Park, 40 Tarpon Ave / 956-943-9323
Del Mar Park, 109 Champion Ave 956-943-1161
Tarpon RV Park, 226 Basin St / 956-943-2040 / www.tarponrvpark.com
The Traveler RV Park, 504 Hwy 100 / 956-943-2040

RESTAURANTS

Church's Chicken, 1748 W Hwy 100 / 956-943-8592 / www.churchs.com
Dairy Queen, 302 Hwy 100 / 956-943-2101 / www.dairyqueen.com
Gabriella's Ristorante, 1506 Hwy 100 / 956-943-2141
Lighthouse Deli, 412 A Queen Isabella Blvd / 956-943-9111
Lost Galleon Seafood Restaurant, 202 Queen Isabella Blvd / 956-943-4400
Pirate's Landing Restaurant, 501 Maxan St / 956-943-3663 /
    www.pirateslandingrestaurant.com
Pizza Hut, 2101 N 23rd St / 956-682-1521 / www.pizzahut.com
Marcello's Italian Restaurant, 110 N Tarmava St / 956-943-7611 /
    www.marcellositalian.com
Pelican Station, 201 S Garcia St / 956-943-3344 / www.pelicanstation.net

SPORTING GOODS

The Shop, 318 Queen Isabella Blvd / 956-943-1785
Quik Stop, 501 Hwy 100 / 956-943-1159

FOR MORE INFORMATION

Port Isabel Chamber of Commerce
    2300 Hwy 35
    800-556-7678
    www.portisabel.org

Port Mansfield
Population: 415
County: Willacy

Accommodations

Fisherman's Motel / 956-944-2882/ 12 rooms
Sunset House, 1144 South Port Dr. / 800-311-4250 / 25 rooms /
   www.portmansfieldsunsethouse.com
Get-A-Way Lodge, 100 West Port / 956-944-4000 /
   www.getawayadventureslodge.com

Campgrounds

Fisherman's RV Park, South Port Dr / 956-944-2653
Park @ Port Mansfield, 1300 Mansfield Dr / 956-746-1530 /
   www.parkatportmansfield.com
R&R RV Park, 901 Mansfield Dr / 956-944-2253 / www.randrrvpark.net

Restaurants

El Jefe's Marina & Cantina, 109 W. Harbor Dr. / 956-944-2876
Fisherman's Inn, South Port Dr / 956-944-2882
Windjammer Restaurant, South Port Dr / 956-944-2555

Sporting Goods

Harbor Bait and Tackle / 956-944-2331 / www.harborbait.com
Port Mansfield Marina, 600 Mansfield Dr / 956-944-2331
The Wright Stop, Hwy 186 / 956-944-2314

Airport

Charles Johnson Airport Port Mansfield / 956-689-3332

RAYMONDVILLE
Population: 9,733
County: Willacy

ACCOMMODATIONS

Americas Best Value Inn, 450 S Hwy 77 / 956-689-5900 / 40 rooms/ $40-$90 /
www.bestvalueinn.com

Antler's Inn, 1800 Expressway 77 South / 956-689-5531

Best Western Executive Inn, 118 N Hwy 77 / 956-689-4141 / 36 rooms / $45-$80 /
www.bestwesterntexas.com

Inn at El Canelo, Canelo Ranch Road / 888-439-3049 / www.elcaneloranch.com

Tall Palms, Business 77 South / 956-689-2850

CAMPGROUNDS

Gateway RV Park, FM 3168 / 956-689-6658

RESTAURANTS

Antojito's Mexicano, 357 W Hidalgo / 956-689-4410

Boot Company Bar & Grill, 205 E Hidalgo / 956-689-3850

Dairy Queen, 534 E Hidalgo / 956-689-5121 / www.dairyqueen.com

Whataburger, 1007 E Hidalgo / 956-689-5578 / www.whataburger.com

SAN BENITO
Population: 23,444
County: Cameron

ACCOMMODATIONS

Best Western Garden Inn, 151 E Ebony St / 956-361-2222 / 43 rooms / $60-$129 / www.bestwesterntexas.com

Days Inn, 1451 W Expressway 83 / 956-399-3891 / 30 rooms / www.daysinn.com

San Benito Executive Inn, 1451 W Expressway 83 / 956-399-3891 / 31 rooms / $43-$69

Super 8, 2340 Hwy 83 W / 956-361-4404 / 54 rooms / www.super8.com

CAMPGROUNDS

Fun N' Sun RV Resort, 1400 Zillock Rd / 956-399-5125

RESTAURANTS

Blue Marlin, 615 E Business 77 / 956-399-6412

Dairy Queen, 801 W Business 77 / 956-399-2850 / www.dairyqueen.com

El Taco Loco, 2480 W Business 77 / 956-399-7152

Longhorn Cattle Company, 3055 W Expressway 83 / 956-399-4400

McDonalds, 1144 W Business 77 / 956-399-6845 / www.mcdonalds.com

Pizza Hut, 1130 W Business 77 / 956-399-1612 / www.pizzahut.com

Ray's Bar-B-Q, 198 W Batts / 956-399-4104

Rosita's, 1651 W Business 77 / 956-399-3320

Subway, 160 W Expressway 83 / 956-399-5151 / www.subway.com

Whataburger, 1110 W Business 77 / 956-399-7440 / www.whataburger.com

FOR MORE INFORMATION

Visit www.sbida.com

SOUTH PADRE ISLAND
Population: 2,422
County: Cameron

ACCOMMODATIONS

Bay View Bed & Breakfast, 12 Laguna Madre Dr / 866-685-8663

Bay View Hotel & Suites, 901 Padre Blvd / 956-761-4884 / 49 rooms / $70-$229

Best Western Fiesta Isles Hotel, 5701 Padre Blvd / 956-761-4913 / 59 rooms / $50-$220 / www.bestwesterntexas.com

Brown Pelican Inn, 207 W Aries / 956-761-2722 / www.brownpelican.com

Casa De Siesta, 4610 Padre Blvd / 956-761-5656 / www.casadesiesta.com

Comfort Suites, 912 Padre Blvd / 956-772-9022 / 74 rooms / $60-$300 / www.comfortsuites.com

Holiday Inn Express, 6502 Padre Blvd / 888-772-3222 / 104 rooms / $60-$200 / www.hiexpress.com

Holiday Inn Sunspree Resort, 100 Padre Blvd / 800-531-7405 / 227 rooms / $80-$300 / www.holidayinn.com

Island Inn, 5100 Gulf Blvd / 956-761-7677 / 26 rooms / $60-$180 / www.islandinnpadre.com

La Copa Inn, 350 Padre Blvd / 956-761-6000 / 146 rooms / $35-$350 / www.lacoparesort.com

La Quinta Inn, 7000 Padre Blvd / 956-772-7000 / 147 rooms / $35-$350 / www.lq.com

Radisson Resort, 500 Padre Blvd / 956-761-6511 / 190 rooms / $125-$550 / www.radisson.com

Sheraton Beach Hotel, 310 Padre Blvd / 800-222-4010 / 250 rooms / $80-$450 / www.sheraton.com

Suntide II, 4400 Gulf Blvd / 956-761-4959 / www.suntideii.com

Super 8, 4205 Padre Blvd / 956-761-6300 / 66 rooms / $40-$250 / www.super8.com

Travelodge, 6200 Padre Blvd / 866-601-6200 / 149 rooms / $60-$429 / www.travelodge.com

CAMPGROUND

South Padre KOA, 1 Padre Blvd / 956-761-5665

RESTAURANTS

Amberjack's Bayside Bar & Grill, 209 W Amberjack St / 956-761-6500 / www.amberjacks-spi.com

Blackbeard's Restaurant, 103 E Saturn 956-761-2962 / www.blackbeardsspi.com

Captain Bob's Seafood Restaurant, 700 Padre Blvd / 956-761-4123

Castaways Restaurant, 823 S Garcia / 943-6880

Dairy Queen, 2401 Padre Blvd / 956-761-1072 / www.dairyqueen.com

Dirty Al's, 1 Padre Blvd / 956-761-4901

Dolce Roma Café, 4200 B Padre Blvd / 956-761-1198
Dorado's Baja Bar & Grill, 5001 Padre Blvd / 956-772-1930
FishBones Pier & Grill, 1 Padre Blvd 956-761-4665 /
www.fishbonesgrillandpier.com
Jake's Bar & Grill, 2500 Padre Blvd / 956-761-5012
Kelly's Irish Bar & Grill, 101 E Morningside Dr / 956-761-7571
La Jaiba Restaurant, 2001 Padre Blvd / 956-761-9878
Louie's Backyard, 2305 Laguna St / 956-761-6406 / www.lbyspi.com
Padre Island Brewing Company, 3400 Padre Blvd / 956-761-9585
Padre Pizza X-Press, 3112 Padre Blvd / 956-761-7273
Palm St Pier, 204 W Palm St / 956-772-7256 / www.palmstreetpier.com
Pelican Station Restaurant, 201 S Garcia / 956-943-3344
Scampi's Restaurant / 956-761-1755 / www.scampispi.com
Sea Ranch Restaurant, 1 Padre Blvd / 956-761-1314 /
www.searanchrestaurant.com
Tom & Jerry's Beach Club Bar & Grill, 3212 Padre Blvd / 956-761-8999
The Lost Galleon, 202 E Queen Isabella Blvd / 956-943-4400
Wahoo Saloon Bayside Bar & Grill / 956-761-5344

FOR MORE INFORMATION

South Padre Island Convention & Visitors Bureau
7355 Padre Blvd
78597
800-767-2373
www.sopadre.com

EMERGENCY MEDICAL 956-943-7829

Jack crevalle are often found behind gulf shrimp boats.

Region 9: Offshore

Light tackle and flyfishing anglers can pursue offshore species all along the Texas coast. Guided trips are available at several different ports. Sabine Pass, Galveston, Freeport, Matagorda, Port O'Connor, Port Aransas, Port Mansfield and Port Isabel all offer offshore fishing opportunities.

Many offshore species like cobia or ling, kingfish, Spanish mackerel, and little tunny can be found just off the jetties that connect inshore bays to the Gulf of Mexico. Inshore species like tarpon, jack crevalle, and redfish can also be found in these near shore areas.

The blue water found offshore often comes inside the jetties along the Texas coast during the hot summer months. Along with the blue water come the larger offshore fish. Tarpon also cruise along in schools within a mile of the shoreline during summer months.

Captain Chris Phillips, based out of the Galveston Bay area, often finds excellent fishing conditions just offshore. Phillips uses a size 2 or 4 white, yellow, or red popper to catch ling around buoys and oil rigs. He makes three quick presentations to the ling, placing the first two on each side of the fish's head and fishing the third. He reports his success rate using this method is almost 100 percent. Use poppers without flash material. When fishing for Spanish mackerel or little tunny, Phillips uses a small baitfish fly usually no longer than an inch and a half long.

Farther south on the Texas coast, Captain Brandon Shuler fishes out of Port Mansfield. Shuler has a military background and is a real stickler for well-tied fishing knots.

Offshore anglers seek out the numerous oil rigs dotting the Texas coast as prime destinations for offshore fish. The oil rigs offer both angler and fish a place to regularly call home. Many Texas off-shore rigs are within 10 miles of the coast, making them ideal locations for anglers wanting to fish for offshore species. Most oil rigs will have some type of fish around them.

There are also numerous shipwrecks found along the coast and, in recent years, outdated military vessels have been purposely sunk to provide man-made reefs. Fish relocate to these reefs within in a short period of time.

Anglers working the rigs need to be prepared with the proper tackle and techniques. As with any offshore angling, the tackle used needs to be capable of handling the fish. Large capacity reels, whether casting, spinning, or fly are a must. The reel drag is more important when fishing for offshore species. Make sure the reel drag is up to the fish you're going after.

Rods also need to be strong enough to handle the larger fish. Fly rods should have a forward fighting grip to aid in lifting large fish. Oil rig legs are often encrusted with barnacles that can quickly cut any fishing line that gets too close and strong rods give anglers a chance to pull fish away from the rig.

Fly anglers will want to have full sinking lines available. A full sinking line will allow fly anglers to keep their line under the waves and in the fishing zone.

Offshore anglers need to understand which knots to use and when to use a metal leader. Captain Phillips recommends 14 to 18 inches of an American Fishing Wire product called 49 Strand 7X7. He reports this brown wire is small, yet strong enough to handle the toothy offshore fish.

Anything floating on the water's surface can provide shelter for offshore species. A floating piece of wood, a bunch of floating bottles or a patch of sargassam weed can provide shelter for small fish. Tripletail, dorado, and ling will often hang around floating patches of debris. These floating homes are quickly spotted by predator species so all the offshore angler has to do is cast to the target.

Take your time looking for fish around the debris. Tripletail will often lie just under the edge of the floating mat and may be hard to see. Fly casters should use small Clouser Minnows in chartreuse or pink and shrimp patterns to entice tripletail.

Captain Phillips shared one tip about catching dorado on flies. He prefers to use a yellow and green or yellow and red popper when casting to dorado. If you are only catching small fish, he recommends trying a larger popper. The largest dorado will often hit the larger popper.

Flies made on circle hooks are always a good idea, but especially for offshore species. Whether it's a baitfish or crab pattern, circle hooks will catch more offshore fish. Basic colors of chartreuse, green, silver, and white often work well for offshore flies. Captain Shuler also likes hot pink flies. Fly anglers will want to have a few topwater poppers in white and yellow on hand.

Many fly and light tackle casters chum an area to get the fish to come closer to the surface. Red snapper can be chummed close enough to the surface to be caught by fly casters with sinking lines.

There are several party or head boats located on the Texas coast that regularly take anglers offshore. These ships don't charge as much as booking a charter trip but they carry several anglers on each boat. Fly and light tackle anglers often use these party boats to get to offshore species.

There are a few things fly and light tackle users need to keep in mind when fishing one of the party boats. First, remember you're not alone on the boat. Each party boat has several anglers on each trip. It's a good idea to discuss fly casting with the captain before you leave the dock. If you're flyfishing, remember to watch your back cast. You can often find a part of the ship where you will not get in other angler's way when casting.

Light tackle fishers also need to remember there are other anglers on the ship. A fish hooked on light tackle will usually take longer to retrieve and you often don't have as good a control of the fish as anglers using heavy tackle.

Take along tackle heavy enough to handle the size fish you will be catching. A quick retrieve and release (due to appropriate tackle) allows most fish the chance to survive. Use the proper tackle.

If you're interested in a record catch, become familiar with the IGFA rules and follow them precisely.

Fly casters can really help themselves by practicing their cast before they get on the water. Offshore fly tackle is usually heavier and often stiffer than the 8-weight you use to cast to tailing reds in the shallows. Be prepared to make a quick cast with only one back cast to minimize interference with other anglers.

There are numerous charter fishing boats that use heavy tackle to catch offshore fish along the Texas coast that are beyond the scope of this book. Excellent offshore fishing guides are located at many of the locations mentioned. Check with local chambers of commerce, visitors and convention bureaus and light tackle guides for recommendations.

Guides

Captain Chris Phillips / 409-935-0208
Captain Brandon Shuler / 956-944-4000

Gag are just one of the many fish found offshore.

The Spot: How and Where to Locate Fish

Not just a good fishing spot, but THE Spot. The one that always has fish. The spot or spots that produce year after year. The spots guides guard and never mention. The spot that everyone wants to be the first to early in the morning.

There are none! This book mentions specific areas to fish, but even specific areas are vast and have many variables both during the day and during the year. A spot that is hot for trout one day is cold the next.

I prefer to understand what attracts fish to a type of spot instead of a particular spot. When I first started fishing on the Texas coast, it always bothered me when I would fish with a guide and he would say, "We're going here", referring to a particular location. It was particularly hard to understand why he decided to fish a vast, long shoreline that appeared to be featureless.

Then I started to fish with a very seasoned coastal fisherman. The places he took me to fish instantly made sense. They had sharp drop-offs from 18 inches deep to 5 feet deep. They had strong tides rushing through with the fish aggressively biting at the start of the tidal change, but not at the peak of the current. They had huge schools of baitfish working the surface and brown pelicans diving all around us.

Spots change, but types of spots don't. Features that attract fish to one location will attract fish to another location with the same features.

The other thing about fishing spots on the Texas coast is that they are always changing. A favorite trout hole one year is just another location for mullet to swim the next year. One of my favorite locations went from being a big-trout-holding, almost automatic sure thing, to a location without any game fish at all within 12 months. The spot had changed due to boat traffic and sand moved by the tides. It no longer held the type of feature that had once made it a place I always wanted to fish.

One year I had several full limits of trout, numerous redfish, sheepshead, black drum, and even flounder from this one spot. The next year I never caught a single fish from the exact same location.

The location was a feeding lane with baitfish of many sizes cruising down the steep drop-off that highlighted the area and prey fish following the baitfish daily. The next year, the water was too shallow for anything but the smallest fish to use as a holding area.

Spots change, but types of spots do not.

What To Look For

If an area is going to hold the fish we seek, it must have something to attract the fish and that usually means food. It has been said thousands of times, if you find the food, you'll find the fish.

One of my favorite types of spots, and the fish's too, is a steep drop-off. Speckled trout especially like a deep drop-off. Locate an area where the water drops off from

12 or 18 inches in depth to 3 or 5 feet in a short distance. This is an ideal ambush location. Large fish want to be able to hide in the deep water. They feel safe in deep water. Any disturbance and they can quickly escape, most often without even being noticed.

To the predator fish, the quick access means quick access to food. The small baitfish and even shrimp stay in the water that is too shallow for the larger predator fish to feel comfortable in.

The prey use the shallow water the same way the predators use the deep water. That is where they feel most comfortable. But large fish know that they can quickly dart into the shallow water, get a meal, and just as quickly be back in the safety of the deeper water they prefer.

Predator fish seek out this type of location and will repeatedly move in and out of the shallow water, taking advantage of a great feeding opportunity. Find a steep drop-off and you've located the type of spot that will produce fish time after time. Just don't get so enamored of the location that you forget to constantly find new spots because "the spot" will change and may someday not even hold enough fish to merit a try.

Another type of location fish prefer is an area with oyster shells on the bottom. Oyster shells provide small homes for the things fish like to eat. There are both large oyster shell reefs and scattered oyster shell areas along the Texas coast. If the reef happens to have deep water nearby, there will be game fish in the area. Oyster shell reefs are some of the most productive areas along the coast.

A fishing guide can help you catch more fish and learn new areas.

Spoil islands are another good type of location to frequent. They are made when channels are dredged for boat traffic, and they dot the entire Texas coast.

Potholes in grassy shorelines are locations that are often overlooked, but readily attract game fish. The sandy potholes located along the flats are great ambush locations, especially for big trout. The big fish will most often hang near the edge of the pothole, instead of in the middle. Potholes can range in size from the size of a hula hoop to a pothole big enough to hold several cars.

When you find potholes, stay in the grass and visually check out the perimeter of the pothole. If you see something that looks like a stick holding within a few inches of the grass surrounding the pothole it may be a fish. Take your time when working potholes because fish know they can quickly and quietly slip back into the grass around the pothole and disappear.

You can often catch several fish and maybe even several different types of fish from one pothole. Make several casts into each pothole before moving on. Try different angles, not just casting from one direction.

Any manmade structure will likely hold fish. Jetties, pilings, boat docks, lighted piers, abandoned boats, and duck blinds are all prime locations for finding fish. Anglers speeding to their chosen fishing spot overlook many of these locations. Many fish like to be around something, and manmade structures are ideal.

When trying to decide on what location to fish, try to find something that is different than the surrounding area. If you're wading and all of a sudden you feel cooler water on your legs, try to remember that location. Did the bottom change from sand to mud? Did you notice a change in the way water flowed in the area? Is there a grass island in one spot along a multi-mile flat? Did the grass change from one type to a different type? Anything that provides a change is a location where you'll find fish.

Another location that will almost always hold fish is anywhere there is bait. If you see lots of bait jumping and splashing early in the morning, there are probably fish nearby. A prime example of a good location is an area where the wind has blown bait along the shoreline. A shoreline that normally has the wind blowing away from the land, but today has the wind blowing into the shoreline, may hold fish. Anytime you see a concentration of bait, mullet, shrimp, or other types, take some time to fish that area.

Fishing Around Birds

Special care should be taken when fishing around birds. Whether casting near birds on land or casting at a place in the bay with hovering birds, this act requires special care. First, try to cast when the birds are not flying near the spot you are casting to. If you see flying birds in the area, wait until you can make a cast without getting near them.

Second, make your cast and immediately lower your rod tip to just above the water surface. With the line low to the water you are less likely to snare any birds flying in the area. Retrieve your lure with the rod tip low and start your next cast with the rod tip low.

If you do happen to hook a bird, be careful. The bird only wants to get away. It is a good idea to place a towel over the bird's head when trying to untangle the bird. It will relax and make removing the snare a lot easier if its head is covered. All birds have sharp beaks and most have long necks that can easily stretch. Try to quickly place the towel over the bird's head at full arms length. Be especially careful around long-necked pelicans.

If you are fishing with someone else, it is best to ask for some assistance. Trying to handle a rod and reel and a struggling bird is very difficult. Untangle the bird and let it fly off under its own power. It will get out of the area as quick as possible.

The Tide Effect

Tides play a major role in the daily lives of all coastal fish. A basic understanding of how the tides work is part of the fishing knowledge required, just like understanding which prey fish the predator fish eat. By understanding how the tides affect your fishing world, you will save time and have a better shot at being at the right location at the right time.

One way to look at tides is to group the two tides with little rise and little fall together, and the two tides with greater rise and greater fall together. The tides go through a week of little movement and then a week of greater movement. Then the two-week cycle repeats.

The tides with the smaller rise and fall are called neap tides. The tides with the greater movement are called spring tides. The way spring is used in conjunction with tides has nothing to do with the time of year, although different times of the year will have greater or smaller tides associated with it.

Also, you need to associate the tides with the moon phases. If you can remember that a full or no moon is associated with a spring tide then you can at least partially predict what type of tide you will have when you go fishing.

There are differences with the tides all along the Texas coast. Tide charts are published in magazines, on the Internet, and broadcast on the NOAA weather radio channel. Check the tides before you plan your fishing trip to the coast.

Within any day there will be a tide change about every six hours. Some areas of the Texas coast will not experience a noticeable tide change, but the change still occurs about every six hours. For most of the Texas coast, the water will only rise about a foot during the normal tide.

Another thing you need to keep in mind is that the tide change occurs about an hour later each day. If you were really catching fish at one spot at 8:00am, the next day the same tidal conditions will occur about 9:00am. Knowing this, you can adjust your arrival time and maybe even get a little extra sleep.

Wind plays a major role in tidal change on the Texas coast. A strong wind added to a big spring tide can shove water into areas not normally flooded and give fish added areas to explore. These flooded areas will also cause a greater than normal outgoing tide when the waters exit the flooded areas. Think not just about the tide movement, but what effect the wind is having on the areas you fish.

With each incoming or outgoing tide, small prey fish and shrimp are flushed along with the water. Predator fish know this and position themselves where the food will be brought to them.

Predator fish will locate inside the mouth of a small lake waiting for the incoming tide and food. Then they will locate outside the mouth on an outgoing tide. The anglers that pay attention to this seemingly small detail will place themselves in a better position to catch fish.

Also think about the temperature associated with the water flooding a shallow area. If the water is shallow, it will heat up very fast. In the warm months, the added heat will detract from the area, but in the cooler months, this warmer water exiting a shallow area will provide warmth to the deeper area where it exits. The warmer water will also attract hungry predator fish.

One feature of tide movement a lot of anglers overlook is the velocity of the tide movement. If the water moves too slow or too fast through a particular area, it may not be the best time to fish that particular spot.

Often, fish will locate in an area right at the start of the tide change. They set themselves in position to grab food that comes by in the tide. Once the speed of the tide picks up, the fish may have to work too hard to stay in that spot and they will relocate to a different area where the water speed is more to their liking. If they stay in the too fast water, they use up more energy than they can replace with whatever meal they might catch.

This is somewhat like the way coldwater trout locate behind a rock waiting on food to be brought to them from upstream. As long as the water flow is not too strong the fish can easily dart from behind the rock and catch food that drifts by. But if the water continues to rise and move faster, the trout will relocate to an area that provides a little shelter from the fast moving water and wait for the water speed to return to the ideal velocity before resuming their position behind the rock.

Saltwater fish do the same thing. Speckled trout will locate where the incoming tide pushes against an island when the tide is just starting to come in. As the tide increases in velocity, the speckled trout will move off to one side of the island and set up in the area just beyond the tide movement protected by the out sweeping current. If the tide continues to increase, the trout may move away and wait for the slower speed of the end of the tide.

Therefore, the best times to fish may be the first and last 30 minutes of the tide change instead of during the peak tide movement. By remembering what the tide is doing when you are catching fish, you can return to the same area when the tide is again at the correct speed for that area.

Tidal movement has a great deal to do with finding fish in any location. Along the Texas coast, tidal change is about a foot in depth. This may not seem like a big change, but one foot of water coming onto or leaving an area as big as Galveston or Corpus Christi Bay is a lot of change.

Tides affect fish and locations differently. Some fish prefer an incoming tide while others prefer on outgoing tide. It can even differ depending on the exact location you're fishing.

284 — FLYFISHER'S GUIDE TO THE TEXAS COAST

There is little doubt that a slack tide is the worst for fishing. Most fish prefer some water movement. Fish that were very active during a slight tide movement can become lethargic during a slack tide and ignore all offerings, natural or fake.

All anglers need to understand how the tide movement affects the areas they like to fish. If a particular area has proven good during the first two hours of an incoming tide you'll most likely catch fish at that location during that type of tide in the future regardless of what time of day. As you gain more experience with tides, you will come to know when to be at certain locations because the tide is right.

Holding Water: A Little Goes a Long Way

An area the size of a car can hold fish while all of the water surrounding the small spot holds nothing. Anglers need to pay attention to small differences as well as big. A small depression can be a fish-holding magnet.

If you're catching fish in a gut, the humps on both sides will probably not hold any fish. If your fly or lure is not landing in the gut, you're probably not catching fish.

If a group of old pilings is holding fish, the surrounding flat may be fishless. Pay attention to small details about the areas you fish. These can often be the best places to fish — the person cruising by in a boat at 30 miles per hour will not know about the small details.

Travel Through the Bays

Many of the boat lanes in Texas bays are marked and many are not. If you're new to an area, it is always a good idea to seek out local knowledge about the best way to travel on the water.

Don't just follow another boat. Many flats boats can maneuver in 6 inches of water, and some in even less. Your boat may not be equipped to run that shallow. Try to stay inside marked boat lanes and learn the area. See if there are any known hazards that a newcomer might encounter.

Also, use the old rule of boat deep and wade shallow. Far too many boats travel in shallow waters that usually hold fish. Try to run your boat in the deeper water and save the shallows for the fish and waders.

General Tips to Improve Fishing

GET SOME SEASONED ADVICE

One thing all anglers can do to increase their knowledge of a particular area is seek seasoned knowledge. If you're new to an area, seek out a senior angler and ask for his or her help. Many will jump at the chance to help a novice learn. A good way to go about this is to go to a boat ramp and find a seasoned angler fishing alone. Ask them to share some of their hard-won knowledge about local areas and local fish. Most will willfully respond to a politely asked question. Don't forget to offer to pay for the gas you use when fishing with someone else.

FISH MID-WEEK

Try to fish some during the middle of the week and not just on weekends. Many of our Texas bays are very crowded for two or three days of the week and virtually empty the other days. Try to take a couple of trips each year to fish during the middle of the week. Parking at the boat ramp will be less crowded and your chances of encountering fish that haven't been harassed by numerous boats and lures increases when you fish during the middle of the week.

GET PROFESSIONAL HELP

The absolute best way to learn about fishing on the Texas coast is to hire a guide. Guides were catching fish yesterday. They have the boat full of gas, have ice boxes packed with cold water and drinks, know what the fish were biting on yesterday, make sure the boat batteries are charged, don't have to worry about parking, tie your fly or lure on for you, and even clean and package any fish you decide to keep. All of this for less money than you'll ever spend per day on any boat you own.

Hiring a guide is your best dollar spent on angling. Texas coastal guides are hard working people that enjoy what they do. They want you to catch fish and will do everything possible to help.

Be sure to have any questions you would like to ask the guide ready before you make your first call, because every guide is different. Most use a variety of tackle and fish many different locations. The more questions you ask up front, the less likely you will encounter a surprise when you get on the water.

Questions to ask a guide include:

- Does the guide fish?
- Does the guide provide tackle? If so, what type of tackle?
- Do we fish from the boat or wade?
- Do you provide lunch? Drinks?
- Is it a half day or full day of fishing? If it's a full day, when does it end?
- How many people can fish on a trip?

- Can the guide recommend accommodations and restaurants in the area?
- Can I keep some fish or is it strictly catch and release?
- Can you help me with my casting?
- Can you provide a couple of references?

These and other questions will help you choose the correct guide. If a guide gets put off by the questions, chose another guide. Most are more than happy to answer your questions and will provide you with an excellent fishing opportunity.

There are only a few fulltime flyfishing guides on the entire Texas coast, but there are many excellent fishing guides on every bay. Discuss the possibility of using fly tackle with the guide if you like to flyfish. If you're going on a shallow-water trip looking for tailing redfish, fly tackle will work as good or even better than casting or spinning tackle. If you are an experienced fly caster and can cast 30 to 40 feet, you can catch fish with a conventional light tackle guide.

Discuss the way you would like to fish and the way the guide fishes before you book the trip. Most guides are open to the idea of using fly tackle even if they don't use it. They will tell you if your day is going to be very difficult using fly tackle and suggest using conventional tackle instead.

Fly anglers willing to learn from casting guides will greatly increase their chances of catching fish.

I cannot say enough positive things about hiring a Texas coastal guide. See the list of guides at the end of this book.

PRACTICE YOUR CAST

It doesn't make any difference if you're using fly tackle or light tackle, practice casting your equipment. The comment I hear most often from guides is, "If they could only cast 30 feet". If you can't deliver your fly, lure, or bait to the correct location, you can't catch fish. Practice casting while you're at home. Most of us can't fish every day so we have to practice whenever we can. Take advantage of the days not spent fishing and practice casting.

If you're a die-hard flyfisher, spend some time practicing casting light spinning tackle during windy conditions. If you use mostly casting tackle, spend some time learning how to cast fly tackle.

Work on making repetitive accurate 30-foot casts with your fly tackle. Do your practicing both when conditions are calm and on very windy days. You never know what type of weather you're going to encounter when you're on the water. If you can accurately make 30- to 40-foot casts, almost any guide will be able to put you on fish you can catch.

Time spent practicing will show when you're on the water.

Fly Versus Light Tackle

Each type of tackle has its place. Many hardcore flyfishers will not even think about using light spinning or casting tackle. Many seasoned casting anglers never use spinning tackle. That's a real shame because all three methods have their place, and the angler that can easily switch between the different types of tackle will be the angler that catches the most fish at the end of the day.

Texas coastal waters experience days where the wind never gets below 20 miles per hour. They also experience days where the only ripple on the water's surface is made by a jumping mullet. Texas coastal waters have all types of weather conditions — from days with 4-foot waves crashing the shoreline to days with the water so calm that it hurts to look at it.

A pure flyfishing trip will be ruined by a steady 25-mile-per-hour wind. If the flyfishers can switch to light spinning tackle, they can salvage an otherwise wasted day.

Learn to use all three types of tackle (fly, spinning, and casting) and you'll be in the game no matter what the weather does.

Fly tackle is not a good searching tool and a lot of Texas coastal angling is searching for fish. If you're able to use a spinning outfit to locate the fish and then switch to fly tackle once the fish are located, you're probably going to catch more fish.

Your arm will not be as tired from trying to blind cast flies in unproductive water. Once you've found the fish, you're not going to spook as many with fly tackle as you will with casting or spinning tackle.

There is no doubt that catching any fish on fly tackle is the most fun, but catching some fish is also more fun than not catching anything. The angler that can easily switch between the different systems will be the angler that catches the most fish at the end of the day. Invest the time necessary to learn to use all three methods of fishing and you'll triple your effectiveness.

Basic Outfits

Fly Tackle

Fly tackle for the Texas coast does not have to be specialized. Most likely, the outfit you use to catch freshwater bass will work for most Texas coastal species. Either an 8- or 9-weight rig works great. I prefer to use a 9-weight system, but certainly an 8-weight will also work well. If you have a 6-weight rod, take it along. There are many situations where a lighter 6-weight will catch more shallow-water fish than a heavier 8-weight. The heavier outfit is often the one to use once the wind starts to get up.

Multiple-piece rods have their advantage. If you're just starting out, consider buying a four-piece rod. Most of the multiple-piece rods made today are excellent casting tools and you'll be able to travel easier with a four-piece rod.

Fly reels need to hold at least 150 yards of backing. Twenty-pound backing doesn't take up as much room as 30-pound backing, but the 30-pound offers a little more strength in case you hook up with a large jack or redfish. Large arbor reels pick up line faster but may offer less backing capacity.

A smooth drag is the most important part of any fly reel. The drag should be easily adjustable and it's a good idea to test your drag while you're still on dry land. Set it to just under the breaking strength of the leader used. A drag that is too loose can backlash and cause line problems. Anglers can also palm the reel spool on super-hot fish. There is generally nothing the fish is going to get tangled in, so letting a fish run for a distance is not necessarily a bad thing. Let the fish run and get your line under control, then fight the fish.

Be sure to back off the drag at the end of the day and trip. Most quality reels use cork for the drag and the cork compresses with time. If the reel is stored for a long time with the drag set, the cork compresses and the next time the reel is used the drag must be adjusted even tighter. Back off the drag once you're done fishing for the day and re-set it the next morning. If the reel is going to be stored for a lengthy period, back the drag well off. Then the cork will be ready for the next fishing trip.

Every Texas coastal flyfisher should have at least two lines: one floating and one sinking. There are certainly merits to having both a sink tip line and a full sink line. If you want to carry both, great.

Modern saltwater floating lines come in many different tapers and colors. Most Texas coastal fish are not line shy except for those in extremely shallow water. Chose a color that works well for your eyes. Light blue lines may help match the sky, but they are often hard to see while casting.

A general weight forward saltwater taper floating line works well. Lines designated redfish taper will also work for most situations. Limp coldwater lines should be avoided.

Use your sinking line. It will help get the fly into the strike zone quicker and let you spend more time actually fishing. Sinking lines work great when fishing for flounder and speckled trout.

Most saltwater fish are not leader shy. Leaders in 2X to 0X work well. Also take along a spool of 12- and 20-pound tippet material. Texas fly anglers rarely need tippets stronger than 20-pound test. Ready-made leaders also work well. Most fishing situations will require nothing longer than a 9-foot leader. Use a shorter 4- to 6-foot leader when casting a sinking line.

A spool of 40- to 80-pound tippet material is required when chasing larger fish like crevalle jacks. If you're not going after a record fish, use a longer section of heavy mono when fishing for these big fish. A 4-foot bite section will prevent most jacks from cutting the leader. A shorter section is often cut by other fish in the school trying to get the fly out of the hooked fish's mouth.

Test the leader several times during the day, especially after catching a fish and when working around oyster reefs. Your fingers can feel most abrasions. Replace any leader or tippet when a rough section is felt. Flurocarbon is not required, but may add a degree of stealth when fishing for nervous fish.

It never hurts to clean your line, especially when used in the saltwater environment. Take along a line cleaning kit and clean your line a couple of times during the day.

Plastic fly boxes won't rust like metal boxes. Modern fly boxes made with foam inserts are great for Texas coastal waters. A box that fits into a chest pocket is about the right size and will hold several dozen flies. Take along three or four of each fly and leave the excess in the boat.

A basic fly box should include shrimp, crabs, spoons, baitfish, and poppers. There are many different patterns and most work well. Redfish are not that picky, so any shrimp pattern will probably work fine.

Baitfish are well imitated by a Clouser Minnow. Take plenty. Also take some classics like Bend Backs, Lefty's Deceivers, Seaducers, and Snapping Shrimp. A basic Texas coastal fly box needs less than 100 flies, but you do need to cover the different zones of the water.

Have flies that are made for fishing the surface, the bottom, and everything in-between. Cover the three zones of water and you'll have the right flies for the Texas coast. A coastal fly list is included near the end of this chapter.

Another reason not to take along unnecessary flies is that they rust. Take all flies out of the fly box at the end of the day and wash them with freshwater. Lay the cleaned flies on a paper or cloth towel and pat them dry with another. Then let the flies air dry. Open the fly box and let it air out also. Taking a few minutes to clean the flies can save the expense of replacing flies with rusty hooks.

One essential tool all coastal flyfishers need is a good hook sharpener. Test the hook on each fly before making the first casts by running the hook point down a thumbnail. The hook should easily dig into the nail. If the hook does not, sharpen it until it does. It is also a good idea to check the hook sharpness several times during the day especially when fishing around oyster reefs. You'll never be sorry you took an extra minute to sharpen a dull hook.

Flyfishers should also learn to use a stripping basket. Stripping baskets help control the fly line whether you're in a boat or wading a long, sandy Texas flat. It's much better to have your excess fly line in a small stripping basket than tangled around a sharp oyster shell.

Stripping baskets are designed to be belted on wading anglers or carried in a boat. Many shallow-water skiffs have built-in stripping baskets. On some models the angler actually stands inside the basket and lets the fly line drop around his feet. Many fly anglers prefer to fish without shoes so they can feel the line with their feet. Keep the line out from under your feet by firmly planting your feet when you first enter the basket and not picking up your feet while casting. The fly line will then land on the deck of the basket.

Other boats have stripping baskets that the angler leans against. Another type of stripping basket is a large cylinder placed on the front deck of the boat. A wet towel in the bottom of the basket helps keep the basket in place and the line wet, making it easier to cast. A collapsible leaf basket or clothesbasket can serve the same purpose. In an emergency situation, a simple five-gallon plastic bucket can be used as a stripping basket.

Another accessory that many fly anglers will find helpful is a small battery-powered light. One of the best models fits just under the brim of a cap. The small light source is great for those early morning, pre-dawn trips. The light adds little weight and can make the difference between a well-tied knot and one that loses a fish.

One cast that all saltwater anglers should know is the speed cast. This cast starts with the fly held in the angler's hand and allows a quick presentation to a fish. The speed cast minimizes false casting and delivers the fly to a cruising fish quickly.

It's best to hold the fly by the bend of the hook. Make a back cast as you normally would and let the line take the fly out of your grasp. I mark all my lines at the 30-foot mark with a permanent marker. Start the speed cast with the 30-foot mark just outside the rod tip. This allows you to load the rod quickly.

If you need to make a longer cast, simply make another false cast, shooting line as the cast is made. Practice the speed cast before making your trip to saltwater.

Texas Coastal Flies

Clouser Minnow — Bob Clouser's Deep Minnow should be in every fly box. The Clouser Minnow, or simply the Clouser, has probably been responsible for catching more fish than any other fly. Clousers and the numerous variations are simple to tie and very effective. One very effective version is Captain Sally Moffett's Foxy Clouser made with artic fox hair.

Texas fly anglers will want to carry Clousers in several different sizes and colors, but be sure to carry chartreuse-and-white Clousers in three or four different sizes. Vary the eye weight to get different sink rates. Other color choices include root beer, black, and solid white.

Lefty's Deceiver — Lefty's Deceiver can be tied in numerous color combinations and sizes. From a small one-inch solid white fly, to a 6- or even 8-inch baitfish-colored version, Lefty's Deceiver is an excellent baitfish imitator. Take along two or three different colors and sizes.

The Half and Half — The Half and Half is a combination of the Clouser Minnow and Lefty's Deceiver. Half and Half variations can be tied very large by using long tail feathers without adding a lot of weight to the fly.

Spoon Fly — The Spoon Fly is a must-have for Texas coastal flyrodders. The Spoon Fly is tied in several variations, but all include a weedguard. The weedguard is a must when casting to redfish cruising the shallow flats of Texas. Captain Tom Horbey makes a good Spoon Fly.

Borski Bonefish Slider — The Borski Slider catches fish. I often use this fly as a go-to fly when nothing else works. There's just something fish-like about its striped tail. Dorsey's Kwan is a similar fly that works well.

Bend Back — The Bend Back is another must-have fly. This fly can be tied in numerous different sizes and colors. Captain Chuck Scates' Hot Butt Bend Back is a Texas favorite. The hot pink version catches ladyfish like nothing else. Other variations include Eric Glass' Mr. Pinky and Captain Corey Rich's Little Black Fly. The similar Rattle Rouser tied in gold works very well for redfish.

Shrimp — Texas is blessed with a healthy shrimp population. Shrimp are one of the prime food sources for both Texas fish and anglers. There are many different shrimp patterns including the Scates Shrimp, Brooks Shrimp, and East Cut Grass Shrimp. All work. Be sure your shrimp patterns include a weedguard.

Crab — Small crabs make up a large part of the redfish diet along the Texas coast, and redfish love them. The Del Brown Permit Crab works great, and an olive crab pattern closely matches many of the crabs in the area. Again, use a weedguard on your crab patterns.

Popper — Almost everything will hit a popper including redfish. Popper sizes range from the very small (like a Dink fly) to large bucktail poppers used offshore. One of my favorite poppers is Captain Scott Sparrow's VIP Popper. This fly is simple to tie and catches many different fish.

Deceiver — The Deceiver is an old fly, but it still catches lots of fish. The classic red and white version is a redfish favorite, but take along Deceivers tied in grizzly red, orange, and root beer. The Deceiver lands softly so you don't spook nervous redfish in shallow water. Tie some of your Deceivers with weedguards for use on the grassy flats.

Crease Fly — Captain Joe Blados' Crease Fly is one of my favorites. It is very simple to tie and very effective. Tie larger versions to catch big redfish or crevalle jacks.

Light Tackle

Light tackle users can be divided into two groups: casting and spinning. Most younger anglers use spinning tackle with the more seasoned coastal fishers using casting tackle. The best anglers learn to use both. Each has its place and each can be more effective than the other under specific circumstances.

Light casting reels need at least 150 yards of line capacity. Speckled trout anglers that happen into a jack will be glad they have that much line. Light casting reels need a smooth drag properly set to handle fish the angler is pursuing that day.

Casting and spinning anglers should back off the drag at the end of the day. If you set the drag and leave it at that setting, the drag washers become compressed and the next trip the angler must tighten the drag a little more to get the desired setting. This process continues until the drag must be set at the strongest setting to get any stopping action at all. Just remember to back off the drag after each day's fishing and the washers will remain at their proper thickness and the drag will work properly for years.

Casting reels with magnetic brakes work well along the Texas coast. There is almost always a wind on the Texas coast and reels that allow anglers to quickly adjust the braking system work best.

Spinning reels should also have an easily adjusted drag. Again, anglers need at least 150 yards of line capacity on spinning reels.

Both casting and spinning reels will be tested by saltwater, so clean all of your reels immediately after a day's fishing. Re-lubricate areas that normally have a light coating of oil, like bearings. Some anglers believe it is best to wash down their reels with freshwater once the day is over. Others believe any water, fresh or salt, inside a reel is bad.

It is best to keep any reel clean of excess water. If your reel gets dunked into the saltwater it is probably best to rinse it with freshwater and oil bearings and moveable parts. A little cleaning goes a long way to keeping your reels in working order.

Reels that corrode after one trip to the coast are probably not the models to use. Find another manufacturer that makes reels specifically designed for saltwater. If you're unsure which models will work, watch boats coming into the boat ramp at the end of the day. Ask a few people which models they prefer and why. You'll soon know which models to buy and which ones to avoid.

Rods for the Texas coast should be between 7 and 9 feet long. Anglers going primarily after speckled trout will most likely want a rod that has a fast, sensitive tip. Those chasing reds will want a stronger rod with more backbone. Light tackle users can get by with one outfit, but it's just like playing golf with one club. It can be done but you won't maximize your enjoyment using only one rod.

There are basically two choices for line for light tackle. Monofilament in either 10- or 12-pound test works great for most Texas coastal situations. With a properly set drag and use of a leader, most anglers will get more casting distance out of 10-pound test line. Extra distance is important.

Learn to add a section of 15- to 20-pound fluorocarbon leader to any casting or spinning rig. By using a strong leader and slightly lighter casting line, anglers can throw almost any lure greater distances.

Many anglers have switched to braided line. They work especially well on spinning reels but be sure to spool at least 20 yards of monofilament on the reel first before filling it with braided line. The monofilament helps prevent the braided line from wandering on the spool.

Lures for the light tackle user are pretty basic. You need a walk-the-dog type topwater like a Heddon Super Spook or Super Spook Jr., Mirrolure TopDog, Rapala Skitterwalk, or Rebel Jumping Minnow. Topwater lure colors include bone, chartreuse, or orange belly with dark back and the classic red and white.

Another hard lure to carry is a Mirrolure Catch 2000 or Classic 52M. Both lures sink gradually, allowing the angler to fish slightly deeper than when using a topwater lure. These hard-bodied casting lures have plenty of weight, making them easy for anglers to throw long distances. The classic red head and white body is a great color to start with. Other colors include pink and chartreuse, chartreuse and blue, and plain silver.

A recent addition to the hard-bodied lure group is the Mann's Tidewater Waker. This lure is designed to run no more than 4 inches deep no matter how fast the angler retrieves it. The lure has a very short diving bill and has proven very effective over shallow-water grassy areas. The lure is heavy enough to cast well and all the angler has to do is make a steady retrieve. The Mann's Waker includes a rattle. The steady rattle sound and shallow movement catches both redfish and trout.

Coastal anglers should also include a saltwater spinnerbait as part of their tackle. Saltwater spinnerbaits like the Strike King Redfish Magic work very well on grassy flats. Fish can feel the big spinner blade in off-colored water. Make sure the jighead hook point is sharp.

Take along at least two spoons: one gold or copper weedless spoon and one treble-hooked silver spoon. If room allows, take along spoons in 1/8-, 1/4- and 1/2-ounce versions. Fall redfish sometimes refuse a 1/4-ounce weedless spoon, but hit the lighter 1/8-ounce version. Speckled trout do the same thing by avoiding the heavier 1/2-ounce and hitting the 1/8- or 1/4-ounce silver spoon. Make sure all of your spoons have very sharp hooks. Test them before you start the day and sharpen any hooks that do not easily dig into your thumbnail.

Jigheads are another basic component of any coastal tackle system. Take along jigheads in 1/16-, 1/8-, 1/4-, 1/2- and 3/4-ounce weights. I prefer a jighead with a small screw on the shank to help hold the soft plastic tail.

Soft plastic tails are as varied as clouds in the sky. Every angler has his or her preference. I recommend a basic group that covers almost any coastal fishing situation.

Every soft plastic group needs to include a color that is very dark. Basic black or black with a lighter belly works well. The group also needs a color at the opposite end of the color spectrum, so be sure to carry either white or some version of white. I like white with a chartreuse tail or smoke with a red tail as my lightest color.

I never fish any coastal waters without fire tiger-colored soft plastics. I don't know why the fish like fire tiger, but they do. Fire tiger, which can be described as having a green back, yellow belly with gold flakes, and fluorescent orange tail, is probably effective because fish can see it. Whatever the reason, they like it and I always have plenty fire tiger soft plastics on hand.

Redflash shad is another color coastal fish prefer. This is red back and silver belly. Fish also like punkinseed with chartreuse tail. This color probably represents the natural color of shrimp and is effective because of that fact. The last color is plum or purple. Plum is one of those colors the fish simply like, sometimes better than any other color.

Many soft plastics are now made with fish-attracting scents further enhancing their fish-catching properties. Some of these are so effective that many anglers have replaced using natural bait with the scented lures.

That's it! Certainly you can take more. There are all types of hard-bodied lures, and soft plastics come in so many colors you could fill this book with just a list of today's favorite hot colors.

The lures and colors I've recommended have produced fish for decades by many different fishermen, fishing many different locations. If there is a just-got-to-have-it lure or color that everyone is recommending, go ahead and buy some. But also be sure to take a basic group like the one I've listed.

STEALTH IS THE WORD

By limiting the tackle you take, you'll be able to move quickly and quietly. Develop a stealthy approach and you'll catch more fish. By limiting the amount of tackle you take, you'll also be able to wade longer without getting fatigued. Watch the birds fishing the shoreline where you wade and you'll see that they move quietly or not at all. When a fish finally comes into range, they make one quick strike.

Also think about the wake you make while wading. Fish have very sensitive lateral lines that tell them when there is movement in the water. Waders make a wake when their legs move forward and fish feel this wake. If you're fishing for tailing reds in shallow water, move very slowly to minimize the wake. The redfish will most likely not see you coming because they have their heads down in a cloud of mud, but they will feel your wake if you move too fast.

Develop a stealthy approach and you'll catch more fish.

Choosing a Boat

Boats used along the Texas coast are as varied as the anglers fishing out of them. You'll see everything from old bass boats to the most modern kayak used to get around Texas waters.

A favorite boat type used along the Texas coast is a deep V bow, center console, fiberglass bay boat. The deep V allows the boat to cut through rough waves, which plague the coast. Many of these boats include a tunnel that allows the boater to carry their motor higher and fish shallower waters.

You'll find bay boats from 16 to 25 feet (and more) in length. Many anglers use these boats to get close to the area they want to fish and then get out and wade the actual fishing area.

It's often said that any coastal boat is a compromise and the center console bay boat is certainly that. These boats are designed to get the angler close to good fishing areas and also to cut through larger waves found in the near-shore waters. The center console design allows easy access to all parts of the boat. Many are equipped with rod racks located on the console. You will also see these boats equipped with bimini tops or T-tops to help shade anglers from the scorching Texas summer sun.

The high bow helps this center console boat handle both rough waves and shallow water.

Fly casters will need to make a few special provisions when fishing out of these larger boats. Try to locate everything your fly line might get caught on before you start casting. A roll of duck tape can cover cleats when fishing and then be easily removed once the day is over.

A simple five-gallon bucket makes a good line holder when fly casting from one of these boats. Place a small amount of water in the bottom of the bucket to help weight it down.

In recent years, the Florida-style poling skiff has made its way to Texas waters. These boats are typically lightweight and allow the angler to pole over shallow-water mud and grass flats, very similar to the way the boat is used when chasing Florida bonefish. Poling skiffs have a poling platform above the motor. Many of these boats include a platform in the bow to increase the height of the angler. This platform may simply be a flat second deck or, in cases of boats used by fly anglers, the deck may also include a stripping basket for holding anglers fly line.

The lighter weight of these skiffs allows the angler to pole them long distances. When casting from the front of a poling skiff, try to stay centered and not rock from side to side when casting. Fish in shallow water can feel the waves created from the rocking motion and will often spook.

Kayaks have become quite popular along the Texas coast. A kayak allows almost any angler the opportunity to fish many of the shallow water areas found along the Texas coast.

There are two major groups of kayaks: sit-on-top and sit-in kayaks. The sit-on-top version is currently the favorite. Kayaks can also be transported by a larger boat to get near the fishing area. Once close to the desired location, the kayak is off-loaded and paddled to the fishing spot. Using a kayak this way allows anglers the chance to fish areas that are often too shallow for a larger boat or too soft for the wader.

Just remember fish can feel every movement in the area. Paddle quietly and try not to make big waves.

Buy a colorful kayak and paddle. Bright colors help other boaters see you. Many of the waters that Texas anglers fish are used by other outdoors-people, including duck hunters. Help them see you by using a bright colored kayak and bright paddles. It is also a good idea to add a warning flag like those used on a kid's bikes to add height to your kayak.

Do some research and try out several different kayaks before you buy one. New kayak models come out every year. There are also several kayak books, including Captain Moffett's Saltwater Kayak Fishing The Texas Way, that offer good tips about kayak fishing.

No matter which type of boat you decide to use, observe all safety warnings. Travel as much as possible in designated boat lanes and watch for other boats, especially kayaks. Use your PFD and kill switch. Take along enough water for the day. A weather radio is a good boating accessory to have on board.

One final tip on boats: Teach your fellow anglers how to ease the anchor into the water before you get to the fishing area.

Landing Nets

I like using a landing net. Numerous catches, especially pesky flounder and soft-mouthed trout, have been saved because I use a landing net. Look for one that will float. If the handle is hollow and the net does not float, inject household sealant into the handle to permanently seal it.

I added an extra rod holder tube to the back of my wading belt for storing my landing net. It stays out of the way until I need it and doesn't pick up any grass that way.

A landing net really helps when you hook a big fish like a jack while wading. Even if the entire fish will not fit into the net, its head will and you can then control the fish while you release it.

Good Quality Sunglasses

I would buy a pair of good quality sunglasses before I would buy a good reel. It's that simple. Good quality sunglasses are worth every penny you spend on them. Sunglasses are as much a part of your fishing tackle as any other component and they'll help you catch more fish.

Buy glasses with amber or vermillion-colored lenses that fit well and do not hurt when you wear them all day. Glasses with side shields help you see more fish. Also, buy a sunglass-retaining string. I like to have a string that is bright red or yellow so I can see it. If you're going to spend the money for a good pair of sunglasses you don't want to lose them.

One other thing: Buy a pair of sunglasses just for fishing. Resist the temptation of using them for other activities. If you buy a good pair of sunglasses, a strong hard case to put them in, attach a visible retaining string, and only use them for fishing, they will last you for decades not just one year.

Cameras

You've done everything right. You did your homework. You chose the correct spot and the correct tackle. You studied the tide charts and were in the spot on the correct tide. You've caught the fish of a lifetime. Great. How about something to remember the catch by?

Take along a camera on every trip to the coast. You never know when you'll catch the fish of a lifetime. Today's small digital cameras don't take up much room and many are even waterproof.

Take plenty of different shots before you release the fish. One thing you might do to help insure you've got a shot worthy of the fish is not unhook it until you're ready to release the fish. If the fish happens to slip out of your grasp it will probably remain hooked and you can retrieve it for another photo.

Another great thing about today's digital cameras is you can actually review the photos you've taken before releasing the fish. Simply let the fish lay in your landing net until you've reviewed the shots.

Be sure to take both vertical and horizontal shots. Get a hero shot with the fish held away from your body and take a second photo with the fish closer to you so you can determine the real size later.

It's a good idea to show someone fishing with you how to use your camera before hitting the water. They may not be the best photographer in the world but any photo is better than no photo at all. Today's point-and-shoot digital cameras take great pictures and even a rank novice will get an excellent photo.

Also, take along a small measuring tape with you when you fish. Plastic tapes cost less than $5 and fit neatly in your pocket. Measure the length and girth of any large fish before releasing.

If you don't have a measuring tape measure the distance between the tip of you thumb and the tip of your little finger. Remember that measurement. Anytime you have a fish you can simply stretch out your hand and get a rough measurement for the length of any fish.

This poling skiff is able to get fly casters into shallow waters.

Health and Safety

Sunblock: Yes I Hate It Too But....

One simple rule about sunblock: Use it! Yes, I hate the stuff as much as anyone, but I use it. There are several good sunblocks on the market. I like one that I can spray on and dries quickly.

I put my sunblock on first thing in the morning, before I leave the cabin. I spray it on the back on my hands and then rub the back of my hands where I need the sunblock. After I have all areas covered, especially the top of my ears and around my nose, I vigorously wash my hands with soap. I wash them like a doctor going into surgery. I don't want any sunblock on my fly line or on my casting or spinning tackle.

If you fish the Texas coast you're going to get sunburned. It's simply a fact. Try to minimize the effects of the sun by using a sunblock.

Personal Flotation Devices: Use Them

If you talk to any game warden he'll tell you he's never picked up a drowned person with a personal floatation device (life jacket) on. Use one; they work. No matter how good of a swimmer you are, use a PFD. It might save your life.

Stingray Shuffle

Texas coastal waters are full of critters with spiny, stingy parts. One everyone needs to watch out for is the stingray. Stingrays have a very sharp barb at the base of their tail. This barb is used by the stingray to protect itself from being eaten.

A stingray can't tell the difference between a wader's foot and something biting down on its back. Anytime the stingray feels any pressure on its back, it curls up and impales whatever is after it. If you're a wading fisherman, that may mean your leg. Being stuck by the barb is very painful. Some waders pass out from the pain. It's best to learn how to avoid stingrays in the first place.

All coastal waders should keep in constant contact with the bottom. Shuffle your feet, never picking the sole off the bottom of the area you're wading. If you never lift your foot, you'll never land in the middle of a stingray's back.

Do not step backwards while wading. Stingrays will often follow the mud trail you make while sliding your feet, looking for creatures you stir up. When you stop, the stingray has a chance to catch up to you. When you step back into the mud trail you just made, you have a chance of stepping on a stingray in your mud trail. Just remember to not step backwards into your own mud trail and you'll be safe.

Another place anglers need to be cautious is when they first enter the water. Anglers have been stung when jumping out of a boat to begin their wade. You may want to poke around on the bottom with something before you jump into the water, especially if you cannot see the bottom.

If you do get stung by a ray, go to the hospital no matter how slight the sting might be. The barb wound gets easily infected. Get the wound thoroughly cleaned. The little time you miss fishing will be well worth it.

Several companies offer wading boots with bulletproof leg protection. These work great but it is best to avoid any area with lots of stingrays. If you start to see many rays in your area you might want to re-think that spot and choose another.

Texas coastal waters get muddier the farther east you go and sandier the farther west you go. The bay systems on the eastern edge of the state receive the most rain. Each bay going west receives less rain until you get to the southern tip where it is the driest.

Planning a Trip

Before you can plan your trip, you've got to make a few decisions. You must decide what type of fish you want to catch. If you want to catch tailing redfish in knee-deep water on a fly, then some locations are better than others. If you just want to catch fish and really don't care what type, the trip becomes much easier.

Most locations on the Texas coast give the angler a chance at several different species on one trip. It is not unusual to catch speckled trout, redfish, and flounder on the same trip or maybe even from the exact same spot. But there are times when it is difficult to catch all three during the same day. Know what you want to do before you start planning the trip.

Some locations are also more conducive to catching certain species than other locations. If you want to catch a tailing redfish on a fly, Aransas Pass may be a better location than Galveston Bay.

Use local guides and fishing reports to plan your trip. If the tailing reds in shallow water are hot in Rockport but not Sabine Lake, take that information into account while planning your trip.

Texas has many excellent coastal guides. Call the guide and don't be afraid to ask questions. Ask for references or seek out other anglers in your home area that have used the guide. A list of guides is provided in this book.

If you do hire a guide, listen to the guide. If the guide tells you to do something, do it to the best of your ability and don't argue. Remember, the guide was fishing yesterday and wants you to catch fish at least as bad as you do.

Some guides offer taxi service to local airports or can arrange for your pickup. Many Texas coastal towns do not have rental cars available. You may have to rent a car at a larger town on the way to your destination.

Some guides have rooms to rent and other do not. Some guides provide all the tackle you're going to need and others expect you to bring your own tackle. Be sure to discuss all of these areas with the guide before you go.

Most Texas guides do not provide lunch, but most will have water on board. If you need a lunch or something special, plan to bring it yourself. It's always a good idea to bring extra water and a lunch for the guide.

If you're not using a guide, review local fishing newspapers, websites with fishing reports, or ask an angler that knows about the area. Don't be afraid to head out by yourself. Texas has plenty of locations made for the angler that wants to discover something new.

Many Texas coastal towns are small and motel accommodations are often limited. If you're traveling with a guest or spouse that is not use to somewhat rough conditions then you may want to book a motel in a nearby larger town and drive to the fishing area. Also, many Texas coastal towns simply don't have a great number of rooms to rent. Weekends can be especially busy. Don't head out on a Friday afternoon without a room reservation and expect to find a room. Book the room well in advance.

Get your fishing license before you leave for your trip. Texas Parks and Wildlife offers licenses over the Internet. Many Texas coastal towns do not have locations selling licenses.

If you can fish during the middle of the week, you will find smaller crowds and often catch more fish.

Use the checklist below to help plan your trip.

CHECKLIST

- ☐ Sunglasses
- ☐ Sunblock
- ☐ Camera
- ☐ Hat or cap
- ☐ Long sleeve Shirt
- ☐ Wading boots
- ☐ Pocketknife

- ☐ Room confirmation #
- ☐ Fishing license
- ☐ Water
- ☐ Cooler
- ☐ Map
- ☐ Rain jacket and pants
- ☐ Weather radio

Tackle

- ☐ Rod
- ☐ Reel
- ☐ Extra line
- ☐ Leader and leader material
- ☐ Flies and lures
- ☐ Nippers

- ☐ Landing net
- ☐ Waders
- ☐ Hat light
- ☐ Hook file
- ☐ Stripping basket
- ☐ Pliers

Catch and Release/Conservation

Texas is blessed with numerous fishing opportunities but there was a time when some of the fish we consider safe today were at a great risk of being over fished. A few brave fishermen gathered and discussed what to do about dwindling redfish and speckled trout populations. That small group soon became the Gulf Coast Conservation Association, or GCCA.

Soon other people thought the conservation ideas GCCA had would work in their state and the organization changed to the Coastal Conservation Association, or CCA. Today CCA has members from Maine to Texas and even new chapters along the Pacific Coast. Membership stands at over 90,000 today.

CCA helps the Texas Parks and Wildlife Department stock millions of redfish and speckled trout along the Texas coast annually. It has numerous research programs dealing with other species like tarpon, flounder, and snook.

CCA takes an active role in areas like freshwater inflows, red snapper populations, off shore species conservation, and other projects. The thousands of volunteers like San Antonio's Mitch Brownlee and Chris Smisek have made a great difference in Texas sport fishing.

You can join CCA at www.joincca.org.

While Texas offers liberal limits on most of its sport fish, anglers can contribute to the longevity of sport fish species. Texas regulations are based on hard data gathered by the Texas Parks and Wildlife Department Coastal Fisheries Division's annual surveys.

The Coastal Fisheries group does gill net surveys twice a year. They also do ramp surveys throughout the main fishing season, quizzing anglers about their catch and fishing experiences. The data gathered has given them a very useful tool to regulate fish limits.

Anglers can also help by only taking fish they need. Fresh fish is best and if you're not going to eat it, don't take it out of the water. Tell your neighbor to catch his own fish. Just because the limit is 10 doesn't mean you have to take 10 fish every day you fish.

Big redfish over 28 inches long are not the best to eat and a fiberglass mount looks better anyway. That jack crevalle you just caught might be a big fish but its better off swimming in the bay to be caught again than kept.

Release your fish in good shape. Be sure to support any fish you're going to release until it can leave under its own power. Use a landing net to help control your fish. Your hands will remove the protective slime found on speckled trout and they may not recover.

Resources

Texas Parks and Wildlife
4200 Smith School Road
Austin, TX 78744
www.tpwd.state.tx.us

Regulates all Texas fishing activities
and maintains state records.

Operation Game Thief:
Call 800-792-4263 to report
illegal activities.

**Coastal Conservation Association
(CCA)**
6919 Portwest Suite 100
Houston, TX 77024
800-201-3474
www.joincca.org

Conservation organization
dedicated to the conservation
and preservation of
our coastal marine resources.

**National Oceanic and Atmospheric
Administration (NOAA)**
1401 Constitution Ave NW
Washington, D.C. 20230
202-482-6090
www.noaa.gov

Current weather information.

**International Game Fish Association
(IGFA)**
300 Gulf Stream Way
Dania Beach, FL 33004
954-927-2628
www.igfa.org

Maintains world records for all
game fish.

Delorme Mapping
P.O. Box 298
Freeport, ME 04032
800-561-5105
www.delorme.com

Texas Atlas & Gazetteer is a
collection of maps showing detail of
the state of Texas including coastal
areas.

Shallow Water Angler Magazine
P.O. Box 420235
Palm Coast, FL 32142-0235
866-512-1105
www.shallowwaterangler.com

Fishing magazine specializing
in shallow water locations of the
Gulf Coast and
Atlantic seaboard.

Texas Fly Shops & Tackle Shops

Abilene

Academy Sports
3950 John Knox Dr
325-698-5490
www.academy.com

Big 5 Sporting Goods
2365 S Danville
325-698-4526
www.big5sportinggoods.com

Dry Creek Anglers
3301 South 14th St
325-690-1350

Amarillo

Academy Sports
Loop 335 & 45th Ave
806-468-6314
www.academy.com

Big 5 Sporting Goods
8004 IH-40 W
806-356-8115
www.big5sportinggoods.com

Gander Mountain
10300 W IH 40
806-354-9095
www.gandermountain.com

RiverFields
2465 I-40 West
806-351-0980

Top Notch Outfitters, Inc.
2617 Wolfin Village
806-353-9468

Aransas Pass

Offshore Adventures & Crab Man Marina
Hwy 361
361-758-6900

Outdoor Texas
259 S Commercial
361-758-1560

Port A Kayak
888-396-2382
www.portakayak.com

Slow Ride Kayak Rentals
361-758-0463

Arlington

Academy Sports
100 W. Arbrook Blvd
817-375-3210
www.academy.com

Dick's Sporting Goods
3891 S Cooper St
817-987-4800
www.dickssportinggoods.com

Orvis Arlington
3901 Arlington Highlands Blvd
817-465-5800
www.orvis.com

Sports Authority
4620 South Cooper
817-467-0090
www.sportsauthority.com

Austin

Academy Sports
www.academy.com
12250 Research Blvd
512-506-6000
5400 Brodie Ln
512-891-4240
7513 North IH 35
512-407-6310
801 E. William Cannon Drive
512-486-6000

Austin Outdoor Gear and Guidance
3411 North IH 35
512-473-2644

Backwoods
12921 Hill Country Blvd
512-263-6310

KC's Outdoors
6800 W Hwy 290
512-288-6001

McBrides
2915 San Gabriel St
512-472-3532

Second Season Outdoors
4402 N Lamar
512-302-4327

Sports Authority
www.sportsauthority.com
13609 N IH 35
512-989-6732
11301 Lakeline Rd
512-331-4892
9600S IH 35
512-291-9423

Sportsman's Finest
12434 Bee Cave Rd
512-263-1888
www.sportsmansfinest.com

Travelfest
9503 Research
512-615-1800

Travelfest Superstores, Inc.
1214 W 6th St, Suite 210
512-615-1300

Beaumont

Academy Sports
6250 Eastex Freeway
409-895-4500
www.academy.com

Gander Mountain
5855 Easter Freeway
409-347-3055
www.gandermountain.com

Bee Cave

Dick's Sporting Goods
3921 Market St.
512-263-2953
www.dickssportinggoods.com

Brownsville

Academy Sports
4305 Old Hwy 77
956-554-6900
www.academy.com

Gordon's Bait and Tackle
7066 E 14th
956-831-4828

Bryan

Sullivan's Outfitters
3602 Old College Rd
817-478-5990

Buda

Cabela's
15570 IH 35
512-295-1100
www.cabelas.com

Carrollton

Fly Tier's Primer, Inc.
1236 Jeanette Way
214-242-0458

Cedar Hill

Dick's Sporting Good
305 W FM 1382
972-291-5530
www.dickssportinggoods.com

Sports Authority
727 N Highway 67
972-293-3594
www.sportsauthority.com

College Station
Academy Sports, 1420 Texas Ave/
979-696-5305 / www.academy.com

Gander Mountain
2301 Earl Rudder Freeway S
979-693-6412
www.gandermountain.com

Conroe

Academy Sports
1420 W. Loop 336 N.
936-788-1888
www.academy.com

Corpus Christi

Academy Sports
5001 S Padre Island Dr
361-986-7200
www.academy.com

Gulf Sporting Goods
3900 Leopard St
361-882-6461

Roy's Bait & Tackle
7613 S Padre Island Dr
361-992-2960

Corsicana

Gander Mountain
3301 Corsicana Crossing Blvd.
903-874-2500
www.gandermountain.com

Dallas

Academy Sports
8050 Forest Lane
214-221-2284
www.academy.com

Dick's Sporting Goods
13838 Dallas Pkwy
972-239-5455
www.dickssportinggoods.com

Fishn' World Inc.
4609 W. Lovers Lane
214-358-4941

Gun and Tackle Store
6041 Forest Lane
214-239-8181

Orvis Dallas
8300 Preston Road
214-265-1600
www.orvis.com

Pocket Sports Company
7235 Syracuse Drive
214-553-0347

Rays Hardware and Sporting Goods
730 Singleton
214-747-7916

Sports Authority
9100 N. Central Expressway, #123
214-363-8441
www.sportsauthority.com

Sports Authority
15490 Dallas Parkway
972-991-3533
www.sportsauthority.com

Tailwaters Fly Fishing
2416 McKinney Ave
888-824-5420

Denison

Daves Ski and Tackle
3714 N Hwy 91
963-465-6160

Denton

Sports Authority
1800 S. Loop Ste. 240
940-783-4100
www.sportsauthority.com

Eagle Lake

Johnny's Sport Shop
101 Boothe Dr.
979-585-8414

El Paso

ATF Fly Shop
1845 Northwestern Dr.
915-225-0570

Big 5
8900 Viscount Blvd.
915-595-4808
www.big5sportinggoods.com
Sports Authority
801 Sundland Park Dr
915-584-6556
www.sportsauthority.com

Farmers Branch

Sports Authority
4245 LBJ Freeway
469-374-9336
www.sportsauthority.com

Flint

The Full Creel Fly Shop
10821 Southern Trace Cir
800-811-8211

Flower Mound

Dick's Sporting Goods
5801 Long Prairie Rd
972-355-1111
www.dickssportinggoods.com

Fort Worth

Academy Sports
6101 SW Loop Blvd.
817-346-6628
www.academy.com

Cabela's
12901 Cabela Dr.
817-337-2400
www.cabelas.com

Backwoods
2727 W 7th St
871-332-2423

Sports Authority
www.sportsauthority.com
4830 SW Loop 820
817-377-1515
1244 Green Oaks Rd
817-731-8578

Texas Outdoors
3821 SW Blvd.
817-731-3402

Fredericksburg

Hill Country Outfitters
115 E. Main St.
210-997-3761

Frisco

Dick's Sporting Goods
2611 Preston Rd.
214-618-0200
www.dickssportinggoods.com

Sports Authority
2930 Preston Rd.
214-387-9215
www.sportsauthority.com

Fulton

Seaworthy Marine Supply
102 S Fulton Beach Rd.
361-727-9100

Galveston

Academy Sports
4523 Ft. Crockett Blvd
409-941-6550
www.academy.com

Garland

Bass Pro Shops
5001 Bass Pro Dr.
469-221-2600
www.basspro.com

Dick's Sporting Goods
205 Coneflower Dr.
972-495-3208
www.dicksportinggoods.com

Fin and Feather
354 E. I-30
972-226-2277

Fisherman's Supply
RR 3 Box 696
972-226-1616

Granbury

Brazos Flyfishers
4412 Waples Rd.
888-200-0364

Grapevine

Bass Pro Shop
2501 Bass Pro Drive
972-724-2018
www.basspro.com

Harker Heights

Dick's Sporting Goods
201 E Central Texas Expressway
254-690-4220
www.dickssportinggoods.com

Harlingen

Hook Line and Sinker
2704 S. 77 Sunshinestrip
956-428-6473

Houston

Academy Sports
www.academy.com
11077 NW Freeway
713-613-6300
19720 NW Freeway
281-517-3800
7600 Westheimer
713-268-4300
13400 E Freeway
713-445-4400
10375 N. Freeway
281-405-4300
13150 Breton Ridge Street
281-894-3700
10414 Gulf Freeway
713-948-4100
8236 S. Gessner
713-219-3500
2404 S.W. Freeway
713-874-6020
14500 Westheimer
281-556-3200

Angler's Edge
5000 Westheimer Rd.
713-993-9981

Canoespor
5822 Bissonnet
713-660-7000

Cut Rate Fishing Tackle
8933 Katy Freeway
713-827-7762

Gander Mountain
19820 Hempstead Hwy
832-237-7900
www.gandermountain.com

Houston Angler
713-953-1079

Orvis Houston
5848 Westheimer Rd
713-783-2111
www.orvis.com

Sports Authority
www.sportsauthority.com
1210 Fry Road
281-599-1944
2131 South Post Oak Blvd
713-622-4940
8625 F.M. 1960 West
281-807-9020
10225 Katy Freeway
713-468-4870
11940 A Westheimer Rd
281-493-9190

Tackle Hut
216 W. Little York Rd #C
713-694-8008

Humble

Academy Sports
9805 FM 1960 E. Bypass
281-446-2013
www.academy.com

Sports Authority
20416 Highway 59 N
281-446-7519
www.sportsauthority.com

Hurst

Dick's Sporting Goods
101 Melbourne Rd
817-590-0740
www.dickssportinggoods.com

Irving

Sports Authority
3524 Airport Freeway W
972-986-1110
www.sportsauthority.com

Jasper

Ann's Tackle Shop
4819 N Wheeler
409-384-7685

Junction

Sonny's Canoes
214 Patricia
325-446-2112

Katy

Academy Sports
1800 N. Mason Rd.
888-922-2336
www.academy.com

Bass Pro Shop
5000 Katy Mills Circle #415
281-644-2200
www.basspro.com

Killeen

Killeen Tackle
1319 E Veterans Memorial Driv
254-634-2020

Lake Jackson

Academy Sports
120 Highway 332 W.
979-373-5700
www.academy.com

Laredo

Arnold Distributing
4520 San Bernardo
956-723-2066
Border Sporting Goods
4610 San Bernardo Ave.
956-722-1007

LaMarque

Creative Feathers & Saltwater Fly Shop
2224 Lake Road
409-935-3733
www.creativefeathers.com

League City

Academy Sports
100 Gulf Freeway N
281-332-2839
www.academy.com

Lewisville

Sports Authority
2325 S Stemmons
972-315-1500
www.sportsauthority.com

Longview

Army Navy Store
1018 W. Loop 281
903-297-7006

Lubbock

Big 5 Sporting Goods
5112 56th St.
806-792-8656
www.big5sportinggoods.com

Fisherman's Headquarters
3823 84th St.
806-793-5822

Gander Mountain
4006 W Loop 289
806-785-1591
www.gandermountain.com
Mountain Hideaway
4816 50th Street
806-797-1064
The Outdoorsman
6602 Slide Rd
806-794-6666

Lufkin

Tri-Lakes Tackle and Outdoor
2208 E. Denman Ave.
936-637-7119

Marshall

Shooter's Sporting Goods
909 E. End Blvd.
903-938-0738

McAllen

Academy Sports
www.academy.com
716 E. Expressway 83
956-632-3000
3901 Expressway 83
956-217-7600

Broadway Hardware
801 W Dove Ave.
956-682-2020

Bud's Fly Shop, Inc.
5509 N Ware Rd.
800-294-0104

Sports Authority
3300Expressway 83
956-631-6501
www.sportsauthority.com

McKinney

Sports Authority
3190 S Central Expressway
972-540-0962
www.sportsauthority.com

Midland

Big 5 Sporting Goods
4100W Loop 250 N
432-699-1595
www.big5sportinggoods.com

H & E Sports
410 N Main St.
915-682-2473

Nacagdoches

Nacodoches Marine
5900 South St.
936-564-3534

North Richland Hills

Sports Authority
8555 Airport Freeway
817-428-5512
www.sportsauthority.com

New Braunfels

Action Angler & Outdoor Center
830-964-3166

Gruene Outfitters
1629 Hunter Rd.
830-625-4440
www.grueneoutfitters.com

Odessa

Big 5 Sporting Goods
3875 E 42nd St.
432-363-9404
www.big5sportinggoods.com

Pasadena

Academy Sports
5500 Spencer Hwy
713-947-4000
www.academy.com

Pearland

Bass Pro Shops
1000 Bass Pro Dr.
713-770-5100
www.basspro.com

Pharr

Rio Grande Outfitters
5510 N. Gage Blvd.
956-782-6746

Plano

Academy Sports
www.academy.com
3305 Dallas Pkwy, Suite 301
972-781-2970
4045 Central Expressway
972-633-4100

Sports Authority
701 Taylor Dr.
972-509-1992
www.sportsauthority.com

Port Aransas

Bilmore & Son Hardware & Tackle
115 N Alister
361-749-5880

Island Tackle
207 W Ave G.
361-749-1744

Port A Outfitters
126 W Cotter

361-749-3474

Port Aransas Ace Hardware
1115 Highway 361
361-749-2004

Woody's Sports Center
136 W Cotter
361-749-6969

Port Arthur

Academy Sports
8453 Memorial Blvd.
409-723-6800
www.academy.com

Port Isabelle

The Shop
318 Queen Isabella Blvd
956-943-1785

Port Mansfield

Harbor Bait and Tackle
956-944-2331

Port Mansfield Marina
600 Mansfield Dr.
956-944-2331

The Wright Stop
Hwy 186
956-944-2314

Port O'Connor

Capt. Marty's, Byers & Adams
361-983-3474

POC Hardware
Hwy 185
361-983-2708

Speedy Stop
16th & Adams
361-983-4411

Richardson

Barlows Tackle Shop
451 N. Central Expressway
972-231-5982

Richland Hills

Sports Authority
8555 Airport Freeway
817-428-5512
www.sportsauthority.com

Academy Sports
7441 N. E. Loop 820
817-514-3140
www.academy.com

Rockport

Pelican Bait
412 Navigation Circle
361-729-8448

Tackletown
3010 Hwy 35 N
361-729-1841

Rockwall

Dick's Sporting Goods
1005 E IH30
972-722-4434
www.dickssportinggoods.com

Sports Authority
920 Steger Towne Rd.
972-961-0825
www.sportsauthority.com

Rosenburg

Coastal Outfitters
1612 1st St.
281-232-3999

Round Rock

Sportsman's Warehouse
3202 S IH 35
512-218-8880
www.sportsmanswarehouse.com

San Angelo

Big 5 Sporting Goods
4251 Sunset Dr.
325-224-4647
www.big5sportinggoods.com

Field & Stream Sporting Goods
3812 Houston Harte
325-944-7094

San Antonio

Academy Sports
www.academy.com
2024 N Loop 1604 E
210-507-4001
15350 IH 35
210-637-2600
2727 N.E. Loop 410
210-871-2630
165 S.W. Military Drive
210-334-6740

Bass Pro Shops
17907 IH 10 West
210-253-8800
www.basspro.com

Dick's Sporting Goods
18103 Rim Dr.
210-558-3444
www.dickssportinggoods.com

Dick's Sporting Goods
5503 W Loop 1604 North
210-680-2288
www.dickssportinggoods.com

Good Sports
12730 I-H 10 West
210-694-0881

Hill Country Outfitters
18030 Hwy 281 North
210-491-4416

Sports Authority
125 N.W. Loop 410
210-341-1244
www.sportsauthority.com

Sportsman's Warehouse
1911 N Loop 1604 E
210-494-5505
www.sportsmanswarehouse.com

Tackle Box Outfitters
6330 N New Braunfels
210-821-5806

Seabrook

Marburgers Sporting Goods
1400 Bayport Blvd
281-474-3229

Shenandoah

Sports Authority
19075 IH 45 S.
936-321-2550
www.sportsauthority.com

Sherman

Gander Mountain
2725 Hwy 75 N.
903-891-8585
www.gandermountain.com

South Padre

Island Outfitters SPI
206 W Swordfish
956-943-2798
www.islandoutfittersspi.com

Padre Outfitters
2400 Padre Blvd
956-761-2322

Spring

Academy Sports
25010 I-45
281-367-1010
www.academy.com

Gander Mountain, 19302 IH
45 / 281-288-2620 / www.
gandermountain.com

Stafford

Sports Authority
12730 Fountain Lake Circle
281-240-3388
www.sportsauthority.com

Sugarland

Academy Sports
16610 U.S. Highway 59
281-276-7400
www.academy.com

Gander Mountain
19890 Southwest Freeway
281-239-6720
www.gandermountain.com

Temple

Academy Sports
1407 Marlandwood Rd.
254-742-7350
www.academy.com

Texarkana

Gander Mountain
2301 University Ave.
903-832-3607
www.gandermountain.com

The Woodlands

Orvis The Woodlands
9595 Six Pines Dr.
281-203-6150
www.orvis.com

Tomball

Academy Sports
28522 SH 249
281-516-4100
www.academy.com

Tyler

Backcountry Fly Shop
3320 Troup Hwy #125
903-593-4602

Gander Mountain
151 Market Square Blvd.
903-839-8205
www.gandermountain.com

Victoria

Academy Sports
8903 N Navarro
361-582-5200
www.academy.com

Tackle Box
3305 N. Ben Jordan
361-575-8700

Victoria All Sports
1902 Houston Hwy
361-575-0655
www.victoriaallsports.com

Waco

Sports Authority
2408 W Loop 340
254-662-0858
www.sportsauthority.com

Watauga

Sports Authority
7612 Denton Highway
817-514-6056
www.sportsauthority.com

Webster

Sports Authority
19801 Gulf Freeway
281-332-6818
www.sportsauthority.com

Wichita Falls

Big 5
3808 Kemp Blvd.
940-691-3628
www.big5sportinggoods.com

Index